BEYOND THE PRADO

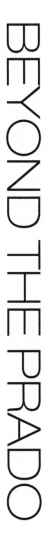

BEYOND THE PRADO

Museums and Identity in Democratic Spain

Selma Reuben Holo

Smithsonian Institution Press

Washington and London

Publication of this volume was supported by a generous grant fromthe Program for Cultural Cooperation between Spain's Ministry of Education and Culture and United States' Universities.

Grateful acknowledgment is made for permission to reprint chapter 5, which originally appeared in slightly different form in "The Art Museum as a Means of Refiguring Regional Identity in Democratic Spain," *Refiguring Spain: Cinema/Media/Representation* (1997), Marsha Kinder, ed., Durham and London: Duke University Press, 300-26.

Editor: Robert A. Poarch
Designer: Janice Wheeler

Library of Congress Cataloging-in-Publication Data

Holo, Selma.
    Beyond the Prado : museums and identity in democratic Spain /
Selma Reuben Holo
        p.   cm.
    Includes bibliographic references and index.
    ISBN 1-56098-925-4 (alk. paper)
        1. Museums—Spain—History—20th century. 2. Museums—Political aspects—
Spain. 3. Culture—Political aspects—Spain. 4 Politics and culture—Spain.
    5. Democracy—Spain—History—20th century. 6. National characteristics, Spanish.
    7. Spain—Civilization—20th century. I. Title.
    AM65.A2H65   1999
    069'.0946—dc21   99-27404

British Library Cataloguing-in-Publication Data is available

Manufactured in the United States of America
05 04 03 02 01 00 99   5 4 3 2 1

I dedicate this book to my husband, Fred Croton,
the true "emperor of ice cream"

CONTENTS

ACKNOWLEDGMENTS

I am profoundly grateful to the University of Southern California, especially to President Steven A. Sample, Provost Lloyd Armstrong Jr., Dean Joseph Aoun, and former Dean Marshall Cohen for believing in me and in my work. A Senior Research Fulbright Fellowship and grants from the Program for Cultural Cooperation between Spain's Ministry of Culture and United States' Universities, the Del Amo Foundation, and the Borchard Foundation helped make this book possible. Certainly, my debts to USC's Fisher Gallery staff, especially Kay Allen, Gymeka Williams, and Jennifer Jaskowiak, can never be fully repaid.

In Spain my most profound gratitude is extended to those who stood behind my efforts from the beginning. Adrian Piera and his wife Estrella Sol, Leticia Azcue, Manuel Blanco, Tomás Llorens, and José Guirao were key figures who opened many doors on my behalf, thereby giving me access to the dozens of people who helped me shape this book. Although it is impossible to mention everyone to whom I owe thanks in Spain, the following were indispensable to my efforts: Manuela Mena, Miguel Angel Cortés and his associate Borja Adsuara Varela, Helena Iglesias, Santiago Palomero, Luis Alonso, Rosina Gómez Baeza, Antonio Saénz de Miera, José Luís Yuste, Martha Peach, José Luis Alvarez Alvarez, Catherine Coleman,

Emilio Marcos Vallaure, A. Fernández-Castañon, Miquel Molins, Manuel J. Borja-Villel, John Zveroff, Consuelo Ciscar Casabán, Juan Ignacio Vidarte, Bartolomeo Ruiz, Luis Monreal Agustí, Ninfa Bisbe, Marta Carrasco, Javier González Durana, Miguel Zugaza, Joan Astorch, Fausto Serra de Dalmases and his wife Marucha, María Victoria Antoñanzas, César Ochoa, J. F. Yvars, Vicente Todolí, Miquel Navarro, Carmen Calvo, Rosa María Malet, Andrés Nagel, José Tasende, Gloria Mouré, Camila González Gou, Margarita Ruyra, Antonio Franco Domínguez, Trinidad Nogales Basarrate, Juan Zozaya Stabel-Hansen, and Ramoncín, our closest neighbor on Madrid's unforgettable Calle de Bordadores.

Outside of Spain my warm appreciation is extended to Thomas Krens, Roy and Ann Boyd, John Suau, Maite Alvarez, and to Professor Leo Steinberg, who taught me, long ago at Hunter College, that if something is interesting, it is probably worth studying. I am grateful to Peter Cannell, from the Smithsonian Institution Press, who first asked me to keep the Press informed of my ideas. And, of course, I owe an immense debt to Mark Hirsch, my acquisitions editor, who took me on, critiqued me along the way, and to Robert A. Poarch, my copy editor. Together they made this book a reality. I want to acknowledge Paul Preston, whom I have never met, but whose books on modern Spanish politics have influenced me profoundly. I am grateful forever to my parents, Ghita and Samuel Reuben, my sisters, Shelly and Linda, and brothers, Mikey and Chucky, my amazing sons, Robert and Joshua, their wives, Chris Holo and Andrea Martíns, and my grandchildren, Sam and Jo. And, finally, a big *abrazo* to my neighbors in Mexico who regularly brought my computer to life with infusions of solar power.

Finally, I acknowledge and thank Fred Croton for his untiring work on this manuscript—for his engagement and inspiration every step of the way. I simply couldn't have done it without him.

When, at the close of 1993, I went to live in Spain for most of the following year, I was expecting to see a country much changed from the one I had last visited six months after Franco's death in 1975. Certainly I had kept an eye on the country's contemporary culture and knew, in much the way that many other Americans did, that the art scene in Madrid had been hot, the Olympics in Barcelona brilliant, and the films of Pedro Almodóvar hip. I anticipated that young people would be completely at home in this lively milieu, but I never expected to see that the whole population—much of which had been born and raised during the Franco regime—seemed to have completely redefined itself as lifelong democrats. Everyone acted and talked as if they had never known any other way of life. Spaniards, who less than twenty years before had felt marginalized by the outside world, now considered themselves to be cosmopolitans, participants, and insiders. I was amazed at how their extraordinary achievement of a peaceful transition—from a forty-year-long dictatorship (with a legacy of many long repressed internal resentments) into a fully intact democratic nation—seemed old hat to them. Almost everyone with whom I spoke with seemed to take for granted the ways in which most of their institutions had so quickly become modernized and accommodated themselves to democratic practices and values.

Notwithstanding their blasé, almost dismissive attitude to what is sometimes called the "Spanish miracle," I probed further about which of those
institutions they perceived as having been especially helpful during the
transition period. Not surprisingly, many credited the press, the media,
and the updated educational system. Others, of course, pointed to the
weakened military and the reduced power of the Catholic church. Some
mentioned the importance of tourism. Repeatedly, in a much vaguer way,
I was informed that a completely "new culture" had evolved. But I was
never told precisely what that meant.

As I inquired still further, I was constantly reminded that Spain is a
country made up of a number of diverse peoples. The suppression of their
cultural diversity during Franco's dictatorship had left a country raw with
unresolved tensions and separatist tendencies. That the exacerbation of
those tensions after 1975 did not prevent progress toward democracy is
largely due to the prevailing post-Franco wisdom that reversed any and all
policies aimed at repressing the powerful expression of Spanish pluralism. The transitional government encouraged the development of cultural institutions that promoted and embraced this diversity—within the
context of preserving the nation-state. Spaniards as a whole supported
their changing political system in direct proportion to the aggressiveness
with which that pluralism and diversity were projected and defended. The
general consensus in Spain seemed to have been that the country's survival depended on a constant striving for an ever more positive and complex, although markedly uneven, balance between the power of the
center, with its culture of "Spanishness," and the powers of the various
autonomous regions, with their distinctive cultures and aspirations.

It is striking to an American how much the need for that balance was
understood by all parties concerned. It is equally striking to see the
degree of financial commitment that both the central and the regional
governments were—and are to this day—willing to make to achieve their
respective cultural goals. Furthermore, an unusually high percentage of
Spaniards, whether highly educated or not, seem to understand the
rights and obligations they have been granted in their 1978 constitution
to create and to own their cultural identities. As a result, there are those
who identify primarily with Spain, those who see themselves as relating
primarily with their regions, those who identify with Europe, and those
who will admit to multiple, overlapping, and competing identities. The
proliferation of orchestras, theaters, dance companies, art schools, festi-

vals, languages, literatures, and museums that have flourished throughout the country since Franco's death attest to how seriously this wide range of possibilities of cultural identification has been taken. The combined result of all of this now untrammeled, often highly individualistic, expression is the "new" Spanish culture alluded to so frequently. This is the culture that proved to be so effective in oiling the machinery of the democracy while it was being created and consolidated.

Beyond the Prado is a meditation on Spanish museums and museum-related entities: about how these museums were affected by cultural and political changes and how they affected the nature of those changes. The book is made up of case studies, some of which find their points of origin years before Franco's death, when certain of the nation's visionaries took advantage of an unevenly liberalizing environment to chip away at the eroding fascist monolith. Others, such as the Museum of Fine Arts of Asturias (Museo de Bellas Artes de Asturias) are products of the transition to democracy, a few including the Guggenheim Museum Bilbao (Museo Guggenheim Bilbao) represent the cultural environment of the last years of the 1990s.

Beyond the Prado is not a history book. Rather, it is meant to provide a nontraditional frame for the non-Spaniard to better comprehend the expanding world of Spanish museums, understand how they relate to each other within the country's larger political transformation, and obtain a sense of their ongoing struggles to assert a broad spectrum of cultural meaning. This frame purposely surrounds entities that usually find it in their best interests to represent themselves as completely unrelated to each other and subject themselves to no framing device other than the minimum requirements of the system and their official mission. While the museums I have chosen to write about certainly do emerge from distinct systems and disparate impulses (the state, the regions, the municipalities, the Roman Catholic church, entrepreneurs, and private and public foundations), they are nevertheless systemic in that they exist within the fluid and porous web of meaning that characterizes Spain today—the very web that permits the state to cohere in the face of daunting postmodern pressures.

This book, then, conceptually and unofficially, links the Prado (Museo Nacional del Prado), the most well-known face of Spain's historical and artistic center, with the Guggenheim Museum Bilbao, the stunning symbol of the flamboyant Basque rejection of the center; the Reina Sofía (Centro de Arte Reina Sofía), the national museum of modern and contemporary art, with the Army Museum (Museo del Ejército), a long-time bastion of ultraconservative values, and ARCO (Arte Contemporáneo Feria Internacional), Madrid's giant international art fair and annual "ephemeral" museum, with the stylish Thyssen-Bornemisza Museum (Fundación Colección Thyssen-Bornemisza). None of these links, or others like them, are in any sense physical or even necessarily structural. They do, however, allow for a way of appreciating that Spain has become a richly democratic country with an intricate mesh of cultural institutions, all of which sustain and nourish extreme divergences of meaning in the most salubrious manner.

These and other case studies are intended to bring to light some of the ways in which museums have functioned as one of the country's influential and, in varying degree, activist institutions in the renewal of Spanish civil society. *Beyond the Prado* tells individual stories while, at the same time, casts each on a stage far larger than any one of them could possibly command on its own. Art lovers casually interested in Spanish culture are, for the most part, familiar with the Prado. Now the Guggenheim Museum Bilbao has exploded into everyone's consciousness, and seeing beyond the Prado has become somewhat easier. This book will provide an analysis of the complex role that the Prado and the Guggenheim Museum Bilbao, and many other less-known museums, have played in the construction of the democratic Spanish citizens' sense of identity. The goal, ultimately, is to provide a better understanding of the unexpectedly powerful and positive force that museums have become in Spanish society throughout the last quarter of the twentieth century.

BEYOND THE PRADO

INTRODUCTION
CENTER VERSUS REGIONS AND THE HISTORICAL STRUGGLE FOR CULTURAL AND POLITICAL IDENTITY

Images of Spain come easily to mind: flamenco dancing, bullfighting, the Prado, the Costa del Sol, the Alhambra, and the Caves of Altamira; or Franco, the Guardia Civil, the Spanish civil war, and its devastating aftermath. A Hemingwayesque mélange would seem to fit most expectations. But another, far more complex, less cliché-ridden picture of Spain has emerged since 1975 after forty years of Franco's repressive rule and isolation—an astonishing group portrait of a nation determined to create a vibrant democratic society within a global environment.

Much has been written about Spain's remarkable transformation from a political and historical perspective. Attention has been paid to the role of the media: radio, television, film, and the press. Scholars have analyzed the shrinking spheres of both the military and the church. Volumes have been dedicated to the expanded choices and rights available to women, to reforms in education, to the adoption of three indigenous languages as co-official with Spanish, and to the evolving relationship with Europe and the Americas. It is now quite clear how each of these aspects played a part in Spain's transition to a liberal Western democracy. But it is far less clear how museums have participated in this refiguring. This book, while recognizing that the vitality and diversity of museums in Spain could not exist without a sustaining democratic environment, proposes that the

1

Regions and cities of Spain.

vitality and diversity of present-day Spain itself owes something to the contributions its museums have made to the active reconstruction of the various identities of its citizens. Those museums, new and renewed alike, have raised fundamental questions about Spanish culture, society, and identity, and by so doing have, in subtle but significant measure, helped create an engaged, open, and stable nation that has regained the respect of the world.

Selected from among the approximately one thousand museums in Spain, the case studies in this book focus on the most prominent institutions in the nation's social drama as well as on some of the more minor characters.[1] A few museums, notably the Prado, the Reina Sofía, the Thyssen-Bornemisza Museum, and, of late, the Guggenheim Museum Bilbao, will be familiar to the reader, either for the fame of their permanent collections or, as with the Guggenheim Museum Bilbao, for its fabulous architecture—which, from its opening day has been on the pilgrimage route for anyone concerned with the contemporary arts. Others, though less sensational, are equally indicative of the society's direction and momentum. Every one of them has a weighty responsibility for the protection or projection of some aspect of Spain's cultural legacy and current political identity. They represent a country that has successfully weathered electoral change and consequent shifts of cultural philosophy. In fact, they mirror those fundamental shifts—often enhancing them as well.

The purpose of *Beyond the Prado* is to encourage the reader to grapple with Spain's museums as dynamic elements in a grand and supple "text," rather than as the discrete entities they often purport to be. Looking at Spanish museums in this way allows them to be understood as organically linked—wittingly or unwittingly, willingly or unwillingly, officially or unofficially—to each other as well as to the past, present, and future of Spain. Furthermore, this approach brings to the surface the range of interpretations of culture prevalent throughout modern Spain—a far cry from what would have surfaced if similarly viewed during the harshest years of the dictatorship and its monolithic ideology, when the Prado alone stood out as the exemplary museum. Today there are a number of exemplars spread throughout the regions of the country. Each competes for attention, press, and audience, all the while affecting the very "meaning" of Spain in ways never anticipated by citizens or foreigners twenty-five years ago. Viewing Spanish museums from this perspective will reveal their unexpected position, beyond the strictly museological, in attesting to, reflecting, affecting, and enhancing the credibility of modern Spain's governing principles of freedom and decentralization.[2]

In effect, then, the reader is invited to make an enormous leap of the imagination and visualize the museums of Spain panoptically—to see them as a kind of macromuseum with approximately a thousand submuseums run by as many directors. To conceive them as such is by no means to suggest that they be considered cogs in a central, official system such as one would find in France. (In fact, Spain's museums, even those that exist under the aegis of the state, are functionally independent of each other; there is no overriding coordinated system.) It *is* to suggest, however, that they can be considered systemically, as functioning freely within a distinctive national reality that accomodates and absorbs them legally and voluntarily. Thus they provide another avenue for comprehending Spain as a country where many cultural identities flourish—especially those that would have been anathema in Franco's day. These museums even flourish when their primary purpose is to promote an identity that would, on the surface, seem to contradict the very idea of a "united" Spanish nation.

The individual case studies focus on the ways chosen to display collections, the strategies of collection building, the responses of audiences to exhibitions, the kinds of buildings constructed or adapted to house collections, the relationships cultivated with Spain's diverse communities, new and evolving systems of financial support, the languages elected to communicate with the public, the legal and political environments that inform policy and even daily operations, and the public relations and educational policies meant to disseminate meaning, rather than on traditional art history or connoisseurship. Although connoisseurship has its own enormous and irreplaceable value when museums are viewed as autonomous units or as members of a group of similar collecting institutions, the purposes of this book are better served by information gained by asking other questions. Asking those "other" questions, coupled with a panoptic view of the universe of Spanish museums, will lead to a better understanding of the reality of their varied and fluid roles in the discontinuous narrative that characterizes today's cultural life.

This book brings to the fore some of the thought and debate, which went on during and well after the "transition" to democracy, about the influence that museums could exercise when encouraged to function freely and actively in society. It was understood that museums contributed to the balancing act among those competing forces that allowed modern Spain to cohere as a nation: some would serve to advance the power and prestige of the state and some the regions; a growing number would feed the thirst for the modern and others would protect a range of traditional values; some would reflect the desire to be international and others appease anxieties about globalism; some would be dedicated to the rehabilitation of forgotten histories, while a few would stubbornly relate the former official story; some would be a by-product of private enterprise, but most would continue to be supported by the state, municipal, provincial, or regional governments and by the Catholic church. Each of these forces would be showcased in one Spanish museum or another, providing every citizen access to some public space where his or her point of view would be visually represented or memorialized. In the new political reality, Spain's leaders accepted that the peaceful existence of the country depended upon the elevation of its deeply fragmented citizenry from that of a threatening liability to that of the highest possible civic asset. Because politicians hoped that promoting museums could be especially useful in convincing the public of the sincerity of their efforts to achieve this profound change, they granted them unprecedented levels of financial support. And, since art museums are so popular and consistently attract the biggest audiences and the most media coverage, they received the most generous support of all—and the bulk of this book's attention.

Some historical background is critical to understanding the importance of museums in Spain and the role they continue to play in the construction of national identity. Spain has a centuries-long history of the regional in conflict with the central, a history that produced a land so scarred by ideology and cultural difference that the Spanish civil war appears to have been inevitable. In the aftermath of that war, in 1939, confronted with the disintegration of the social fabric, the victorious Generalísimo Francisco Franco imposed a harsh dictatorship on the exhausted population. He rationalized his regime and its often brutal policies by returning repeatedly to the rhetoric of state and church unity. Franco used every resource at his disposal, including language, the educational system, the church, the press, and, of course, the military, to impose that ideology. Although never a lover of the arts, he recognized their symbolic power and occasionally turned to them in his efforts to impress his supporters and, when he thought it to his advantage, the outside world.

The Valley of the Fallen is a haunting example. This immense architectural and sculptural monument celebrates his regime, which like all such regimes needed specific, literal, and accessible symbolic forms to illuminate and commemorate it. Franco intended the structure to be an aid to reinforcing the bitter myth of absolute national unity on Spain's stubbornly dissimilar peoples, but to this day, the Valley of the Fallen, its gigantic cross looming over the Sierra de Guadarrama mountains outside of Madrid, is apprehended as a glorification of the Right, recalling the price that each citizen paid for the civil war. Still, it is most searing for those who were on the losing side of that war, bringing to mind the many workers who served out prison sentences there as forced labor, some dying in the process. Conversely, as we will see later in this book, Franco was not averse to exploiting contemporary abstract art, when it suited him, in order to distract the international community from the harsh substance of his regime.

Even before Franco's death in 1975 an undeniable undercurrent of ideas diametrically opposed to the dictator's had begun to swirl about in certain elite circles. The idea of a monolithic Spain was already atrophying in the face of the unprecedented economic growth and increased contact with the outside world that occurred in the 1960s. During the transition to democracy after Franco's death, new governing principles not only acknowledged and encouraged, but astonishingly, also mandated Spain's essential diversity and regionalism. They became guideposts informing statesmen presented with the daunting task of crafting the foundations of a civil society. As a result, they developed a democracy in which the state's constitution actively supported varying levels of autonomy for the regions. These regions, exercising newfound freedoms and civic responsibilities, set themselves to reestablishing (or in some cases establishing for the first time) distinct identities within the new state structure. The political leadership of the transition bet that even the most belligerent regions would find it in their best interests to remain connected to the traditions that held Spain together for the last five hundred years. They recognized that simply advancing freedom would not be sufficient to keep their country together in a time of resurgent ethnic pride. Thus, they needed to encourage the creation of civic institutions that would contribute to the construction of the identity of a "new Spaniard" — a citizen who could accept that the country as a whole would work in everyone's own best interests. Like Franco, the founders of the modern Spanish democracy, without always appreciating aesthetics per se, accepted the power the arts possessed to advance that goal and to implicate the whole country in its achievement. The cultural policies developed by the new government were strategically designed to aid in the important task of convincing the populace that the emerging democracy was, in the name of Spain, endorsing the country's heterogeneity.

One of the reasons that Spain may not be widely appreciated for avidly embracing democracy is due to the lingering misperception by the outside world that it is a homogeneous country. Partly this misperception was encouraged because of Franco's insistence on the domination of the regions by the center. To conceive of Spain as a country composed of a number of fractious peoples, all of whom look at the world very differently, would have been difficult for any outsider conditioned by decades of Franco's propaganda. It is not common knowledge, for example, that Andalusians from Seville in the south differ as much, in some ways, from Barcelonans in the north as they do from Germans; that residents of Santiago de Compostela identify more with the Portuguese than they do with Madrileños; that there are at least three mother tongues in Spain other than Spanish; and that the Basques consider themselves an entirely separate ethnic group from other Spaniards. Due to extraordinary efforts since Franco's death, the idea of a diverse Spain is no longer so unbelievable. The planning and intelligence behind these efforts can be better appreciated now that the world has witnessed just how difficult it has been for other countries to transform their own authoritarian forms of government into mass liberal democracies.[3] More and more, it appears to be something of a miracle that the Spanish people, the large majority of whom had grown deeply cynical regarding the likelihood of controlling their own fates after forty years of Franco's rule, were able to transform themselves so quickly, so deeply, and so broadly across the land. Bluntly put: it looked easier than it was.

To properly gauge the enormity of the Spanish journey into democracy, it is necessary to consider not only the decisions and actions of a people reimagining themselves politically with an emphasis on a number of regionalisms but also to consider that they were doing this while dealing with a simultaneous and overriding powerful will to retain the physical and political integrity of the nation-state. It became in the late 1980s and throughout the 1990s commonplace to witness revisions of borders and/or allegiances in those countries undergoing change. In the rush to democracy, the reinstatement of pre–World War II borders and the subsequent renaming of lands became a frequent occurrence. In 1995 alone, over one hundred battles were fought within countries, rather than between them. Many of these battles (wars, really) had as their end the creation of a culturally homogeneous country. Local leaders became experts at manipulating ethnic, religious, and racial fears, igniting the repressed anger of decades of suppressed identity. Accepted ideas of sovereignty and nationalism were being challenged by long-repressed ethnicities, tribal loyalties, and regionalisms while, at the same time, and often in the same place, there was a seemingly unstoppable impetus toward greater globalism also working to undermine those traditional ideas. Given the evils perpetuated in the name of nationalism in the not too distant past, one might not be inclined to lament its apparent decline. However, abandoning the principles of nationalism also threatened to reduce the shared sense of responsibility to societal coherence, to *solidaridad,* as it is called in Spain.

Spain's leaders, with most of its citizens behind them, looked at this contradictory situation directly and tried to deal with it without trivializing it. What Spain did was to come to grips with the demands for ethnic and regional empowerment—along with the desire for global engagement. It confronted the challenge of redefining the old and tired dream of absolute, exclusive sovereignty and the unquestioned unity of the nation-state in light of the uneven demands for autonomy.[4] Spain was the first country with a highly diverse population, extremely complex regional allegiances, and at least some of the same potential for ethnic violence and territorial dispute, later seen in the ex-Yugoslavia, to emerge as a full democracy from a long and repressive post–World War II dictatorship. Still, this is not meant to suggest that Spain fully escaped the rending zeitgeist. The Basque Country in the north, a longtime bastion of secessionist sentiment, was and remained a fertile breeding ground for anti-Madrid and "antiterrorist terrorism," while Catalonia in the east and Galicia in the west also retained strong antipathies to the center. And, without a fully articulated plan for the future and no sure path into the next phase of the country's history, there was no reason to believe that the young King Juan Carlos I, Franco's chosen successor, would succeed in leading the country into the modern world as stable, free, and worthy of international respect. There were even mutterings, when the king assumed the monarch, that his nickname was likely to be "Juan Carlos the Brief." Four years after Franco's death, historians were still writing lines such as these:

Until the long-awaited event actually occurred, most observers of Spanish politics felt that Franco's death would be followed by considerable upheaval and instability leading eventually either to a military coup or a resumption of the Civil War after a forty-year hiatus. . . . As these lines are written, we are still too close to the beginning of Spain's new experiment with democracy to know for certain whether or not the post-Franco reforms will be ephemeral or long-lasting.[5]

Soon, what had been a single party state now enjoyed over one hundred political parties freely assembling. Spaniards, understandably jaded about politics, became enthusiastic participants. The public mood remained optimistic, if occasionally guarded, throughout the process. Foresighted leadership, enlightened self-interest, and a combination of new blood plus holdovers from the old regime who had been anticipating change for years allowed for the conceptualization and articulation of a democracy where both center and periphery could feel they were achieving their own goals. For all of its competing claims and desires, this leadership held in common the realization that Spain's most daunting challenge was to sustain Madrid's claim to the center, to allow the periphery their autonomy, and to create a political and cultural rationale for it all to cleave.

One of the most visionary elements in Spain's victorious leap into democracy was the mainstream renunciation of the politics of revenge. There were no Czech-style "lustrations" or "truth and reconciliation" commissions such as those later created in South Africa. The fascist period was, in effect, relegated to oblivion, but not without the discourse and analysis, books and articles about the forty preceding years that would permit the country to learn from its past and avoid living in a state of total denial. This rapprochement allowed for what the whole population uneasily knew anyway: that the great majority of those who had pursued successful lives during the Franco years had (tacitly or vociferously, implicitly or explicitly, willingly or unwillingly) enabled the totalitarian regime's lengthy hold on its power. At the same time, it explains the lack of any real resistance to the inclusion of able individuals from the old leadership in the transitional government. As a result, some politicians who had possessed immense powers under Franco remained in positions of considerable influence well into the 1990s—proving themselves to be just as valuable to democratic Spain as they had been to the dictatorship before it.[6] It was immediately evident that it would be unprofitable to waste time uncovering all of the possible collaborations of the past. Even King Juan Carlos I, chosen by Franco himself to be his successor, could have been denigrated. But, when he renounced the traditional Spanish model of authoritarian heads of state in favor of the modern European constitutional monarchic model, he surprised many. That gesture was an especially resonant signal to both conservatives and liberals alike to move ahead, to avoid the quicksand of recrimination, and to begin in earnest the creation of a democratic state.[7]

None of this is to insinuate that those who had suffered under the dictatorship simply forgot their pain and rage. The anger against Franco, symbolized by Picasso's long, self-exiled antifascist painting *Guernica,* was palpable. Tales of executions and torture flooded back into the collective memory as new and frightening information was disclosed about those long years under the dictatorship. The natural urge to punish those who had been in charge was, without a doubt, in the air. But the other consciousness, the one that kept reminding of the need to break the cycle of violence, dominated. Personal memories of civil war and post-civil war traumas remained and will, undoubtedly, never be totally eliminated. In Spain, however, the private and the public spheres were effectively separated. No longer was the rhetoric around "victors and vanquished" considered appropriate to the public arena.

To their credit the leaders of the transition not only survived a grim event that could have set back, or even obliterated, all of their progress, but turned it into a moment of opportunity. On February 23, 1981, Lt. Col. Antonio Tejero took control of the Parliament Building in Madrid while the Cortes was in session. A silence descended on the streets in anticipation and fear of an armed struggle. Defying most expectations, King Juan Carlos I took charge of the situation. First, he made private calls to loyal generals reconfirming their pledges of allegiance to him, effectively isolating those generals behind the parliamentary takeover. He then addressed the entire nation on television, reassuring all of his people that democracy would prevail. The coup d'état failed, the plotters were arrested, and the following day, approximately one million people marched in solidarity through the Madrid streets toward the palace. Photographs show the leaders of every political party, arms linked, at the head of the crowd. Democracy had, six years after Franco's death, definitively come to stay in Spain.

To this day, almost two decades later—after contending with Basque ETA (the Basque terrorist group) terrorism, state terrorism against ETA, tensions between center and periphery in Catalonia and Galicia, and several harsh economic crises—Spain persists in pursuing its future as a loosely united constitutional democracy. There was a recurring need to adjust and revise political agreements made early on because political environments inevitably evolved. That there will be a constantly shifting balance, rather than stasis, between the center and the periphery has now been accepted by a preponderance of the populace. It has also been accepted that Spain's inspired synergy between culture and politics provided much of the basis for the present success.

Beginning with the 1978 constitution, the leitmotif in the building of the new society has been the twinned theme of personal liberty and decentralization. The constitution also grants to all of Spain's citizens, as their natural right, a full cultural life, and it specifically requires public powers at all levels, from the state to the municipalities, to develop their own cultural plans. It is a mark of its preternatural maturity that the constitution expresses no concern that these various levels of government might have conflicts. The framers believed that, if encouraged, regional cultural expression would build self-confidence and would ultimately raise the educational and economic levels of those locales and that this would be good for Spain as a whole. The transitional governments also provided for the promotion of culture at the state level. They had every intention of preserving a sense of the shared national patrimony and engaging more with the international world of art and ideas.

Culture, in its various manifestations and aspects, became food for lively discussion in Spanish media, at the ubiquitous bars, at home, and at influential conferences.[8] Subjects like censorship, recuperation and construction of identities, education of creative and critical citizens, and receptivity to the outside world were all grist for the mill. Leaders in both the private and the public sectors were trying to understand just how the cultural obligations demanded of the society and written in the constitution could be best fulfilled. Museums, especially art museums, held a high profile in the cultural debates and emerged as one of those institutions expected to play a starring role in Spain's addressing of the current challenges. Politicians considered it their duty to fund museums since they reach a large and mixed public of citizens and tourists. They also recognized that Spaniards take a special pride in their collective artistic patrimony, and that they frequented in far greater numbers their museums than their public libraries, theaters, or symphony orchestras.[9] As a result, all levels of government from the state to the municipalities, made, from the start of the cultural debates, substantial investments in their museums. So, too, did an impressive number of institutions from the private sector—businesses, foundations, and banks—begin to spend large sums sponsoring museums and museum-related activities. All of this was undertaken with little or none of the tax relief associated with similar efforts in the United States.

Museums immediately proved to be reverberant arenas for advancing culture. Modern and contemporary art museums could be, as in all Western democracies, safe venues for oppositional and antiestablishment attitudes, attacking authority and tradition. In newly democratic Spain they were appreciated as special sites of celebration of the new freedoms. They were also effectively employed as antidotes to isolation. By the early

1980s exhibitions in Spain from New York, Paris, and Berlin had provided exposure to the latest and most exciting art-world trends. Museums of contemporary art, which were springing up everywhere, also came to be evidence of sophistication in cities usually branded as merely folkloric and provincial. By the mid-1990s they were flourishing not just in Madrid but also in Valencia, Extremadura, Santiago de Compostela, Majorca, Andalusia, Barcelona, San Sebastián, and Asturias. At the same time, museums showcasing the art and archaeology of specific regions, single artists, and the old masters were renovated, expanded, brought up-to-date, or built from scratch. Museums and their policies were known to affect people who never crossed their thresholds. They were a constituent part of the general frisson. The Prado, for one, always seemed to be in the news. Every Spaniard who read a newspaper or watched television seemed to have an opinion about Picasso's *Guernica* once it had come home: should it be moved from the venerable Prado to the upstart Reina Sofía? should it retain its protective glass shield? should it be allowed to leave Madrid for loan to exhibitions as close as the Guggenheim Museum Bilbao or as far as Paris?

Museums have thus emerged as one of the emblems and engines driving Spain into democracy. Individual museums such the Prado and the Guggenheim Museum Bilbao have done their parts, but it is the broader-based institution of the museum that has succeeded most in normalizing the culture of pluralism. *Beyond the Prado*, written from the point of view of an outsider with no stake in any individual project, is dedicated to exploring how the links, overlaps, and intersections, the erasures, addenda, and palimpsests, the subtleties, excesses, and harmonies make that institution such a serious contributor to life in contemporary Spain. Within these explorations are lessons that can be especially useful to those in the United States who are presently struggling with the problem of how that country's cultural life can be reenergized—fragmented and fearful as it has become. Studying Spanish museums in their relatively new democratic setting might provide clues in that effort to reimagine a national cultural identity that better affirms and more joyously celebrates America's diversity and uniqueness as it meets the new millennium head on.

1 THE LONG ARM OF THE CENTER

Madrid is the geographical midpoint of Spain. As the capital city, it is also the political and administrative center of the country. Although it has a population of approximately five million people, it sometimes seems that everyone who lives and works there has deep roots elsewhere—Andalusia, Galicia, Castile, Extremadura, the Canary Islands, or one of the country's other autonomous regions. In Madrid, more than any other city in Spain, one hears constant boasts of its willingness to absorb strangers. These characteristics, passionately cultivated since the rebirth of democracy often surprise visitors who have not traveled to Madrid since the Franco years. During that period, Barcelona was considered to have the more expansive environment, while Madrid was described as oppressive and closed. Contemporary Madrid, however, is generally recognized as the most broad-minded, tolerant city in the country. Furthermore, because the principles fundamental to Spain's democracy have mitigated the requirement for a stifling insistence on the symbolism of capital as national unifier, Madrid no longer has to hammer home messages trumpeting its overarching power. Thus the halls of Parliament, long the source of edicts limiting the regions' abilities to mobilize and assert themselves, began in 1979 to support regional efforts to recapture their own centrality and autonomy, which they had not possessed in over forty years. Nevertheless, it still falls on Madrid's shoulders to knit together a convincing image of "Spanishness" for its citizens and the world. This image is one that must be crafted out of the crazy quilt of "national" identities that Spain has nurtured in recent years.

In Spain as in many other countries, the state museums (especially those focused on art and archaeology) are among the key institutions constructing and nurturing the sense of national traditional identity.[1] They are expected to participate in this task by collecting and preserving essential pieces of the cultural and historic patrimony from every region of the country. They also need, of course, to display and interpret their material so as to provide what is in effect a visual text that will be read as "proof" that there was a shared past and, by implication, that there will be a shared future. Because Madrid is Spain's capital, the objects in that city's museums are expected to be construed as belonging to, and in some measure representing, every Spaniard. On the other hand, there are also treasures belonging to every Spaniard that are housed in state museums located outside of Madrid. They are, even if primarily representative of a specific region, the property of the state and belong not to that region alone, but to the nation as a whole. Despite the redistribution of power to the regions, the apparatus of the state museums, although discussed often and supported differently by the major parties, was never dismantled. In the end they persist precisely because they are understood to be one of the strategic counterbalances to entropy and to the dissolution of consensual values in Spanish society.

Notwithstanding all of the changes, it is still in Madrid, in the galleries of the country's richest museums, that visitors from all over the world find themselves in the presence of a coherent Spain. Even if that coherence is to some extent a fiction, and has never been fully realized in any sustained way, it retains its value as a stabilizing metanarrative in a potentially unstable situation. By 1996 only 50.1 percent of Spaniards identified themselves as being as much Spanish citizens as citizens of their region; indeed, fully 49.9 percent perceived themselves as having their first allegiance to their region. At the same time, 55.7 percent still did think of Spain as their country.[2] Since all museums, Spain's included, are "sites for the *bodying forth* of imaginary histories,"[3] it is the very serious business of the museums of the capital to present visual evidence that there is—in spite of the radical decentralization of the nation and in the face of a precarious sense of Spanish identity—a nation-state worth claiming. The museums must do this even if the threads that bind some of the regions to the center are frayed. And they will continue to be charged with the same mission as long as a majority of Spaniards finds the idea of "Spanishness" worth preserving. The museums of the state are in the business of reminding and convincing those fully identified Spaniards, and those only marginally identified as well, that they have more in common with each other than they do with anyone else (or, at least, that they are better off belonging to the nation as a whole than not belonging to it). They are also responsible for projecting the most stable picture possible of the country to the outside world—a necessary function when it comes to foreign policy issues, to the progress of a united Europe, and to matters related to economic investment.

As far as art is concerned, the Prado is by far the richest of the Spanish state museums. With masterpieces as important and numerous as those in comparable institutions in New York, Berlin, Paris, and Vienna, it is a rare traveler who comes to Madrid and does not at least pay homage to their favorite Velázquez, Rubens, Goya, or Titian paintings. Despite the fact that Spain is no longer an economic, political, or military force of the first rank, the Prado is a firm reminder that Spain retains powerhouse status in the world of culture. It is also one of the few Spanish institutions that contains so many objects of such inestimable value and importance. Spaniards of every region, whether or not they have ever set foot in the museum, are eager to lay claim to its treasures as their own.

Madrid also is home to Spain's internationally acclaimed modern and contemporary art museum, the Reina Sofía (Centro de Arte Reina Sofía), which opened officially in 1988. The Reina Sofía museum became the permanent home of Picasso's *Guernica,* the twentieth century's one masterpiece universally associated with antifascism. Beyond claiming that work for the Spanish people as a whole, the Reina Sofía has committed itself to communicating and enhancing the role of the Spanish people as primary participants in the most important creative movements of the last century. Its job is to underline the point that Spain's modernist artistic patrimony includes seminal contemporary figures, such as Picasso, Dalí, and Miró, that Spain's creative days were not extinguished with the death of Francisco Goya in the nineteenth century. The Reina Sofía, as it evolved during the socialist period, was also intended to expose Spaniards to the broadest range of recent artistic trends, thereby dispelling, for citizens and tourists alike, the seemingly intractable impressions of provincialism attached to this nation, marginalized and isolated from the world for so long.

Physically very near the Prado and the Reina Sofía, the Thyssen-Bornemisza Museum (Museo Thyssen-Bornemisza) opened to great international fanfare. The Thyssen-Bornemisza Museum has filled yawning gaps in the state art collections, making up for time once thought irretrievably lost by Spain's not having collected art seriously during much of the last century and a half. With these three museums, along with those others financed by the state, Spain could honestly boast that, like other culturally influential European nations, it was deeply connected and committed to most of the major art movements that form the corpus of Western art history.

Beyond those three giants, one also finds in Madrid the country's pri-

Medieval galleries of the National Museum of Archaeology (Museo Arqueológico Nacional). Courtesy Servicio Fotográfico, Museo Arqueológico Nacional.

mary archaeology museum. The National Museum of Archaeology (Museo Arqueológico Nacional) is the classic identity-construction institution, crammed with glorious objects from every region of the Iberian Peninsula, all exhibited to relate Spain's official story. This is not a museum that troubled itself throughout the transition to democracy with multiple perspectives or alternate histories. Beginning with pre-Iberian times, its narrative is presented as a unified, linear, and unambiguous march to the present day, all battles and victories leading to the ultimate oneness of Spain. Sculptures, decorative arts, and funerary objects are used to underline the historical construction of the nation-state through all of its explorations, conquests, and reconquests. Throughout the first twenty years of the democracy it was the platform for the telling of the traditional story presented in the traditional way. That the struggle to foster, preserve, and, indeed, create a sense of national identity is a continuing one and that it plays itself out with urgency in the museums of the country as a whole became evident in 1997 in this very museum owing to a highly publicized controversy over *La Dama de Elche,* one of its most renowned icons.

La Dama de Elche. Courtesy Servicio Fotográfico, Museo
Arqueológico Nacional.

La Dama de Elche, certainly the famous work of art in the National
Museum of Archaeology and one of the most celebrated pieces of sculpture in the history of art, has had an unusually politically charged journey
to Madrid. A sublimely beautiful pre-Iberian stone head and torso, the
sculpture is usually considered to be about 2,500 years old although questions do, on rare occasions, arise about its antiquity. It was excavated in the
town of Elche in 1897 and sold to France where it was prominently displayed in the Louvre. While there, it was sorely missed in Spain and efforts
were made in scientific and literary circles to expedite its return, all of
which were short-circuited by the Spanish civil war. But in 1941, during
World War II, Franco was able to bring *La Dama de Elche* home. Once back,

it resided in the Prado until 1971, when it was finally transferred to Madrid's archaeology museum.

This was not, though, a mere cultural exchange. In bringing *La Dama de Elche* back to Spain, Franco took full advantage of the rich symbolism that had grown up around the sculpture to enhance his nationalistic rhetoric. It became especially useful to him in representing the perfect manifestation of the pre-Roman roots of the great Iberian civilizations, an indispensable tool in validating his Spanish fascist ideology. *La Dama de Elche* provided an early opportunity for Franco to enhance his political stature and the stature of Spain with the help of art museums. That opportunity presented itself in 1941 when Marshall Pétain, head of the Vichy government in France, sought a way to appease the ostensibly neutral Franco after he had been denied his territorial ambitions in French Morocco and Gibraltar by Hitler. *La Dama de Elche* became the goodwill gesture that Franco accepted, hoping he could use the recuperation of lost Spanish treasures to mitigate his political humiliation. In fact, *La Dama de Elche* did reenter Spain triumphantly, accompanied by much pomp, ceremony, press coverage, and many crates of other returned Spanish art.[4]

La Dama de Elche took up residence in Madrid without further incident until 1997. At that time the city of Elche, wishing to have the work exhibited in its own archaeological museum for a two-month period during the celebration of the 2,000th anniversary of Elche's founding, petitioned to borrow it. The loan was at first denied by the National Museum of Archaeology, supposedly for conservation reasons, shocking the residents of Elche and many others. Their shock was a direct result of their reading of their democratic rights as guaranteed by the constitution. On the other hand, for those who believe in the need to protect a strong sense of Spanish identity, lending *La Dama de Elche* was seen as a sure way of upsetting the delicate balance so recently established between center and periphery. The latter camp, concerned about the stature of the center, unabashedly expressed its anxieties that Madrid's museums would soon be emptied out as the regions "take home their cultural properties."[5]

It seemed that the periphery had lost this battle, until later in the same year the National Museum of Archaeology's decision was overridden by the state. Parliament, unexpectedly sympathetic to the demands of Elche, reversed the museum's decision, insisting on the rights of the locality to exhibit its patrimony in order to enhance its sense of local identity. Then, oddly, Parliament reversed itself, using the conservation reports as reasons for refusing the loan. But they were not able to do this before the exhibition catalog was published announcing the appearance of *La Dama de Elche* in the Elche Archaeological Museum (Museo Arqueológic de Elche).

It will never be known whether concern for the sculpture's conservation was the determining factor in this case or whether it was the politics of centralism versus localism. It can, however, be safely inferred that such controversies will not be eliminated as long as Spain is made up of increasingly self-confident and aggressive regionalisms. The Elche affair was one unsettling reminder that the state and the museums of the state tread on unsteady ground when they involve themselves in questions relating to the disposition of works of art with historical and symbolical meanings. It is also a strong reminder that Spain's citizens believe it is their right and duty to defend their political positions, with art as their weaponry.

Other state museums in Madrid, such as the Museum of the Americas (Museo de América), originally created in 1941 but not opened until the mid-1990s when the Spanish government had begun in earnest to reestablish close relationships with the Americas, do try hard to present Spain's colonial history from a nuanced point of view. Displayed in the galleries in the most beguiling manner are objects of silver and gold from the former Spanish colonies that attest both to the artistry of the conquered peoples and Spain's wealth as a result of its extreme exploitation of those civilizations, a recreation of the original "cabinets of curiosities" that reveals the distinct worldview of the colonizers themselves while beautifully contrived didactics explore the Spanish assumptions about Spanish "civilization" and its encounter with America's native peoples. However, when trying to present more than one perspective, particularly when it would diverge too much from the state's, even this museum still occasionally falls short. For example, one soon realizes, in the rooms dedicated to religion, how deeply the old ways are entrenched. While purporting to have a "liberal" view of the indigenous religions, the museum never even begins to deal with Spain's attempt to eradicate them and to impose Catholicism as the region of "New Spain." The state's most profound historical assumptions are therefore never essentially examined.

Outside Madrid the state fully owns and operates twenty-three other museums, including the Museum of Ceramics and the Sumptuary Arts (Museo Nacional de Cerámica y de las Artes Suntuarias) in Valencia, the Sephardic Museum (Museo Sefardí) in Toledo, the Museum of Roman Art (Museo Nacional de Arte Romano) in Mérida, the Museum of the Caves of Altamira (Museo de las Cuevas de Altamira) in Altamira, the Museum of Polychromatic Sculpture (El Museo Nacional de Escultura de Valladolid) in Valladolid, and the Museum of Pilgrimages (Museo de las Peregrinaciones) in Santiago de Compostela. The state also partially controls (owns the contents and the buildings while granting management to the regions) eighty-one more museums. Furthermore, it retains the ownership of the contents of eighty-eight other museums, having relinquished their actual management to more appropriate ministries or governmental bodies. And finally, it has twenty-five museums related to it by still different agreements. Set as counterweights to the many hundreds of museums controlled by regional, provincial, and municipal governments, these 215 state-associated museums are interleaved throughout much of the society. They appear to be ubiquitous, if unequally weighted, links in the chain of the general narrative of Spain as nation-state. They are vehicles for telling the center's side of the story, a side that, since the democracy has been established, is regularly beset by forces successfully relating their own tales of cultural difference while manifesting little or no concern for the narrative of a nation indivisible.[6]

Since the defining tension in Spanish postmodern democratic life is a product of the constantly shifting balance between the center and the periphery, it should come as no surprise to witness that tension mirrored in the cultural policies of the two principal political parties: the Socialist Party (Partido Socialista Obrero de España), which ran Spain for fifteen years (1981–1996), and the Conservative Party (Partido Popular), which won national elections in 1996. The split between major parties in Spain is not like the harsh one in the United States, where liberals believe that culture should be at least partially supported by the government and conservatives contend that it should stand on its own. In Spain, as in much of Europe, it is thought that the government should directly finance culture, and that the fruits of that funding should be available to all. Although there is a growing desire on the part of Spanish conservatives to encourage private support of culture, they have not considered abandoning the public responsibility for it: the politics of Spanish culture are not about whether, but rather about which elements and to what degree, the government should support the arts. When the socialists were in power, there was, not surprisingly, a very strong flow of direct government financial support for the immense patrimony. At the beginning of their rule there was almost no tax relief to support private giving to the arts. By the end, though, there had been significant acceptance, even among many socialists, of a changed legal and political climate that encouraged private funding. Nevertheless, the most important socialist distinction was its prideful advancement and encouragement of the autonomous regions to explore, produce, and then publicly present their own cultural heritage. Already in the air when Franco died, this regionalism picked up considerable steam once the socialists took control in 1981, coinciding with the transition to democracy and with the regions' assumption of previously unheard of responsibilities for managing their own lives.

Conservatives were concerned that the socialists spent fifteen years reinforcing the cultures of the margins to the point that they threatened the country's equilibrium and the ideal of Spanish unity. They feared that an ideology of "parts" had gained in prestige over the ideology of "the whole." Conservative Party members worried, for example, when the socialists began to talk publicly of turning over the management of some of the national museums outside Madrid to the regions in which they were located. Andrés Carretero, head of the state museums in the socialist Ministry of Culture in 1994, defended this strategy, convinced that material in certain museums would be better suited to local control.[7] For example, as Carretero explained, the Socialist Party did not recognize the value of maintaining a museum of the Spanish Roman heritage in Mérida, a museum of Valencian ceramics, or a museum of the Jewish heritage in Toledo. He explained that members of the party believed that the art and artifacts in those museums were regional manifestations, ultimately, and a burden on the state.[8] By early 1995 this type of rhetoric—supporting the notion of cultural divestment by the state—had subsided somewhat as it became clear that a vocal public was taking sides with the conservatives on this issue. In 1996 the conservatives took power. And none of the museums mentioned above ever lost their national status.

The extent to which the Conservative Party differs from the Socialist Party in its policies was made unambiguous to me in an interview I had on May 17, 1995, with Miguel Angel Cortés, then a delegate to Parliament, Conservative Party member, and spokesman for culture, (and one year later, after the conservatives won the national elections, secretary of state for culture). Cortés pointed to Catalonia as a prime example of the cultural and political debate in Spain simmering between the nation and the regions. To enhance its separate identity, Catalonia was trying to recapture items of cultural interest held in state museums and house them regionally. He explained that the Catalonians were demanding that "their share" of materials relating to the Spanish civil war be placed in archives in Barcelona. The archives, located in a regional library in Salamanca, have always made available information on the war to scholars for research purposes. When, in 1995, Catalonia made this demand, most of the general public (outside Catalonia) reacted negatively, insisting that Salamanca should never let the archives go because the material belonged to the nation as a whole. Catalonia's demand was not met. Cortés felt this demand, and others of its kind, were extremely destructive to Spain's identity.

Early in the Conservative Party's reign, money was designated for removing the archives—not to Catalonia, but rather to a separate state archive of the civil war in Salamanca. Cortés hoped that, by taking the material from any one region and putting it under the jurisdiction of the state, the debate would end. Philosophically, the "differentiating factor" between the conservatives and the socialists, he explained, can be summarized in the Salamanca archive situation: conservatives believe in the primacy of Spain as a shared community where the socialists do not. Cortés stressed that this did not mean that his party denied the value of the essential pluralism of Spain. Rather, he feared that pluralism, if pushed too far, could lead to Spain's fragmentation. As Cortés said at that time and on numerous other occasions: "Either Spain is all or it is nothing."

Cortés also spoke of his interpretation of the laws requiring that objects comprising Spain's national patrimony be held together forever. Royal treasures could not, legally, be turned over to the regions. Management might, he believed, be turned over but never the ownership of the property. Transferring the control of national museums to the regions was ultimately illegal and unconstitutional. Indeed, he insisted, one could never transfer the ownership of Velázquez's *Las Meninas* (or any other of the Prado's treasures) to the autonomous regions. His fears were, as it happens, not entirely far-fetched, since it was reported to me by Manuela Mena, then vice-director of the Prado, that Catalonia had, before the Salamanca archives incident, once requested its "share" of the Velázquez collection.

When I asked Cortés, before the general elections, what the conservatives would do should there be a change in government, he said that they would, more than the socialists had ever done, aid those museums that nurtured the so-called "Spanishness" of Spain. There would be less interest in subsidizing either internationalism for its own sake or in elevating local cultural identity at the expense of the whole. Furthermore, he indicated that the Conservative Party was interested in encouraging increased tax relief for donations to museums. The Conservative Party, he said, would be especially helpful to those museums that contain royal, ecclesiastical, and provincial collections developed from the appropriation of church properties in the nineteenth century. Above all, the conservatives wanted to disseminate a sense of shared historical culture. Cortés expressed fear that the public could no longer understand Velázquez, "the most accessible of Spanish painters"—and that this had to be remedied. His party, he went on, was less interested in contemporary or radical art of any kind than the socialists had been. And they were convinced that in the socialist years money used to promote "spectacular" events had been spent at the cost of neglecting the more serious infrastructural needs of museums, libraries, and archives.

Cortes also wondered why none of the socialists had thought to combine programs and policies between the ministries of education and culture. In fact, within months of assuming power the Conservative Party actually joined those two ministries. Although combining the ministries reminded many liberal Spaniards that Franco had also envisioned education and culture as possessing a single mission, the Conservative Party appears to have made the two ministries one without extremist messages or overtones. Rather, the move provided a means to increase the budget for traditional culture, exactly as promised. It allowed for the agglomeration of funds in the budget to save crumbling cathedrals and better protect

the royal patrimony. Work on the Museum of the Caves of Altamira pro-
gressed rapidly, and funds were put into the Romantic Museum (Museo
Romántico), the Escorial (El Escorial), the Lázaro Galdiano Museum
(Museo Lázaro Galdiano), and other long-neglected institutions. The
Socialist Party had linked the idea of "Spanishness" with the nurturing of
a contemporary internationalist identity. Now, the Conservative Party was
determined to spend every effort and an enormous amount of money
reinforcing the Spaniards' sense of historical identity and their connectedness to the idea of "Spain." The conservatives were fully prepared to
accomplish this through museums and other cultural and educational
institutions. And they were prepared to export that idea as passionately as
the socialists had imported international cultural trends.

Chapter 1 concentrates on the power triangle in Madrid of the Prado,
Reina Sofía, and the Thyssen-Bornemisza museums. These, the most visible of the Spanish state museums have come to epitomize the successes
and failures, strengths and weaknesses, idealism and cynicism, vision and
blindness of the politicians who grant them existence. They endured the
most public struggles to define and present a positive picture of the Spanish patrimony in this country's post-Franco era. And, these three museums
were microcosms of the paradoxes of the center-periphery relationship in
the first two decades of the democracy. Hence, the focus on them in the
opening of the book. Chapter 2 is dedicated to the Sephardic Museum in
Toledo as a special case showing how progressive national values were formulated in a state museum located outside of Madrid. Chapter 3 is dedicated to the museums of the formerly powerful military and religious
cultures, which no longer control the national narrative but cannot be forgotten for their historical contributions to it. The last chapter in part one
relates the stories of two of Spain's most influential art foundations. Both are
based in Madrid and both have contributed to opening and modernizing the
environment of Spain by means of their museum and museum-related activities. One represents the purely philanthropic impulse and the other the

entrepreneurial impulse. The case studies in part one demonstrate that the center is, indeed, no longer insidious or repressive, but, over the twenty years of the transition and consolidation of democracy provided varied and multifaceted responses to the ongoing and complex needs for the representation of Spanishness through the arts.

1

1 INSIDE MADRID

THE PRADO

Founded in 1819 under the reign of Carlos III, the Prado is at times referred to in Spain as "The Magnificent Invalid." The building, the Villanueva Palace, is named for its architect, Juan Villanueva. It is often considered the best example of neoclassical architecture in Europe. The Prado houses thousands of works, including, not surprisingly, marvelous Spanish paintings, but also superlative examples of the Italian, Dutch, French, and German masters, along with lesser-known ancient sculpture in its galleries. Its art has been collected by some of the keenest curatorial minds in European history. The Prado deserves to be called magnificent, as it is a treasure trove of incalculable value.

Many talented and passionate artists have influenced the Prado's collections. Velázquez not only served as royal painter but also as museum curator for Philip IV and was charged with traveling to Italy to seek out and purchase the finest art of his day. Others who have worked at the court included Rubens, Tiepolo, and Goya, who indelibly stamped the

Grand Gallery of the Prado (Museo Nacional del Prado). Courtesy Manuela
Mena.

museum with their own values and personalities. For over 175 years the
Prado's role has been to transmit its aggregate sensibility to a general
audience. But during the last quarter of the twentieth century there has
been much lament over the Prado's inability to do so. The consensus was
that, owing to neglect during the socialist period, the national museum's
ability to transmit that artistic sensibility to today's audiences was badly
impaired and in need of serious attention.[1]

The creation of a democratic society is a philosophical as well as a
political act. It involves subjectivity, personal and collective agendas, and
constant shifts of power. Museums become weapons in these struggles as
disparate factions struggle to create their own version of society. In that
process, some win and others lose. The Prado was a loser during the
1980s and 1990s when the Spanish democracy was in formation because
its essential mission was not interpreted as being consistent with the prevailing agenda. Long a domain of educated art lovers, the Prado presented
dual problems for the governing socialists. It became uncomfortably
apparent to them that the country's most prominent cultural institution
represented the old centralism and was inextricably bound up with an

elitism against which they were ideologically opposed. They had no idea how to democratize and, at the same time, decentralize the Prado. It seems they were daunted by an institution aptly characterized by Philippe de Montebello, director of New York's Metropolitan Museum of Art, when he talked about its "two natures which are in great measure irreconcilable: it is a democratic institution at the service of the aristocratic hauteur of the artistic experience."[2]

Accepting Montebello's observation, José Luis Alvarez Alvarez, former mayor of Madrid and essayist on legal aspects of museums, has argued convincingly that the Prado's duality could have been reconciled by conceding that modern national museums shoulder a double responsibility: the democratic one being educational and the traditional one being to conserve for all time the aristocratic taste that first formed the collection. To fulfill that responsibility, he writes, these two opposite functions must be brought into line. Then they must be adapted in a way that is both vital and embracing of the larger society, while still protecting the contemplative nature of the galleries.[3] But, as anyone could observe who visited the Prado during the twenty years that followed the demise of the dictatorship, this was not undertaken with any degree of commitment.

Surface gestures were certainly made. The Prado added air conditioning and repainted and relit the galleries. A fine restoration facility was built. Halfhearted reinstallations of the permanent collection were made. It would be unfair not to recognize that the museum was nowhere near as dark or uninviting a place during the 1990s as it was during the 1970s. But aside from those minimal concessions, the greater task of communicating broad dimensions of cultural meaning to a diverse, increasingly art-ignorant public was relegated to other state museums. The Prado, during the first two decades after Franco's death, was not considered politically fertile enough to go beyond its old, supposedly discredited meanings. It was simply not allowed to enter the new era with vigor and relevance.[4]

In the early years of Spain's democracy the socialists called for as pervasive as possible a recasting of the old image of the domineering power of the center in order to encourage a more engaged, more empowered citizenry. When it came to expressing the new, more benign centralism in a museum setting, it was perceived as easier and more politically wise to invent a goodly number of new museums than to reinvent the oldest one of all. To the socialists, the Prado must have been a reminder of the drab

Franco values, and to invest major resources into it would seem to have gone against the grain of the shining, hip, 1980s Spanish identity they were so vividly constructing. Thus they dedicated their minds, money, and time to developing what were determined to be more appropriate projects. They never developed a complete and viable plan, taking into account architecture, art, and programming, that would assure the Prado's future as one of the principal democratizing institutions.

Most strikingly, the Prado completely failed when it came to education and public outreach—the best means of communicating values to the "nonelite." Madrid newspapers frequently railed about the need for cloakrooms, for enlarged bookstores and restaurants, and for auditoriums and conference rooms in the Prado to make it an accessible institution. More fundamentally, though, visitors who entered the Prado, even in the 1990s, were not offered anything as a means of orientation to the collection to grasp its greatness. No proper information desk provided a sense of what is in the museum, where certain works of art are located, or how the museum was organized. Visitors were approached by individuals offering to guide them, but because it was usually unclear whether they actually worked for the museum, such encounters usually generated anxiety rather than welcome and ease. Signs and labels were totally inadequate. In fact, there were hardly any useful extended explanatory labels on the paintings themselves, making it almost impossible to glean anything beyond the most rudimentary information. Thanks to a private support group, Friends of the Prado, a few of the galleries began to be stocked with informational sheets. Throughout the socialist period, however, the majority of visitors left the Prado confused, guilty, and unenlightened—never having received those essential experiences one has come to expect from a museum, especially a museum with one of the world's finest collections.

That great works of art should "speak for themselves" has worn itself out as a defense for the lack of a good museum education program. With art education in a general decline, museums have come to be essential educational institutions. A number of other museums in Spain initiated increasingly sophisticated education programs by 1986. And while other museums began to let their audiences in on the "secrets" of their paintings, the Prado left them mute for the uninitiated. This neglect of the nonscholarly public was irresponsible, unfair, arrogant, and, in the end, oddly elitist for a socialist government. It is no wonder that the Prado's

Spanish attendance declined in the first twenty years of the democracy—only 40 percent of the audience in the last year of socialist power was Spanish.[5]

The Prado never received enough financial support from the government—neither during Franco's years nor throughout the socialist period. It probably functioned with the smallest permanent curatorial and education departments of any major museum in the West, barely able to perform its most elementary duties. National museums in Great Britain, Germany, Mexico, Canada, New Zealand, and Australia, all smaller in size, have larger staffs. Where the Metropolitan Museum of Art has at least one hundred curators on staff and the Louvre has seventy, the Prado never had more than five full-time curators during those first twenty years of the democracy. Instead it relied heavily on contract curators to work on temporary exhibitions and research projects. The socialist bureaucracy repeatedly undermined all modest attempts to expand and modernize the Prado's activities.

During 1993 and 1994, the art world was scandalized as it became public knowledge that the physical plant at the Prado was being terribly neglected. The roof was leaking perilously close to masterpieces, including Velázquez's *Las Meninas,* and no one seemed able to get the situation under control. Much of this was because of impotent directors vulnerable to dismissal for real and imagined political reasons. It is no accident that between 1991 and 1996 the Prado had five directors, and morale in the institution was at a nadir.[6] How could any sustainable vision be implemented by a director with so insecure a tenure, which could end due to political whim, no matter how distinguished his or her record? Directors continually expressed concern about shortages of space, inability to hire qualified staff, constant and inappropriate governmental intervention, and insufficient financial support. His ability to affect the infrastructure having shrunk to almost nothing, the last socialist-appointed director, José María Luzón Nogué, seemed to confine his complaints to his concern over the lack of a cloakroom in the entry of the museum.

No director has been able to deal effectively with the conundrum of the so-called *Prado disperso* (dispersed Prado). There are at least 3,500 paintings owned by the Prado that are spread throughout museums in the autonomic regions on permanent loan, either for exhibition or for storage. Although there is supposed to be a collection's management system in place, in reality the location and condition of the works of art has often been unclear and unverifiable. A number of them (around 20 percent of the total cache of objects that were transferred to the Prado since 1819) have been lost or destroyed; some just cannot be accounted for. Furthermore, the loan policy from the Prado to the participating museums has never been a rational one. Manuela Mena, who as vice-director of the Prado during the final socialist years seemed to understand the policy better than anyone else at the time, believed that some loans, such as those to the Fine Arts Museum of Asturias (Museo de Bellas Artes de Asturias) in Asturias and the Museum of Fine Arts (Museo de Bellas Artes) in Valencia, were put to good use, but that most were not. She indicated that a museum in Seville, for example, actually asked the Prado to take back the works it had received; one in Granada kept approximately forty paintings it had received in storage rather than on display; and, after requesting the loan of some masterpieces, a museum in Barcelona was not satisfied with what it considered the "second tier" paintings that it received and asked for "better" ones. Furthermore, Mena feared that there could be serious danger to the museum's integrity if plans being discussed to put trustees representing the autonomic regions on the board of the Prado were implemented. Such a tactic, she worried, was part of a strategy to allow the regions to make yet additional inroads into the Prado's holdings.[7] Her concerns (valid or not) reveal the depth and breadth of emotion surrounding the issue of the dispersed Prado and underline the requirement that any solution about them must reflect and balance both autonomic and centralist aims.

The key questions, then, with regard to management of the Prado during the first twenty years of the democracy were more complicated than they initially appeared. The socialists might have been confused (or in denial) about the "real" ownership of the collections within the Prado. Some of the autonomies truly believed that they were entitled to claim parts of that patrimony. And, if they were to get those parts what would that mean? Would those autonomic regions then be further encouraged to see themselves as mininations? One begins to see the nuances and problems that emerge when attempting to deal with the Prado in a holistic manner: it rapidly becomes clear how much the museum functions as a metaphor for the central issues around the "wholeness" of Spain itself.

By the end of the socialist period, virtually shamed into dealing with the Prado, an international group of advisers convened to discuss critical issues and to look for an architect for the desperately needed expansion.

The search, not surprisingly, failed. It will always be evident, because so little was done on their watch to improve it, that the Prado was never a socialist priority, nor was a wide-ranging vision created that could bring it into the twenty-first century so that it could positively affect the identity construction of the emerging citizenry. The fundamental steps of developing a long-range plan, acquiring an adequate curatorial staff, training for such a staff, shaping an education and outreach program, providing reasonable visitor services, developing a more modern approach to the installation of artworks, and finding a positive approach to the *Prado disperso* congruent with Spain's centralist needs *and* its now less-centered political life were simply not taken. As a result the Prado, even with all of its great paintings, did not begin to approach the functional reality of today's national museums in other parts of the world.

Excuses made during the socialist years always boiled down to the argument that there was no money available to properly care for the Prado. But a look at state-funded museum activities other than those for the Prado reveals that insufficient political will, not insufficient funds, within the Ministry of Culture was the problem. The ministry repeatedly supported the contemporary over the traditional as the preferred path to the creation of the "new Spaniard," a person open to and engaged with the world. The Socialist Party was more interested in formulating a "with-it" image of Spain by creating institutions than in reformulating the Prado so that it could fit into their agenda. And so, the government made generous provisions for its spectacular new national modern and contemporary art museum, the Reina Sofía, and for the old master museum, the Thyssen-Bornemisza Museum, each created in the party's own image.

Not including the enormous cost of renovating the old hospital that would become its home, the Reina Sofía was to receive four times the annual budget of the Prado and was given a substantially larger professional staff. These budgetary decisions were rationalized by the argument that the costs for the Reina Sofía represented the necessary expenses of setting up the operation of the museum. Nevertheless, it was always apparent that the budget for the Reina Sofía was inequitable, and the distribution of resources could have been much more balanced. After the Reina Sofía was in operation, the building of the Thyssen-Bornemisza Museum further drained funds *and* space from the Prado. Over $300 million were spent to acquire the Thyssen-Bornemisza Collection and many more millions to renovate the Villahermosa, the palace across the square from the Prado that (adding insult to injury) had been promised for Prado expansion. The Prado was clearly a cultural stepchild during the consolidation of Spain's democracy, its budget often frozen during the socialist reign. It was the loser in a political gamble that the mood of the people would favor new and contemporary institutions over a rethought and reborn Prado.

Unsurprisingly, the Prado became one of the rallying cries of the Conservative Party when it sought to discredit socialist achievements. Elected in 1996 the conservatives began at once to involve themselves with the museum: with what it represented and what it might become if it were reconsidered. They regarded the museum, with all of the aristocratic characteristics that had been spurned by the socialists as irrelevant and as the potential embodiment of their own opposing democratic political philosophy.[8] But the Conservative Party's task in preparing the Prado for the twenty-first century was formidable due to so many years of neglect. Still, for the first time there was hope that the Prado would finally gain some of the budget and independence of political interference it needed in order to properly function.

Claiming it as the symbol of its own values and ideology, the Conservative Party took immediate steps to strengthen the Prado. Changes in the laws were instituted guaranteeing that its director appointee, Fernando Checa (and his successors) would have more job security, and that he would report to a board of trustees, not to politicians.[9] Checa, a highly respected art historian who had worked in recent years as an influential exhibition curator, inspired hope in the new government that he would be able to understand and promote the values of the museum as long as he was permitted to do his job without political interference. So as to make that more likely, the Conservative Party introduced a modern management structure, one which separates the museum's business and art leadership responsibilities. In effect, they decided to continue the successful experiment initiated at the Thyssen-Bornemisza Museum (described below). They also increased the number of curators, restructured the professional staff for efficiency, and promised more training of professionals and increased resources. Promises were made to acquire more office space and for future gallery expansion in an adjacent cloister—as well as in the palace long occupied by the Army Museum (Museo del Ejército).

By the end of 1996 the Prado did acquire, at no cost to its own budget, over 15,000 square feet of desperately needed office space, clearing exhibition space in the Villanueva for works that had been in storage to be seen by the general public. In 1997 the new director had already submitted a thoroughly revised plan to bring the Prado into the twenty-first century as a healthy institution. The work on the roof had begun. By the end of 1998 Rafael Moneo, Spain's most renowned architect, was awarded the commission for the Prado's renovation and expansion, beginning with the incorporation of the seventeenth-century cloister. Restoration has started throughout the institution. Ultimately, the Palacio del Buen Retiro (home to the Army Museum) will be incorporated into the expansion. Hopes were running high by the end of the century that the recovery of the ailing institution was now a distinct possibility. With the rejection of the Socialist Party, the time was right for the Prado to reclaim its power symbolic of the center: to bring together its aristocratic and democratic qualities. Still, in order to be successful the Conservative Party would have to find a way that acknowledged Spain is not as it was when unity could be presumed as the prevailing national myth. At the same time it is now widely accepted that the country does need a national museum of which it can be proud and that operates with contemporary "best museum practices." The Prado, both in its remodeling and its policies toward the *Prado disperso* can be a vessel for meaning in today's Spain if it stays the course with its ambitious plans for the future.

THE REINA SOFÍA

The socialist government, having turned its back on Spain's regressive past and, by extension, on the Prado, looked toward an optimistic future in Europe and the world. The Reina Sofía (Museo Nacional Centro de Arte Reina Sofía), the second national museum in Madrid's cultural triangle, offers one dramatic example of the Socialist Party strategy to use modern and contemporary art to demonstrate Spain's participation in an international dialogue. Flashy, huge, and definitely trendy, the Reina Sofía has attracted millions of visitors after opening on May 27, 1988, under the patronage of the popular Queen Sofía. With a dynamic cycle of German, Italian, and American exhibitions to its credit, the Reina Sofía rapidly succeeded in putting Spain on the contemporary museum circuit, taking its place as a ranked player in the "art scene" and signaling the openness of Spain's reborn society. Nevertheless, for all of the activ-

The Reina Sofía (Museo Nacional Centro de Arte Reina Sofía). Courtesy Museo
Nacional Centro de Arte Reina Sofía.

ity, the Reina Sofía became, for a while, a problem within the most elite
group of Spain's state-run museums. There were some who saw its very
creation as a political indulgence, its operations marred by governmental
caprice, its budget exorbitant, and its mission incoherent. But it began
with great optimism.

The Reina Sofía was initially envisioned as a total rejection of Francoist
values, through art, and was meant to be "emblematic of Spain's integration in the modern era."[10] An outgrowth of the Spanish Museum of Contemporary Art (Museo Español de Arte Contemporáneo) situated in the
outskirts of Madrid in a nondescript building, the Reina Sofía was conceived to be located in one of Madrid's oldest and most lively in-town
neighborhoods, and to occupy the former General Hospital (Hospital
General)—one of the capital's largest and most venerable landmark
buildings. A well-know architect, Antonio Fernández Alba, was commissioned in 1980 to restore the General Hospital building and convert it for
use as a major exhibition center. He completed his work and the center
opened in 1986. Alba succeeded in balancing the historicity and the

poetry of the building with its future purpose (in combination with the new landscaping and restoration of the grand inner courtyard) and the building made a great impact on Spanish society. The Reina Sofía was intended to be the flagship institution representing the convergence of Spanish and international artistic creativity. It was to be a site for activity generated by the world's great modern art hubs, offering both original exhibitions and joint projects. The Reina Sofía's ambitious mission was to offer a vision of twentieth-century art from a Spanish perspective while simultaneously covering the whole spectrum of modern art. The museum was projected as an important way of compensating for those decades of isolation during the Franco era. It was expressly articulated that the Reina Sofía should not be oriented from a local perspective nor be parochial but rather should allow Spaniards to catch the prevailing winds of contemporary creativity.

The early years for the Reina Sofía were extraordinary. From 1986 through 1988, under the inspired leadership of Carmen Giménez, director of exhibitions, more than thirty shows were organized, which wholly realized the original mission. A balance was achieved between the national and the international. Major Spanish artists who had not received exposure in Spain, while being recognized the world over, finally were given their due in their native country. Joan Miró, Julio González, the artists of the renowned 1937 Spanish Pavilion in Paris, and, of course, Pablo Picasso were given major exhibitions and introduced, often for the first time, to their fellow citizens. Visitors were exposed to contemporary and international postwar artists, including Jasper Johns, Carl André, and Christian Boltanski. Several contemporary collections, like those belonging to Count Panza di Biumo and Patsy and Raymond Nasher, were also shown. The Ministry of Culture translated and made widely available numerous museum catalogs and critical texts from international exhibitions that never made it to Spain to appease the hunger for word of the new. Finally, in order to give the Reina Sofía more prestige, it was officially declared a museum rather than a "center" by Royal Decree 535/88 on May 27, 1988. Carmen Giménez is universally credited with having bridged the gap between isolation and engagement in the artistic affairs of Spain.

The elevation from a center or "kunsthalle" (an art gallery for temporary exhibitions) to museum was a clear indication of the hopes the government had for the impact of the Reina Sofía on Spanish society. The socialist government had wagered that the long-repressed craving for participation in the larger world would find an immediate response in those Spaniards who had an interest in the global debates about creativity and its ramifications for a dynamic public. The government considered it important to build on the new museum's popularity and provide an arts forum with even more serious intent than a center for exhibitions could fulfill. As a museum the Reina Sofía would now be required to continue enhancing the permanent collections while beginning to provide the kinds of services expected of a modern museum. These services include preservation, restoration, scholarly research, and public education programs.

In anticipation of these added expectations the museum hired architects Antonio Vázquez de Castro and José L. Iñiquez de Ozoño. Their most obvious contribution was a bank of three elevators on the outside of the building. These elevators give access not only to upper floors but also allow views, linking ancient and modern in a single panorama, of the surrounding city in the tradition of *miradores* so prevalent in Old Spain. These elevators also recall the Pompidou in Paris and inspired the nickname, sometimes affectionate: "Sofidu." Less obvious was the work that architects Vázquez de Castro and Iñiquez de Ozoño did in the behind-the-scenes spaces, transforming an old building into a "smart one." When they were finished the total area of the museum was immense: approximately 500,000 square feet, occupying all six floors of the old hospital had been thoroughly adapted to its changed use.

For reasons never adequately explained, Carmen Giménez was dismissed, and in June 1988 the first director of the museum was appointed. Tomás Llorens, a well-known art historian who had been the founding director of IVAM (Instituto Valenciano Arte Moderno) in Valencia, the country's most brilliantly conceived and managed regional museum, took Giménez's place. Llorens brought the intellectual resources of a highly trained scholar and an experienced museum professional to the operation of the museum. Reiterating the mission of the Reina Sofía, he stated that this twentieth-century art forum would be dedicated to the presentation of international movements but also to the country's own artistic partimony—to local artists relevant to the development of Spanish art and international art throughout the modern and postmodern periods. Hence, the exhibitions of Giacometti, Matisse, Dada, constructivism, and Spanish artists such as the *Equipo Crónica,* along with collector-based exhibitions emanating from the Phillips Collection in

The *Guernica* by Pablo Picasso. Courtesy Museo Nacional Centro de Arte Reina Sofía.

Washington, D.C., and the Beyeler Collection in Switzerland. Llorens also supported the ongoing acquisitions program, the development of a research library, and the creation of a modern collections management infrastructure. Nevertheless, Llorens only served until September 1990 when he, too, was unceremoniously removed from his post.

After Llorens was fired, María de Corral was appointed director. A curious choice, de Corral had no serious scholarly qualifications or public museum experience to speak of. She managed her own commercial art gallery before she had assumed the responsibility of purchasing art for the wealthy, essentially private La Caixa Foundation based in Barcelona. She was therefore well-known to art dealers in Spain and throughout the world. Given a substantial acquisitions budget, de Corral became the sweetheart not just of dealers and artists in the United States and Europe, but of directors on the international museum circuit, largely because of her ability to rent their major, expensive exhibitions. Under de Corral's leadership the museum also secured gifts of Spanish and international artists; key twentieth-century works were requisitioned from the Spanish Museum of Contemporary Art and the Prado; and, most significantly, works by Picasso, Miró, and Dalí were formally transferred to the Reina Sofía. This activity created a corpus of classical modern material upon which the state museum could be built.

During de Corral's tenure, the one deed that was to have the most ringing repercussions was the decision to move Picasso's *Guernica* from the Prado to the fledgling institution. The original idea to do so had actually been Llorens's, but his insistence on moving the work had caused enormous tension between him and then minister of culture, Jorge Sem-prún. According to Llorens, this was probably the reason for his own removal.[11] With a new minister, Jordi Solé Tura, and the passage of two years, moving the *Guernica* now seemed feasible. The ministerial change of heart owed less to sympathy with the idea of moving the masterpiece than the fact that, after the initial stampede of visitors, it had become painfully apparent that the Reina Sofía would not be able to maintain the attendance levels that would justify its enormous budget. It was clear that the museum was not generating enough excitement. The museum did not possess the great icons that could press the point home of the magnitude of Spain's impact and influence on modern art history. Something needed to be done.

Part of the solution to the attendance problem, though extremely controversial, was to proceed with Llorens's plan for the appropriation of the *Guernica* for the Reina Sofía. To some Spaniards the ministry was "robbing" the Prado of the one true Picasso masterpiece it had in its holdings. There were vociferous discussions about the physical dangers of such a move. To others, it was unethical and even illegal. This faction argued that Picasso had had a relationship with the Prado in his lifetime, even functioning briefly as its honorary director during the civil war. Furthermore, Picasso had made a symbolic token sale of the work to the Prado in order to guarantee that his wishes for its final ownership and display would be honored once Franco's dictatorship had ended. It was housed—self-exiled—at New York's Museum of Modern Art until Franco's death, with the understanding that it would not be returned to Spain until democracy was restored.[12] Nevertheless, it was finally moved, and the transfer sent shock waves throughout Europe and the United States as well. The decision had positive identity ramifications: to keep the masterpiece in the Prado would have seemed to imply that Spain's creative growth had come to an end with the greatness of Picasso. To bring it to the Reina Sofía would have implied the opening of a new chapter of creativity—with the same great Picasso. The transfer took place under the greatest security and without mishap and, as the ministry had hoped, caused an immediate boost in attendance at the Reina Sofía. At the same time, it must be noted, the loss of the *Guernica* did contribute to the Prado's declining visitorship.

There can be no denying that during de Corral's tumultuous years the Reina Sofía's collections grew. The substantial body of work that was transferred from the former Spanish Museum of Contemporary Art included material that had been acquired over the past eighty years. Including material from other government and private sources, there were 8,900 pieces, mostly Spanish, some quite significant, plus a few non-Spanish pieces of importance accessioned after Franco's death. Contemporary sculptures by the Spanish Basques Eduardo Chillida and Jorge Oteiza and paintings by Catalan Antoní Tapies were acquired, and demonstrated a strong Spanish presence in the international art world. At the same time, through de Corral's term, the Reina Sofía became perhaps too closely associated with conceptual and abstract art. De Corral's taste was in complete synchronicity with the fashion of the moment and overpowered any possible oppositional trends. She was especially resistant to highlighting Spanish contemporary realism, an integral element of the Spanish aesthetic. This brought her to the point of alienating a major segment of the Spanish art world when she tried to resist giving a retrospective exhibition to Antonio Lopez, Spain's premier realist painter.

The balance of the Reina Sofía was finally thought to have completely tipped in favor of fashion and trendiness when it began to look as if the contemporary artists promoted by the most powerful 1980s art dealers dominated the best spaces in the museum. For example, Richard Serra, Mario Merz, Ellsworth Kelly, Julian Schnabel, Jannis Kounellis, Anish Kapoor, Dan Flavin, and Bruce Nauman received what many thought to be disproportionate gallery allotment. It was believed by many that fine Spanish artists who were not key figures in the current international art market were completely ignored. Visitors to the Reina Sofía in those days could only shake their heads in wonder at the relatively low profile given to those Spanish contemporary artists, who were, paradoxically, being lauded in Europe and America. Without a doubt de Corral appeared to be unwilling to move away from what seemed to many to be an internationally promoted artistic hegemony at a time when Spain needed to switch over to a more open, more permeable and locally responsive aesthetic environment in order to better represent its own emerging reality.

Perhaps because of a fear of a recurrence of *españolización,* the inwardness imposed on culture by Franco, the exhibitions at the Reina Sofía had begun to lean too heavily on this internationalization. Under de Corral the leadership of the museum had missed a subtle but important moment not only in the consolidation of democracy but in the history of art itself. After over twenty years of a diet rich in art as defined by the international culture, power, and business structures, contemporary art in Spain was now ready to be presented and promoted as an active agent in that discourse, and many believed that the Reina Sofía should assist in this. The perception was growing that de Corral was short shrifting the art of her own country at the very moment when both art historical and museological theory and practice were beginning to favor the deconstruction of the outworn linearity of the monolithic contemporary narrative that had reigned for so long.

The Reina Sofía was becoming a bland experience for both Spanish and foreign visitor. The Spanish accent was missing. As a machine of cultural identity, there was simply no imaginative integration and contextualization of the country as a whole with the world. Local had lost out entirely to global. The Reina Sofía had become obsessed with, and some might say submissive to, dominant market judgments. Paradoxically, it was seen as an institution depleting or discouraging Spain's creative potential, not as a unique partner in the evolving history of its art. After a few years under de Corral's "followership" the Reina Sofía had begun to resemble a client state of the international museum circuit. Established in the hopes of nurturing Spanish cultural identity, it was beginning to fail in that regard. Spanish citizens had reached the point of seeing themselves as thoroughly modern and thoroughly international. Ironically, because of this change, they no longer believed that *all* of their values and ideals needed to be universal or international. With the confidence of a country connected to the larger world, they now wanted their national museum to encourage and reflect their distinctive creativity and their own independent, sometimes anarchic, ways of making and judging art. They also wished their national museum of modern and contemporary art to reflect their special and eccentric relationship to the many ideas of centeredness that marked democratic Spain. The center could be New York; it could be Madrid; but it might also be Barcelona or Oviedo or Santiago de Compostela or Bilbao. Subtly, it had become a mark of the provincial rather than of the cosmopolitan personality to need to turn so frequently to those outside cultural arbiters. The Reina Sofía had missed that moment. And, now, many museum goers were asserting that Spaniards were able to be in charge of their own artistic destinies. They did not need to be so deferential anymore.

As a result of de Corral's failure to comprehend this important shift in Spanish attitudes, she was fired in September 1994 by the Socialist Party that had hired her. To the party's credit it recognized the nature of the failure of her leadership. For José Guirao, her successor, Spain's national museum was a special type of institution that needed to better showcase the country's artistic contributions in a dramatic and impressive way. The Reina Sofía, he said in a long conversation we had after he took office in 1994, needed to make clear to everyone that Spain is a country with special qualities. Unlike France, he pointed out, "Spain produces monsters of creativity—Goya, Velázquez, El Greco—and, in the modern day, Picasso, Miró, Dalí."[13] He believed that nothing about the previous exhibition program had communicated the major creative force that Spain was when at its best. Guirao wanted to highlight the best works of younger Spanish artists as well as the more classic contemporaries and to promote artists from the regions. Furthermore, Guirao was planning to remedy the relative neglect of Spanish realists by purchasing their work for the permanent collection whenever possible. He would encourage the collecting of Spanish photography, almost completely unacknowledged as an artform yet, and quickly named a curator with that sole responsibility. Guirao then went on to talk about shows that the Reina Sofía could originate to enhance the sense of the Spanish contribution to world art. For example, he asked, "there have been many exhibitions about Spaniards influenced by going abroad, but why not have one of artists who came here and were 'contaminated' by Spain?"

Guirao was, even during his first year, universally acclaimed for his refocusing of the museum and for balancing Spain's cultural identities, making the museum a confident participant in the world of modern and contemporary art. For all his need to emphasize the "Spanishness" of the Reina Sofía, Guirao carefully maintained a balance of local and global engagement by continuing to present international contemporary art exhibitions. His philosophy could never be called parochial. These exhibitions proved to be as controversial as most contemporary shows might be in any large city and as lively. In January 1997, for example, an exhibition of Jannis Kounellis's work created a society-wide debate about censorship. A live parrot, which had been part of the exhibition, was removed by Guirao when it became apparent that the bird was neither eating or drinking. A huge flap between animal rights people and arts people ensued, and the artist proclaimed the show a disaster because the artist's work had been censored. The museum became a forum for lively debate over values, over the relative importance of art and life, and over the limits of freedom and responsibility. Later in 1997 Guirao teamed up with the Institute of Contemporary Arts in London to put on an exhibition of the American Vija Celmins, an artist whose technically and imaginatively brilliant work is known in some sections of the United States but is relatively unknown in Europe. Also in 1997 Guirao chose to feature the work of Vicente Roja, a Mexican artist of Spanish descent who had abandoned Spain during the civil war. That these artists, and others outside the mainstream, were now on the Reina Sofía's roster was further indication that Guirao wanted to lead Spain's national modern museum in fresh, unexpected directions. He redressed the balance, and localism and globalism gained the energy and the synergy it had been previously losing.

The Reina Sofía, as is the case with most contemporary art museums, is still in the throes of self-definition. Because its mission is to represent the modern and the contemporary, this will remain the case as long as society in Spain keeps changing. One can feel secure, though, in predicting that in the free-wheeling democracy that Spain has become, the Reina Sofía will need to reexamine and redefine itself every few years and that it will grow. In the process, it will fight battles that reflect the country's evolving personality. Wise leaders such as Guirao and the conservative government that (uncharacteristically) retained him long after they assumed power will know that this is not a negative phenomenon, but rather that the intensity and openness of those battles and the redefinitions that result from them will be the markers of the museum's success and relevance. They will also be markers of the openness to debate and dialogue, to contradiction and ambiguity that characterize today's central Spanish government as it accommodates the changing dictates of society through its elected officials.

THE THYSSEN-BORNEMISZA MUSEUM

The Thyssen-Bornemisza Museum is a celebration of Spain's positive sense of its place in today's world through the reclamation of its lost prestige as a significant art collecting nation. The Ministry of Culture, always seeking credit and recognition, proudly noted in a slick report memorializing the opening of the Thyssen-Bornemisza Museum in 1993 that Spain, which found itself on the front page of the *New York Times* after the purchase of the collection, had not been considered so newsworthy since the victory of the Socialist Party in 1981. The fact that this cultural coup attracted prominent coverage by one of the most influential newspapers in the world proved to the party the value of the purchase.[14] The celebration that followed was genuine. It was understood by all that the Spanish government had taken a big risk in committing the funds for this collection and that the gamble had paid off handsomely.

It all began when the Baron Hans Heinrich Thyssen-Bornemisza contracted in 1988 to lease the collection to Spain for nine and a half years, at a cost of $5 million per year. Although there was some concern about the deal, the government proceeded. The Villahermosa, a palace virtually catercorner from the Prado—which had been promised for its own future expansion—was then renovated for the purposes of housing the new "rented" collection. But it was not the mere opening of a museum of leased art that so impressed the *New York Times* and attracted the admiration of the world. Rather it was the decision in 1993 of the baron to actually sell the collection of 775 paintings to Spain for the reasonable price of $350 million. Spain had received this respect because it had beaten out numerous suitors by strategizing wisely and positioning itself to appear to be the most appropriate party to acquire this vast cache. The Thyssen-Bornemisza Collection is widely recognized as one of the finest private collections assembled in the second half of the twentieth century, and its incorporation into Spain's cultural patrimony was recognized as a sign of national vitality and promise. Its acquisition will be recorded as a high-water mark and as a point of pride for Spaniards as it reflects on its cultural achievements.

Whereas the Prado continued to present itself throughout the last years of the twentieth century as an antiquated museum of old-master paintings, the Thyssen-Bornemisza Museum was intended, from its earliest days as a state-run museum, to represent something else entirely. It radiates cool, corporate modernity and efficiency and functions as a virtual advertisement for the new Spain; it heralds the country's full participation in the world of culture in a businesslike way. In fact, the Thyssen-Bornemisza Museum presented a remarkable contrast to the Prado across the street: understaffed in its deteriorating facility and largely out of touch with its public. Much to the dismay of those who love the Prado (and other long-suffering state museums) the Thyssen-Bornemisza Museum opened with sufficient staff, a perfect facility, and the government's commitment to permanently safeguard the identity, unity, and international prestige of the collection. The public loved the Thyssen-Bornemisza

Museum from the first—just as the politicians had hoped they would. Everyone was dumb struck at how efficiently and definitively the government acted to get the immense job done.

The Thyssen-Bornemisza Collection is the product of three generations of active collecting, beginning with the Baron August Thyssen, the grandfather of Baron Heinrich Thyssen-Bornemisza. Baron August Thyssen was a friend of Rodin's and commissioned a number of important pieces of sculpture from him at the end of the nineteenth century. That collecting passion gathered considerable steam under the influence of his son Heinrich, fueled by funds from the iron and steel empire his family had created. Heinrich and his wife, Baroness Margrit Bornemisza de Kaszon, left Germany and settled in Hungary in the early years of the twentieth century, but after the Russian Revolution, moved to Holland, where Baron Hans Heinrich was born in 1921. The family moved again, settling in Lugano, Switzerland, where they bought the Villa Favorita. Enormous energy was put into expanding the collection between the world wars when, tragically, many private collections came on the market. Subsequent to his father's death in 1947, Baron Hans Heinrich became the collector in the family, purchasing what he could from his siblings and continuing to acquire avidly from around the world. The collection, as it took shape under him, seemed in its cohesiveness to have always been destined for public enjoyment. The baron had an illustrious history of making it generously available, either at the Villa Favorita or when he loaned it to numerous museums.

The focus of the Thyssen-Bornemisza Collection is Western art, roughly speaking, from the fourteenth century until the present. It includes paintings from the German pre-Renaissance and Renaissance, Dutch, Italian medieval and Renaissance, English, French, and the occasional Spanish. The present baron made a huge contribution to the collection by acquiring modern masters: he bought impressionist and postimpressionist works along with paintings by the German expressionists, especially those the Nazis had deemed degenerate: Grosz, Beckmann, Heckel, and Kirschner. He purchased pictures from the Russian avant-garde—examples of cubism, futurism, and other such works. He bought postwar English paintings, and most surprisingly, acquired North American nineteenth- and twentieth-century works. This section is especially dear to the baron.[15] More importantly, it fills significant gaps in European museums and has become an essential point of reference for anyone interested in this period, since it is one of the rare collections in Europe that gives an idea of how some influential American painters saw their own century. In sum, the Thyssen-Bornemisza Collection resembles the Norton Simon Museum in Pasadena, California, and in the frequent comparisons of the two collections they are considered of almost the same quality. Even if history will not judge it as being as consistently rigorous as Simon's collection, no one with any knowledge of art could ever doubt the wisdom of having acquired the collection.[16] Although the quality of the works varies, they fill gaps in Spain's notoriously spotty art holdings in English, French, Russian, and American painting and, as a whole, qualify as a coveted collection.[17]

Once the collection outgrew the walls of Baron Hans Heinrich's Villa Favorita, it began traveling. In Spain the modern masters were exhibited in the Spanish National Library (Biblioteca Nacional) and the old masters were shown in the Royal Academy, both in Madrid. When the decision to lease the collection to the Spanish for nine and a half years was made, Spanish architect Rafael Moneo was commissioned to redesign the Villahermosa. He was an astute choice, not only because of his universally acknowledged talent, but also because he possessed the right experience, having recently designed the National Museum of Roman Art (Museo Nacional de Arte Romano) in Mérida and the Davis Museum and Cultural Center at Wellesley College. Since then Moneo was awarded the Pritzker Prize for architecture in 1996. He has received other world-class commissions, including the new Roman Catholic Cathedral in Los Angeles. As dean of Harvard's School of Architecture, Moneo was able to bring the requisite internal and external reputation to the Thyssen-Bornemisza project.

Moneo and a highly skilled team of architects, technicians, and subcontractors proceeded to turn the Villahermosa into a state-of-the-art museum. This mid-eighteenth-century example of domestic architecture, which had already experienced various transformations, most recently into a bank building, would regain, to the greatest extent possible, its original forms. From the start, the goal was to give the impression that it had always been as it would appear in 1992. Any Spaniard or foreigner passing by was to feel that this building was proof that Spain had lovingly shepherded its past, so as to produce a vibrant present. Moneo was thoroughly successful. The exterior of the building is a welcoming invitation to view the collection in a contemplative and serene space. The

The Thyssen-Bornemisza Museum (Museo Thyssen-Bornemisza). Courtesy Fundación Colección Thyssen-Bornemisza.

interior architecture contributes to this intrinsic pleasure without being either distracting or egocentrically involved. It flatters the works of art so gently as to make them glow.

The art glows because of the generous space each work is allotted and the combination of natural and artificial light the building provides. Protected from overexposure to ultraviolet rays by the most sophisticated technology and from changing humidity and temperature by a climate control system that is both efficient and environmentally responsible, they are conserved in the most advanced manner. Looking outside, the visitor is treated to views of the most charming parts of old Madrid. To help in the appreciation of the art, signs are clearly written and color coded. Labels with generous information accompany each painting. Tranquility and information coexist in ways rare in any museum. At the Thyssen-Bornemisza Museum there are always free brochures describing the museum's services; all materials are produced in several languages. A corps of volunteers provides docent and tour services. An effective education program has been developed with the schools, guaranteeing attendance and participation by the nation's children. Library, archive, and reproduction services are up-to-date and accessible. Public relations are superb. The comfort of the visitor is enhanced by a restaurant, a cloak-room, a welcoming and informative reception area, and a good museum shop. A number of temporary, well-publicized exhibitions ranging from the old masters to the modern masters encourage repeat visits. Thus, great crowds of people have come to the Villahermosa to see the perma-nent collection, but also repeatedly return to study the *Golden Age of Dutch Landscape Painting*, a revised view of André Derain, or Baroness Carmen Cervera Thyssen-Bornemisza's own trove of paintings—as a former Miss Spain, she played a special role advocating for her country throughout in all negotiations. One enters the Thyssen-Bornemisza Museum and feels welcomed. One leaves feeling informed.

In its first year 800,000 people came to the Thyssen-Bornemisza Museum. That year, 1992, was an auspicious one for Spain in many ways. The Olympics in Barcelona, the World's Fair in Seville, and the opening of this new museum in Madrid coincided with the half-millennium cele-bration of Spain's epic explorations. A sense of history combined with an optimism about the future filled the air. As they did at all 1992 events in Spain, lines at the Thyssen-Bornemisza Museum formed around the block and the anticipation was immense. Most of the visitors were Span-ish (78 percent), while the bulk of the rest came from Europe and Amer-ica. Attendance naturally went down after the first year and has vacillated between 460,000 and 580,000 annually since then, depending on whether or not there have been temporary exhibitions.[18]

The Thyssen-Bornemisza Collection also offers a new formula for the private management of public funds in state museums. Examination of the financial structure reveals that it would be a mistake to assume that the Thyssen-Bornemisza Museum is, fundamentally, not a government supported museum. But it does differ from other state museums in that there are explicit expectations that this one will attract significant reve-nues to offset the cost of operations. After the state's purchase of the col-lection, ownership of the museum and its collection was transferred to the Thyssen-Bornemisza Collection Foundation, which has been charged with managing the collection and with paying off the full purchase price. Technically, the foundation borrowed the money still due the Thyssens (after the rental fees paid by the state during the period of the loan were deducted and the interest fees for the upcoming payments added) and is responsible for repaying that loan. In actuality the repayment of that loan is guaranteed by the state. In an agreement signed between the foundation and the Spanish Ministry of Culture, it is absolutely clear that while this museum would try to pay its own way in the future, "the Spanish government will remain responsible for covering the budgetary deficits of the Foundation, enabling the Foundation to meet its expenses at all times."[19] The museum's governance is a mix of public and private: the board of trustees consists of eight members of the Spanish government and four appointees named by the Thyssen family. The Thyssen-Bornemisza Museum was thus the first major Spanish museum to create and sustain the much-desired modern corporate image. This accomplishment has been securely and comfortably backed by the Spanish government.

Undoubtedly, the Thyssen-Bornemisza Collection Foundation tries, to the extent that it can, to pay its own way. As its published reports demonstrate, it has undertaken many successful efforts to offset its expenses with income. The foundation charges a substantial admission fee and runs the gift shop and chic café very much for profit. It also engages in spirited fund-raising for special exhibitions, trying to imitate the American model. The museum produces and sells beautiful, original scholarly and general-audience exhibition-related publications. It sells objects relating to the collection, has membership programs, rents out conference rooms, markets its spaces for special events, and offers paid private tours. It was the first state museum allowed to keep the money it earned in order to offset expenses rather than returning that money to the state. Since the museum has such an active marketing strategy, it has carved a distinct niche for itself and is thought of as a highly unusual effort for a socialist-inspired institution. Although its income still does not meet its expenses, it does do quite well.[20] That the effort is so well thought of is a measure of the taste for modern, entrepreneurial thinking that was in the air even during a time almost totally dominated by the socialist mentality. Certainly, the future of the Thyssen-Bornemisza Museum under the conservatives is secure, since it represents at least a surface push toward the self-sufficiency and fiscal responsibility that they so admire.

The Thyssen-Bornemisza Museum has made a genuine effort to overcome the kind of administrative logjams that plague other state museums. Unlike the traditional public museum throughout the Mediterranean, the Thyssen-Bornemisza Museum does not run on a Napoleonic system—professionals are contracted and can be both employed and fired based on rational criteria, rather than the more normative paralysis at the lower levels and political hiring and firing at the top.

A managing director and an artistic director have been put at the helm. Modeled on the Metropolitan Museum of Art in New York, where a two-headed leadership seemed to have been working well at the time, this type of leadership was a bold experiment for Spain. It was later extended to the Prado, but not until the conservatives won the 1996 elections—an indication that the Thyssen-Bornemisza Museum's organizational structure was considered by both parties to be a success. Furthermore, the Thyssen-Bornemisza Museum's annual report, *Memoria*, would be the envy of any high-powered American corporation. Replete with colored bar and pie charts and a pledge to openness in the use of funds, it provides financial data, numbers and profiles of visitors, and detailed breakdowns of expenses and revenues. It includes an organization chart showing that the museum is headed by the minister of culture, Thyssen family members, Spanish royalty, other appropriate ministers, and some private citizens. The report also includes information about the internal management structure, the human resources philosophy, and personnel profiles, which includes "years of service with the company." The report makes every effort to establish for the readers that the Thyssen-Bornemisza Museum is the very model of a corporate enterprise whose bottom line is the preservation of great art for the pleasure of its visitors.

The Thyssen-Bornemisza Museum has proven also to be a model of collection care, marketing, planning, and public education. It has raised the expectations of the Spanish citizen in regard to what their cultural patrimony deserves, helping both museums and Spain take several giant steps forward in reconciling notions of the preservation of the past with equally powerful notions of a lively democratic present. The Thyssen-Bornemisza Museum has been one of the signs that Spain is not only up-to-date, but also a good place to visit and spend tourist dollars. It represents one of the most effective illustrations that Spain can counteract its reputation for being old-fashioned, folkloric, and enmeshed in a crippling administrative culture that prevents efficient decision making. The state, via this museum, has proven itself able to be flexible, sensitive, and swift. This is a model not wasted on its citizenry, which it both affects and increasingly reflects. It is not surprising that in 1999 plans to expand the museum were announced. It had done its job exceedingly well.

The Spanish socialists made decisions about all the major state museums based on whether or not they could be useful to the country as seen through political and populist eyes. They made museums society's darlings. But certain state museums were favored over others because they were flamboyant reminders that the country really did have a modern center. When the conservatives came to power in 1996 one of their most pressing cultural challenges was to demonstrate that they could preserve and update the older values they still treasured without negating the newer ones symbolized most extravagantly by the Reina Sofía and the Thyssen-Bornemisza Museum. A balance was needed to weave a new Spanish narrative supporting and inspiring a revised vision of the ideal democratic citizen. The Conservative Party took to this task with enthusiasm. Vast resources were put into restoring the balance. It remains for history to show to what extent it was able to meet the challenge successfully, to remedy what was broken and not break what had already been fixed.

2 OUTSIDE MADRID: THE SEPHARDIC MUSEUM IN TOLEDO

Question asked of the ticket taker at the Synagogue of Santa María la Blanca in Toledo, Spain: "Are the Jews of Toledo funding the restoration of this old synagogue?" Answer: "There are no Jews left in Toledo."

Question asked of the mayor of Toledo and president of the museum's Friends Association, Juan Ignacio de Mesa Ruiz, at the reopening of the Synagogue of Samuel He-Levy: "Why are you, a non-Jew, so committed to funding the restoration of this old synagogue?" Answer: "Because we are all Jews in Toledo."

There is an enormous gap separating the citizens of Toledo when acknowledging or denying one of the most shameful episodes of their shared past—the expulsion of the Jews from Spain in 1492. The size of the challenge assumed by those who, over five hundred years after the Inquisition began, took it upon themselves to bridge this chasm by educating the Spanish citizen to their many cultural and, in some cases, genetic links to that discarded Jewish history, is just as enormous. Government officials, professional museum staff, and private individuals have decided to reincorporate that past into the present consciousness. There was agreement among them that the most effective way to achieve that goal would be by completely renovating a languishing museum—the Sephardic

Museum (Museo Sefardí). This updated museum was to have the greatest possible national and international prestige. It was envisioned from the beginning not merely as a local effort but as a priority project of the Spanish state, and it was intended to be recognized as a metaphor for the renewed relationship of all of Spain to its Jewish heritage. The museum is housed in the beautiful and ancient Synagogue of the Samuel Ha-Levy (also known as the Sinagoga del Tránsito), once the grandest Jewish house of worship in the city. This project's realization would involve restoring that synagogue to reflect its former grandeur, collecting archaeological objects to illustrate that history, and providing education to a variety of audiences, Spaniards and foreigners alike.

The city of Toledo, designated as one of the "Seven Cities of Humanity" by the United Nations because of its medieval architecture and its continuity as a living city, has a legacy that extends far beyond the aesthetic. Important as Toledo is for its cathedrals, palaces, and plazas, it once possessed a spiritual dimension that set it apart from other beautiful European cities of its period. To this day, the Catholic aspect of Toledo's spiritual dimension survives. Religious celebrations, such as the Feast of Corpus Christi with its colorful, highly ritualized processions of the faithful through the cramped streets, seem to belong here as they do to no other place. The overwhelming smell of dried thyme, the sight of treasured heraldic banners draped outside the windows, the flowing robes of the participants, and the mesmerized crowds attest to, at the very least, the living memory of religious fervor. It was not only as a Spanish center of Catholicism that Toledo earned its distinction. Toledo was also a locus of *convivencia*—a place where for centuries, until the advent of the Inquisition, peoples of the Jewish, Catholic, and Muslim faiths lived and worked together in relative harmony.

CONVIVENCIA

Contributing their skills and talents, Toledoans created sacred and secular spaces that shaped for its time one of the most elegant and sophisticated cities in the world. By 1492, when the Jews were expelled during the Spanish Inquisition, *convivencia* suffered a fateful blow; after 1609, when the Moors were expelled, it was for all intents and purposes forgotten. Centuries later, with the death of Franco and the withering away of his dictatorship, wise men and women in Spain's young democracy recognized the value of reincorporating the memory of *convivencia* into the ideals of the emerging society. They saw Toledo as a Spanish city that could function as one of their vehicles for teaching tolerance and pluralism to Spaniards who had been brought up, for the most part, in a closed-minded and homogeneous world. The mayor of Toledo, Juan Ignacio de Mesa Ruiz, supported this plan. His role as president of the Friends Association of the Sephardic Museum was a strong signal to his constituents that he wanted to restore his city to its noblest period.

The lessons learned in Toledo have become especially poignant as the twentieth century draws to a close. They consist primarily of the costs to a city and a nation when it engages in the equivalent of ethnic cleansing. Without doubt, expelling the Jews and Moors from Spain contributed to the country's decay and diminishing impact in the world. Their absence affected agriculture, administration, economics, and culture. Spain came to think of itself as a single people united by a single faith. Toledo, a capital city for hundreds of years before the expulsion, became a symbol of a civilization's self-imposed loss of a complex and rich identity in its eagerness to be homogeneous. Educated citizens of Toledo once led their lives nurtured by the philosophies of saints, rabbis, and imams. They could boast of being comfortable with contradiction in spiritual and mundane matters, of being unthreatened by paradox or difference, and of taking pride in being sophisticated citizens of the world. After the Inquisition, these same Toledoans turned into fearful, closed-off human beings whose attitudes and relationships were prescribed and circumscribed by the strict theology of the church, and who could not admit other religions or perspectives into their worldview. Nor would they deviate from mainstream spiritual attitudes for fear that heretical opinions would sully (or even endanger) them. Over the years, as Toledo became cut off from the rest of the world, so too did the rest of Spain. One could argue that it was precisely because of this centuries-long, more or less continuous pressure to compress the Spanish identity into a unity of church and state that it was possible for the nation, after the country's horrific civil war, to endure its modern forty-year-long dictatorship.[1]

Franco had aspired to reconsolidate Spain's divided and diverse population into a single people with a united political, cultural, and historical identity resonant of Spain under Ferdinand and Isabella once he assumed power. This dictatorship encountered resistance, surely, but for the most part there was acceptance and complicity with its goals. It was clear to

Franco and to his immediate circle that reinforcing the history and culture of what they considered to be mainstream Spain would be an important element in the education of the citizenry. Policy decisions made in the historical past, insofar as they agreed with Franco's regime, needed to be validated. The issues of *convivencia* and the expulsion of the Jews seemed irrelevant and were consequently ignored. The expulsion of the Moors was taught as an unambiguous victory called the Reconquest. There was never, during the dictatorship, a national call to critically reexamine Spain's official narrative. Typically, the standard response, should the question of the expulsions even arise in social conversation, was that it may have been an unfortunate event, but the Catholic kings surely had their reasons, probably economic ones. Franco did deviate once from the standard story by rescuing several thousand Jews from the Holocaust. But, that is another story for another book.

With the advent of democracy and a fresh look at the nation's history it became apparent that more needed to be said about Spanish Jews and their pre-Inquisition lives. Both intellectuals and politicians were aware that Spain's population had always been much more heterogeneous in its makeup than modern convention had allowed. The expulsion of the Jews and Moors had only created a myth of homogeneity: Basques, Catalans, and Gallegans may have shared a religion, but, in truth, they differed profoundly in language, culture, attitudes, and education. Those who crafted the democracy realized that stressing, rather than papering over this diversity, could be key to the democratic education of the citizenry. It became obvious to them that the values of pluralism and tolerance had to be reinforced. These intellectuals and politicians agreed that action had to be taken on a number of cultural fronts, especially those that encouraged public debate and the expression of differing opinions. Therefore, it followed that it would be useful to reexamine a time when Spain had acutely emblematized those values. Reclaiming the pluralistic nature of pre-Inquisition Spain became one of many positive educational goals.

Those in charge of reconstructing a civil society all hoped to instill values that would minimize the Spanish willingness to follow an authoritarian figure in the way that Spaniards had followed Franco. If they were successful in their leadership, they reasoned, no one would be able to simplify the national identity or forcefully homogenize their lives again. Spaniards would understand themselves—sometimes as individuals and certainly as citizens—as the possessors of multiple, often contradictory identities. One of the largely unheralded victories of the last twenty-five years of the twentieth century is the successful creation of this "new Spaniard" in so short a time after the demise of the dictatorship. Spanish citizens have absorbed revised definitions of their best selves and turned that understanding into a guide for their new reality as a democratic country. A full participant in the affairs of the world, Spain is now, more often than not, credited with being a tolerant, generous, proactive, and helpful voice in the community of nations. Spain is, furthermore, one of the most peaceful countries in Europe. Indeed, its infrequent, if deadly, bouts with Basque terrorism (the extreme test of the country's tolerance) are handled by the majority of people in a remarkably restrained and civilized manner. They have even made it clear that they will not accept death squads as a way of countering the Basque assassins. No matter what happens, there are no calls for capital punishment or even for extremely long jail terms, regardless of the severity of the crimes the ETA may have committed. The once venerated military is shrinking away, in part owing to the huge number of conscientious objectors—the largest number in Europe. It is often remarked that no one can recall the names of the generals any more; in the old days many of them were among the most well-known members of society. On a familiar level one sees the pervasiveness of this attitude in that one has to search far and wide to buy toy guns in stores, not because they are outlawed, but because parents simply don't want to purchase them for their children.

This taste for nonviolence can only have come about because Spaniards have been taught both directly and indirectly how to avoid repeating some of their past mistakes—as well as how to gauge some of the mistakes they see made in the world around them. The nation has decided to avoid ethnic prejudice for the most part, balance the extremes of regionalism and centralism and to be acutely conscious of the pitfalls of isolation. Spanish citizens are taught to esteem openness, to explore their own past more critically than ever before, and to appreciate the experiences of the outside world. These reformed ideals have been and are being transmitted in many ways—in schools, by a free press, and by exposure to uncensored arts and entertainment. It has also become accepted in Spain, as it has in so many other parts of the world, that one of the most effective and proactive means of informally educating a wide cross section of people is within the setting of a museum: hence the willingness to bring the Sephardic Museum in the city of Toledo back to life in an extremely significant way.

Spanish intellectuals have a large effect on those politicians who form

the cultural policies both of the central government and of the autonomous regions. This is not to say that Spanish thinkers are always successful
in influencing politicians to do as they wish. But it is undeniable that in
some cases, especially when intellectuals and politicians share party
affiliation, they have shown the ability to telegraph their ideas to each
other. The example of the Sephardic Museum of Toledo is telling. No
doubt, some of the self-examination that Spain underwent would have
occurred automatically during the nation's transition to democracy. Still,
much in the refining and enhancing of this process materialized because
of a deep connection of the political to the intellectual impulse. Before
we begin to explore how intense that reexamination was, and how the
Sephardic Museum was a reflection of it, it would behoove us to digress
for a moment and recall the furies that were unleashed in the United
States when some intellectuals considered it appropriate to turn to museums as the means to achieve their cultural and political ends.

THREE EXHIBITS IN THE UNITED STATES

Three events figure prominently in the American national consciousness: the terrible treatment of African Americans; westward expansion;
and the Allied victory over Japan and Germany in World War II. Until the
1960s the cultural history of African Americans had been largely neglected
or stereotyped in the classrooms of America, their wide-ranging accomplishments unheralded. Westward expansion was explained to every
student in grade school as the fulfillment of the Manifest Destiny of the
United States and was always taught as a good and noble thing. World
War II is remembered, interpreted, and explained as one of our greatest, certainly most unambiguous triumphs. For a variety of compelling
reasons, which range from changing demography to the rise of alternate methods of critical analysis, American intellectuals began to see a
need for rethinking these events in American history. Soon, there was a
desire to "go public" with these reinterpretations. In each case a major
American museum presented a revised perspective for these events to
general audiences by means of an ambitious exhibition concept. The
directors and curators naively expected that the public, including those
most affected by the new interpretations, would be convinced, merely by
virtue of the museum's authority, to revisit these matters and willingly
accept the curator's recasting of them. All three efforts were resounding

failures, largely because the American curators worked in a vacuum, seemingly having no political consciousness. Their miscalculations, however, highlight the success of the attempt to revise the normative history that took place in Toledo.

Harlem on My Mind, an exhibition mounted at the Metropolitan Museum of Art in New York in 1969, presented high points of African American culture to large museum audiences, which were, then, mostly white and middle and upper class. Underlying this effort was the hope that audiences that had been unaccustomed to attending the Metropolitan Museum of Art would not only come to the exhibition but would also become regular museum goers. *Harlem on My Mind* was conceived as a celebration of the Harlem Renaissance, an extraordinarily creative and influential period in African American history. It was installed using daring, innovative multimedia techniques, which have, by now, become standard fare in museums. It opened to much fanfare. However, what had started with seemingly the best intentions had proceeded without sufficient thought and ended as political disaster. The museum was picketed and vilified for being elitist and condescending to the very people it wished to reach. The director of the museum, Thomas Hoving, had hired a young curator, Allon Schoener, who had no expertise in African American culture and did not choose to engage African American experts for advice. Worse even than his lack of rigor were his unsophisticated political sensibilities, which caused him to introduce controversial subject matter about African American–Jewish relations and thereby to set off a shocking, and probably avoidable, explosion of rage from both groups. In retrospect Schoener admits that he made a fateful mistake by thinking he, an outsider, could identify totally with the African American experience. There was also resentment against the museum's decision not to include painting and sculpture in *Harlem on My Mind.* Since painting and sculpture were still then considered the "high" arts, African Americans came to the conclusion that their creative work in the visual arts was not considered appropriate for the halls of the Metropolitan Museum of Art. *Harlem on My Mind,* for all of its positive goals, ended up heightening racial tensions. It remains one of the haunting reminders that cultural institutions are, and have always been, "crucibles for the shaping of our national identity."[2] In this case, because the museum tried to shape national identity but did so in a political vacuum, it badly miscalculated its affect on the American public.

The West as America, held at the National Museum for American Art (Smithsonian Institution) in 1991, was another example of a naive underestimation of the potential power of the museum. Should anyone question the effect that museums have on their visitors and the world in general, this exhibition would erase all doubt. The curators of *The West as America* used beloved images of the Old West to challenge the myth of Manifest Destiny by subjecting it to a highly critical, Marxist analysis of westward expansion. They used American nineteenth-century landscape, history, and genre paintings to support their thesis. They interpreted the paintings as having aided the capitalist powers in the United States in creating and perpetuating untruths about their activities, which included the rape of the environment and the destruction of Native Americans and their culture. This exhibition, twenty-two years after *Harlem on My Mind,* caused another storm of discontent. In the case of *The West as America* the problem was less one of faulty scholarship than of a lack of empathy on the part of the curators for their audience. To most of the people who wrote in the Smithsonian's comment books, the museum was guilty of simply substituting one ideology with another in what seemed to them to be an arrogant, patronizing, and unilateral way.[3]

The West as America was so disturbing to so many people that some legislators entered the fray (the most influential of whom had never seen the exhibition) threatening reduction of funding for the Smithsonian and suggesting that the organizers were not loyal Americans. Curators, in trying to dismantle a myth, had gone about their business in a way considered to be so arrogant and so one-dimensional that they antagonized the very population they had hoped to engage in critical thinking. No doubt they left the myths more entrenched than ever. Certainly, they helped to deepen the suspicion of intellectuals in the United States by politicians and the public. The lack of willingness to admit and deal empathetically with the political complexities of the curatorial premise certainly hurt the museum's ability to have a positive influence on American national identity construction throughout the succeeding decade.

Finally, the *Enola Gay* was an exhibition planned as a fiftieth-anniversary remembrance of the atomic bombing of Japan that ended World War II. It was scheduled to be held at the National Air and Space Museum (also a part of the Smithsonian Institution) and proposed to analyze that defining military event from a new critical perspective. This critical perspective was meant to break the taboo surrounding the questioning of many of the national assumptions, most of the textbooks, and the still vivid memories of surviving veterans and their contemporaries. One point of the proposed Enola Gay exhibition was to open up for debate the statistics regarding the high numbers of casualties that would have occurred in the event of the invasion of Southern Kyushu in Japan; these numbers have long been the justification of the decision to bomb Hiroshima and Nagasaki. Instead the plans for the *Enola Gay* inspired the equivalent of a cultural riot. Once again, curators had insensitively questioned an ingrained idea in American history, had been indifferent to their audience, had ignored facts that might have created problems for their own arguments, and had left their audience with nothing in exchange for their consideration of a revisionist inter-pretation. The curators, wanting to undertake something fundamen-tally political, neglected to do the requisite political work that would have allowed their ideas to be heard. They thus found it impossible to influence public opinion—even though that is precisely what they hoped the end result of their work would be. The curators thus kept the museum itself from being an arena for conservative debate. The exhibit that was finally mounted simply displayed the historical artifact—the Enola Gay fuselage—and allowed for no platform for intellectual inquiry or persuasion.

As a result of the three exhibitions mentioned above and a number of others as well, American museums, especially those supported by public funds, are increasingly finding themselves little more than treasure houses or, in the case of historical or military museums, homes to arti-facts. This sad situation has emerged because those responsible for the programming of some of our major American museums have handled controversial ideas clumsily, without any political acumen or communal empathy. Consequently, these institutions, it seems, are now acceptable to society only insofar as they function as affirmers of the mainstream cul-ture or presenters of essential aesthetic ideas. They have lost their oppor-tunity to reshape the national identity in a way that was much needed.[4]

THE SPANISH RESPONSE TO THE RECUPERATION OF JEWISH HISTORY

There is, I believe, something to be learned in the United States from the Spanish experience as Spanish cultural leaders so successfully wrestled with reinterpreting a lost part of Spain's history. Juan Ignacio de Mesa Ruíz has written, in the bulletin for the Friends Association of the Sephardic Museum, a kind of warning to Spanish society. Recognizing that the Spanish Inquisition is still an extremely sensitive subject and that he could easily offend his constituency, he treads gently but surely, never putting himself above or in opposition to his public. He carefully describes how the museum's support group is committed to disclosing and publicizing the true nature of Spain's culture before 1492, comprised as it was of differing beliefs and cultures. Mesa Ruíz goes on to write about the association's work in trying to apply history to the present so that it may serve Spaniards and the world as a permanent lesson. He expresses the hope that Spain and other nations will avoid policies of homogenization. In the same bulletin Mesa Ruíz writes about the construction of the identity of a responsible democratic citizen, the "new Spaniard," and the obligation of the private individual in a free and civil society to understand his or her own history. Still, he does not blame; he does not separate himself from the public; and, he does not condescend. Rather he enlists: "We, who have for so long been prevented, by our economic and political situation, from participating in those very matters which affected us most directly, find it extremely difficult today to fully understand that it is we, those of us in the civil society, not just the government, who must participate in reaching a true understanding of our own cultural patrimony."[5]

That a museum can be one of the truly effective means of excavating identity makes sense because museums function best as loci of informal learning. Since it has reopened in 1994 about 250,000 people a year visit the Sephardic Museum in Toledo. Those visitors are Spaniards and foreigners, adults and children, Jews and non-Jews, rich, poor, and middle class, casual tourists and committed scholars—people of all types interested in all manner of historical material. Unlike other kinds of formal learning situations—classrooms, for example—museum audiences usually are members all of the above-stated categories and more. Furthermore, they are all in an enclosed place at the same time—a kind of *convivencia*. Learning takes place not only by reading didactic labels and looking at objects, but also by experiencing the space itself. Merely by entering the Sephardic Museum visitors absorb the message that the Spaniards were a diverse people before the Inquisition. Gazing at the Arabic architectural ornamentation and the Arabic script, they begin to sense that there was at least a working relationship between Jews and

Arabs. Since many people erroneously consider Jews and Arabs always to have been enemies—genetically to be enemies—this is usually a surprise. Although most who visit the city of Toledo have not come for the sole purpose of seeing the Sephardic Museum, the visitors who do come are deeply moved.

Comment books are used at the Sephardic Museum as they were in *The West as America* to gauge visitor's thoughts and feelings. Curator Santiago Palomero describes the entries as "love letters" and talks about how they reflect the transformation that the museum has wrought upon much of its audience, especially upon the non-Jewish Spanish segment of it.[6] The comments are written in Spanish, Catalan, Gallego, Euskera, English, French, German, Hebrew, Japanese, Dutch, Italian, Greek, Polish, Russian, and other languages and range from the moving to the mildly critical. (All following quotes from the comment books are author's translations from Palomero's Spanish.) "To the city of our fathers. . . . Many generations past you persecuted our ancestors who went out from here. Our family arrived in Turkey, and from there went to Rhodes; from

The Sephardic Museum (Museo Sefardí) in Toledo before 1971 restoration. Courtesy Archivo Moreno, Instituto de Conservación y Restauración de Bienes Culturales, Ministerio de Educación y Cultura de España.

there we arrived in Jerusalem, the holy city, and from there we have come to visit Toledo. All of this was transmitted to us by our ancestors, from generation to generation, and we have not forgotten," signed by the "Family Calvo Toledano," was written in one book.

The comment books also allow for a larger debate in the safe confines of the museum, like the entries that refer to issues of tolerance: "Dios, Yhavé, Alá, please make us all live in peace"; "The Jewish culture left much wisdom in Spain"; "The visit has touched me. With the hope of a better world, with tolerance and love among nations"; and, in Catalan, "Everything here is different from our culture, it is not better nor is it worse from our form of life. This is an homage to there being tolerance and understanding of all of humanity. One day it will so be." At the same time there are occasional calls for the return of the museum to the Jewish people, such as (in Hebrew), "Now is the time to return the synagogue to the Jews so that it will cease to be exploited commercially." Sometimes these claims are answered in the comment books themselves: "On the contrary, for those who do not understand the long history of oppression, it is worth presenting a thesis as legitimate and complete as this one so that we realize and gain more awareness. Enough with bitterness!" Then there is the more political remark such as, "My respect to the Jewish people and my wish that they would respect the Palestinian people and give them their liberty." And, occasionally the confused visitor will write something like, "I don't get it! First we throw them out, and then we make them a museum. I just don't get it!" The children come and go, leaving their traces, which range from "This museum is very pretty. I am also very pretty" to the more freighted, "It is incredible that Arabs, Jews, and Catholics could live together in Toledo." Lovers leave projections of their own feelings: "I am here with my love. Toledo and this synagogue are marvelous." The multitude of thoughts crisscross in the Museum—daily, openly, constantly, with thousands of people—in ways that reflect and encourage the construction of the identity of today's Spaniard—and deconstruct yesterday's.

THE FORMER SYNAGOGUES OF TOLEDO

The Synagogue of Samuel Ha-Levy (later known as Sinagoga del Tránsito) was built in 1357 by Samuel Ha-Levy Abulafia, a private philanthropist and treasurer to King Pedro I of Castile.[7] The great room of the synagogue is decorated in elegant Hebrew calligraphy, which was, along with all of the ornament, created by Arab artisans. The calligraphy contains Hebrew phrases that are mostly in praise of God and taken from the Hebrew Bible. There are also words of praise to the donor and to Allah as well. After the expulsion of the Jews from Toledo the synagogue was taken over by the Christian military Order of Calatrava. Then, after the order ceased to exist, the building was consecrated as a church and renamed Nuestra Señora Santa María del Tránsito. At the beginning of the twentieth century it had devolved into a half-abandoned warehouse. Despite these changes and the subsequent deterioration, the building was declared a national monument by King Alfonso in the early years of the twentieth century. During the Franco regime, although visited by some Jewish pilgrims, it deteriorated like many other neglected monuments throughout the rest of Spain. Formally designated a museum in 1971, while Franco was still alive, it remained disorganized and without professional guidance. The museum had no scholarly underpinnings, educational programming, library, archives, acquisition policy, or security system. And, it had no objects. Visitors had no means of understanding where they were or why the synagogue had a Christian name. Only after 1981, with the advent of democracy, did it receive any attention and begin to advance, in several stages, to its present status as a fully modern museum, which was inaugurated as the Sephardic Museum (Museo Sefardí) in 1994.

The neighboring Synagogue of Santa María la Blanca, although not yet officially a museum, will likely receive that status when its own renovation is complete. Nevertheless, unofficially, and in the minds of the visitors, the Synagogue of Santa María la Blanca functions as a kind of annex to the Sephardic Museum. Built before the Synagogue of Samuel Ha-Levy, the Synagogue of Santa María la Blanca has an even stronger Arabic architectural style. It must have become too small for the Jewish population because it became a Christian church well before the Inquisition, and a number of Christian architectural elements still remain today. At the June 1994 press conference celebrating the reopening of the Sephardic Museum in the former Synagogue of Samuel Ha-Levy director Ana Mária López said that the future of the Synagogue of Santa María la Blanca would be linked to that of the newly opened museum. She indicated that the Synagogue of Santa María la Blanca might become an arm of the Sephardic Museum itself, perhaps as a research center where Sephardic family histories could be researched by computer and other sophisticated investigatory techniques.

In López's statement one could see, if alert to the relationship between the intellectual and political in Spain, a significant moment transpire. The director of the museum, an archaeologist of imposing qualifications, made her declaration about the future for the museum. She did so in front of highly visible politicians and powerful representatives from the Ministry of Culture. Evidently, the politicians had, as yet, no idea of the extent of the director's expansion plans. Nor were they ready to accept and take on the project as an obligation, morally or budgetary, of the ministry. Nonetheless, her dream had been articulated in front of the media from all over the country. The process of linking museum activity to the political will had been furthered, but not naively, nor in a vacuum.

RETURN OF THE MEMORY OF THE JEWISH TRADITION TO TOLEDO

That process was undoubtedly helped by King Juan Carlos I's decision to preside over the opening of the renovated synagogue and museum. The importance of his presence cannot be overestimated when assessing the eventual impact the Sephardic Museum might have on the national consciousness. It was Juan Carlos I who had gone to the modern Madrid Synagogue to confront expulsion issues with the Jewish congregants, saying to them, in 1992, "Spain is no longer only nostalgia for you; rather, it is a home." And it was he who, in the name of Spain, made an official trip to the recently recognized state of Israel, winning the hearts of the Israelis. He continues to gain the respect and admiration of Jews all over the world as he performs major symbolic acts signifying the desire for a national reconsideration of the shared Spanish-Jewish past. At the reopening of the Sephardic Museum in Toledo, celebrating what had already been accomplished, one could watch and hear the next steps already being taken toward a more profound investigation of the past and of its meaning for modern Spain. One could almost predict the inevitability of a new budget being granted some day so that the Sephardic Museum could annex the Synagogue of Santa María la Blanca. The convergence of intellectual inquiry and political will are at the heart of this project and that convergence helps to fulfill legitimate needs in the society because it involves groundwork that has been so effectively prepared.

Still, one has to wonder just who was pressing so hard for the success of the Sephardic Museum. Certainly not Jews, because, as the young girl at the ticket booth to Santa María la Blanca correctly replied to my query, "There are no Jews in Toledo." Yet, as Juan Ignacio de Mesa Ruíz said, "We are all Jews in Toledo," on some at least poetic level. Both are right. The Inquisition, either by expulsion or conversion, wiped out Toledo's Jewry. Nevertheless, for years after it is said that there were secret Jews and Jewish rituals practiced throughout Spain, especially in and near Toledo. There was the perpetuation of Jewish memory and kinship, and then there was also betrayal and assimilation. Eventually, the Jews who remained in Spain intermarried. But peculiar family recollections, certain names and patterns of obfuscations of those names, and some documents preserved in various archives still indicate Jewish lineage to canny Spaniards. The former Jews (new Christians) have assimilated into every level of society—the highest orders of the military, religion, and aristocracy being no exceptions. The literary, scientific, and political arenas also absorbed the former Jews, as did the ordinary citizenry.

None of this was at all easy. There was an undercurrent of resistance and suspicion of the new Christians, called *conversos*. Many of these ex-Jews found themselves repeatedly needing to prove the sincerity of their Christianity. Most just tried to stay alive while assimilating into an increasingly homogeneous Spain. The desire of the more rabid *conversos* to be thoroughly Christian resulted in some of the most shocking anti-Jewish arguments, many made by them and their descendants, as they entered positions of power in the churches and elsewhere. These ex-Jews developed irreproachable means to proclaim their separateness from the tribes of Israel, which were so hated throughout Spain at that time. And some of them were, no doubt, the ancestors of the "Jews" of modern Toledo.

Even for those Spaniards who do not suspect that any Jewish blood flows through their veins, the contributions of the Sephardim in the ways and degree to which that culture helped form their country are worth exploring. Assuredly, most people, as short a time as twenty-five years ago, knew little, if anything, about that legacy. But now archaeologists, art historians, and cultural and intellectual scholars are delving into that history. Some of them work for, or in collaboration with, the Sephardic Museum. Others are professors on the faculties of Spain's many universities. These researchers have struggled to bring new perspectives to what they see as the significant task of rescuing the Jewish contribution to

Spain from irrelevance, if not oblivion. They have developed an empathetic relationship to the Jewish experience, which they have projected into all of the museum's work: its brilliant architectural restoration, exhibitions, publications, conferences, labels, educational programs, and the overall pervading attitude.

The story of Santiago Palomero, vice-director and curator of the Sephardic Museum, is emblematic of the new scholarly interest in the subject. Palomero is an archaeologist by training. When he took the state examination to enter the museum profession, he never dreamed that he would be placed at the then inchoate Sephardic Museum. He knew no Hebrew and had no Judaic studies to his credit. Nevertheless, he was appointed to the museum in Toledo. He settled down to work, studied Hebrew and Judaeo-Spanish and began a passionate investigation of the culture. He asked a colleague, Leticia Azcue, then the vice-director of the Museum of the Royal Academy of Fine Arts of San Fernando (Museo del Real Academia de Bellas Artes de San Fernando) in Madrid, one of Spain's best art museums, for help. Working pro bono and in her scant spare time, she agreed to help the museum in aid of her colleague and because she loved the city of Toledo. Ultimately, she, too, became captivated by the material. Coincidentally, at an international meeting of museum professionals in France, she met Rachel Hachlili, a prominent Israeli archaeologist and oft-published writer on the history of ancient Jewish art.[8] Once Azcue discovered the access that Hachlili had to Israel's Department of Antiquities, she began working with her to gain Israeli help in stocking Toledo's museum with artifacts.

Help from Israel was badly needed because of the ferocity and success of the Spanish Inquisition. Little is left in Spain of the material culture of the Sephardim. In Toledo there are the two synagogues, a few stone fragments, and some grave markers. There are remnants of architecture and a few objects in Gerona, Córdoba, and scattered throughout other cities. At least 1,200 years of life have virtually disappeared. Of Spanish Old Testament and related Judaeo-Spanish materials, the most complete are found in the Holland, New York, Cambridge, Oxford, and London. A small number are in Madrid, and several can be found throughout the Iberian Peninsula. Illuminated manuscripts are particularly rare in Spain, with one *Scroll of Esther* in the National Library being a precious example. There are more and better scrolls to be seen in London and elsewhere in the Sephardic diaspora. The only documents that seem to have survived in any quantity in Spain itself are legal papers in municipal archives. These papers contain the laws describing what Jews were allowed to do and buy, what their rights were and were not. There are records of civil suits and taxation. Extant documents attest to when and where Jews had to dress differently than Christians, were not supposed to eat among them, and were prohibited from dwelling in certain cities. What is apparent, finally, is that almost no works of art, or even artifacts fashioned for the daily and ceremonial lives of the Sephardim survived — there is almost no material culture that would bear witness to their long residence in Spain and to their lives as the highly productive and creative members of Spanish society that they were.

But even though they knew that the synagogue itself would always be the most important element of the museum, Azcue and Palomero were determined to have some artifacts from the Sephardim in their museum — at the very least some pieces that could cast light, in ways that only objects can, on the Jewish presence in their land. In order to do this they needed to secure international cooperation. Having met Hachlili, Azcue and Palomero convinced the Ministry of Culture to let them embark on a mission to Israel with director López. It took them three days and three nights in Jerusalem to identify seventy-four antiquities and to secure permission to borrow them on long-term loan for the Sephardic Museum. By sheer dint of their passion and an ability for wakefulness, seemingly known only to Spaniards (whose normal schedules keep them awake late into the night), they cut through mountains of red tape and succeeded in securing the objects they wanted for the Sephardic Museum.

Because Spanish-Jewish objects of the Sephardic period were, with a few exceptions, nonexistent, those that they obtained were almost all archaeological items from the ancient Near East, dated from the Bronze Age to the Roman domination. They demonstrate daily life and are important because no such collection of objects from that area and period exists in Spain. They contextualize territorially, historically, and geographically the origins of the traditions of the Jewish people, whose customs were perpetuated by those Jews who ultimately became Spaniards. This loan from Israel has further resonance for Jews all over the world because it attests to the good diplomatic relations that now exist between Spain and Israel, made possible by Spain's democratic government when it recognized Israel as a state.[9]

The "Garden of Memory" at the Sephardic Museum (Museo Sefardí). Courtesy Museo Sefardí, Ministerio de Educación y Cultura. Dirección General de Bellas Artes y Archivos.

Once the objects arrived, Palomero researched them and presented them in a dignified and highly didactic display that linked Spanish Jewry to its biblical roots. They formed a visual and intellectual foundation for the museum. The sensitivity that Palomero and the museum's director brought to this enterprise was extraordinary. Care was taken in the interpretation of the objects and in the significance endowed upon them. Furthermore, Palomero and López decided early on to use consultants (including Hachlili) from all over Spain, Europe, America, and Israel. Their objective was to present the most important information and to be certain that they not overlook anything key to the Sephardic Jewish culture. They repeatedly insisted that, although they wanted to present the past as completely as possible, they also wished to avoid, to the extent possible, losing themselves or the objects in subjective considerations or side matters that were not central to their goal of reincorporating the history of the Jews into the modern Spanish identity. In other words, they protected themselves by not assuming that a perfect empathy could be attained with a people whom Spain had grievously persecuted in the distant past. They did not make any of the mistakes that had ruined *Harlem on My Mind.*

The success of this highly consultative process cannot be overestimated. There were many difficult decisions to be made regarding policies and presentation of material in the museum. The curators could have moved off track and offended both international Jewry and institutional Catholicism had they made insensitive decisions. For example, there were requests from the Jewish community that the synagogue be occasionally used as a house of worship—as had occurred in Gerona, another old Jewish center. In Toledo, with the advice of their consultants, the museum decided to deny that request. They reasoned that, like it or not, the synagogue had also been consecrated as a church. If it were allowed to function as a Jewish house of worship, one would also have to allow Catholic worship services to be performed there. The decision was made that since the former synagogue is now a museum; it is no longer a house of worship. As one might imagine, coming to this decision posed difficulties for those who had already begun to empathize with the Jews who would be entering the old synagogue. But they knew that they could neither deny nor undo their country's history. They could, however, face that history, try to understand it, and confront its ramifications with as open a mind as possible.

Another difficult problem surfaced concerning the placement of several surviving gravestones from ancient Jewish cemeteries in the area. At the opening reception of the museum some knowledgeable Jewish guests remarked that the presence of these stones immediately adjacent to the synagogue was markedly un-Jewish. They pointed out that according to Jewish law a cemetery had to be located outside the precincts of the town—never on the grounds of a synagogue. López and Palomero, having made the basic decision about the nature of the building, explained to the guests that the area with the stones is not a cemetery. It is, rather, a "garden of memory" within the precincts of a museum. It was not easy for some of the guests to accept this. At the same time they could see that the explanation was an honest, considered, and consistent attempt by the museum to retrieve the memory of those Jewish Spaniards who spent their lives in Toledo so very long ago. Even though the old synagogue can no longer function as a sacred space it still reverberates with meaning and does retain a spiritual dimension. Many difficult choices such as these were made that required taking into account numerous contradictory considerations. Decisions were taken without being overly ideological, accusatory, defensive, or arrogant. Yes, the curators knew that Spanish history could not be undone. At the same time, they were determined that it could be made to serve their compatriots better than it had until then.

Any modern museum professional knows that the art and artifacts, and indeed the mission, for which they are responsible will not reveal their secrets without help. It is the museum's duty to introduce its collection to the public by means of brochures, labels, and other materials. The Sephardic Museum pays a great deal of attention to that responsibility, pointing out in its didactic labels that its fundamental objective is to demonstrate the magnitude and importance of the Jewish presence in Spain and that, without that Jewish presence, the formation of Spanish society would have turned out quite differently.

The introduction to the museum itself on its text panels is quite basic, unashamedly asking and answering such fundamental questions as "What is a synagogue?" It takes nothing for granted and is, nevertheless, written without any condescension. Temporary exhibitions demonstrate the extent of the dissemination of Spanish-Jewish culture throughout the world. Much of what the Sephardic Museum has been able to accomplish is owing to the museum's Friends Association. With the central government providing the core support for restoration and staffing, scholars providing the research, and an enthusiastic audience, much of the success of this project was predictable. But it was also necessary, if the intended effect on identity formation was to be profound, to engage both the local elites of Toledo and the royal family, representing the nation as a whole. The Friends Association, formally created in 1991, has taken it upon itself to fulfill that task, putting its prestige and financial resources behind the endeavor. All major museum events have had the Friends Association's imprimatur, have been covered by the media, and have attracted the most influential citizens. The association encouraged the king and queen of Spain to give their annual Royal Toledo Foundation (Real Fundación de Toledo) award, in 1993, to an involved Sephardic family. The prize is awarded to persons or institutions who have performed outstanding work on behalf of the historical patrimony. It was, as a part of the association's effort, awarded to Don Morris Pinto on behalf of the extended Sephardic Pinto family for their substantial contributions of property, objects, and funds to the Sephardic Museum. This was a strategically important gesture. The attention by both king and queen ensured that any remaining stigma in the air surrounding the recuperation of the Sephardic legacy in Spain was obliterated. It also ensured that the museum's intellectual goals would become one of the priorities of the overall social enterprise.

With the museum as the visible beginning, the process for the recovery of the lost Jewish identities in Spain has gained its face and body. Realizing that they had created a thirst for more knowledge, the Sephardic Museum began collaborating with the local university in the Castilla–La Mancha region to create educational programming to slake that thirst. The first courses took place in 1991 and were taught by Spanish and European professors in the following subjects: "Spanish Jews in a Historical Context," "Jews in the Lower Middle Ages," "The Converso Phenomenon," and "Inquisition and the Jewish Spanish Conversos." A curator from the Jewish Historical Museum in Amsterdam was invited to give a lecture on Holland, which had become one of the new homes for Jews who left Spain. There were lectures on Judaism as a culture of resistance and on the Synagogue of Samuel Ha-Levy and the archaeological excavations that were taking place there. After these initial offerings a professor from the University of Tel Aviv was invited to speak on Judaeo-Spanish languages, and Spanish professors were also invited to speak on medieval Hebrew and Judaeo-Arabic languages. There were lectures on medieval Hebraic-Spanish literature, secular Hebrew poetry in Spain, religious poetry, narrative, prose, and women in Hebrew medieval literature.

Demand was such that the courses continue to the present day. In 1992 and 1993 the summer courses were concentrated on the expulsion of the Jews from Spain and its aftermath. They also dealt with the antecedents to the expulsion, specifically the pogrom of 1391 in Castile, the 1492 Decree of Expulsion, and the consequences of that decree. Recent offerings have turned to the basics of Judaism. The 1994 course, inaugurated by the archbishop of Seville, was simply titled "Judaism, Practice, and Belief." It included lectures on textual sources in the Talmud and prayer, death and birth in Judaism, and Judaism in daily life. There have also been classes on Jewish cooking, the Sephardic wedding, as well as the holy days, feasts around the Wandering, and minor feasts. Finally, there have been classes on the Jewish neighborhoods in Toledo and the medieval synagogue. To quote from one of the brochures for winter courses:

The Sephardic Museum of Toledo tries to show, by means of its collections, not only the history of the Jews in Spain and the Golden Age of culture that developed in Islamic Spain and in the Christian reigns throughout the Middle Ages, but also the birth of said culture in its place of origin with the influences that adjacent cultures of the Near East had on it. At the same time the museum wants to make available information on the later expansion of Spanish-Jewish culture to other parts of the world so that the legacy of that culture can become integrated as an essential part of the historical Spanish patrimony.[10]

In so doing, the museum has reached beyond its borders, out to the international community, where the Judaeo-Spanish language, Ladino, is still spoken and where exiled Sephardic Jews still preserve living memories of their beloved Spain.

By recovering one part of Spain's non-Catholic history, the Sephardic Museum has done an excellent job in educating the modern Spaniard. It is ironic and surely not accidental that the decision to exhume this past focused on Toledo, the city that, during Franco's day, was chosen for the creation of the Museum of the Visigoths (Museo de los Concilios y de la Cultura Visigoda), a site where the earliest origins relating to the ideology of the unitary identity of the Spanish people were to be documented and displayed.[11] By thriving in the city so recently and blatantly used to reinforce the closed nature of fascist Spain, the Sephardic Museum plays an especially instructive role as the metaphor chosen by the democratic state for the reopening of the country and its cultural renewal. By dramatically reminding all visitors to Toledo that Spain, like other democratic nations, can confidently absorb the "other" into its national identity, the state and its museum argue for the country once again becoming a place of *convivencia*—as it so proudly had been over five hundred years ago.

3 MILITARY AND ECCLESIASTICAL MUSEUMS INSIDE AND OUTSIDE MADRID

The institution of the museum resists definition. Elusive and fluid, its part in the construction of the identity of the new Spanish citizen twists and turns unexpectedly, forever squirming out of the neat boxes any cultural historian might have prepared for it. Multiple in form and seemingly the possessor of infinite personalities, the museums of Spain are ever-present reminders, even warnings, that there is no longer either a reality or an ideal of a unified Spanish cultural identity. Since the death of Franco, as we have seen in the preceding chapters, many of Spain's museums have gone far beyond their missions as vessels for the preservation of precious artifacts, lobbying discreetly or indiscreetly for their desired impact on the attitudes of Spaniards. Separately, each museum has exercised its own brand of meaning-making by developing its own message. When viewed as the "grand text" upon which this book is predicated, they can be seen and understood as embodiments of the competing and conflicting political and cultural debates that surround and infiltrate Spanish lives. These museums are homes for attitudes that represent every point on the identity compass; they are safe havens for centrists and regionalists, progressives and conservatives, moderates and, occasionally, even extremists.

Spain's museums are refuges where ostensibly incompatible value systems can represent themselves safely within the larger context of official cultural institutions. They contribute to a sense of inclusion, even for the small minority of the population that would have preferred that Spain had retreated into a traditional, authoritarian society. Spanish museums have not only seized the opportunity and the obligation to function as stages for progressive ideas about culture; they have also served a larger, less transparent role of supporting internal stability by acting as preserves for the relatively silent, ever smaller group of ultraconservatives. In the latter context a small percentage of military museums and some religious museums have provided protected, public settings that allowed for the expression of Spain's most intransigent old-fashioned, even regressive values. During the two decades following Franco's death, one could still visit a number of these military and ecclesiastical museums, only to be confronted with haunting glimpses not normally projected at the forefront of the "new Spanish culture." Although both the military and the church have lost a great deal of their once enormous prestige in Spain, they too have been allowed their museums and their freedom of expression. In fact, these museums have played idiosyncratic roles in assuring those liberties across the whole spectrum of society during its metamorphosis. Thus, in this chapter we will consider the effects that a few special but significant military and Catholic church museums have had on identity construction throughout the transition and consolidation of democracy in today's nonmilitaristic and secular Spain.

MILITARY MUSEUMS

The most important of Spain's military museums continued to echo the history and values of the dictatorship long after the country was democratic. Nevertheless, they also played an unheralded, nearly imperceptible, paradoxical, and telling role in shaping the narrative of the national drama as the country rushed (carefully) along the road of democratization. Walking into the Army Museum (Museo del Ejército) in Madrid and the Museum of the Alcázar (Museo del Alcázar de Toledo) in Toledo, perhaps the grandest and most important of Spain's military museums, one's first reaction was simply shock, especially after visiting other new and renovated museums that flourished in the 1980s and 1990s.

Most national museums had, at least, been physically updated by the end of the century. Even the Prado had received some attention to its physical plant. And a number of contemporary art museums had been built. Regional museums sprouted up all over the country proudly expressing up-to-date aspirations, touting their local cultural autonomy, and calling for integration into the modern Western world. Scores of museums had been subjected to some level of public discussion about purpose, and their staffs had been engaged in some debate about how best to express their evolving missions during the country's dynamic period of redefinition. Yet there were some museums that fell completely out of that mainstream. Among them, Madrid's Army Museum and Toledo's Museum of the Alcázar are the most dramatic examples, and their postdictatorship survival the most informative with respect to the focus in this book. With Franco's portrait still staring down on the visitor in the former and the story of the Spanish civil war siege told by the right in antiquated heroic terms in the latter, it seemed as if they were stuck in time capsules. These museums in no way resembled what most Spanish museums became or were becoming. One was compelled to ask: "What is it that did *not* happen to them? What exactly is going on?"

What was going on was the overt commemoration of Franco's version of history. That these institutions were not significantly altered during the two decades after Franco's death is an irrefutable sign of just how opposite the new regime was from the dictatorship. Their perpetuation is part of that tacit societal agreement, the "pact of forgetfulness," which was such a significant factor in the Spanish transition's success in quickly achieving its democratic goals. Unlike other fully articulated and legally binding agreements about the economy, social welfare, and politics, this "pact" was a never-spelled-out social covenant in which Spaniards collectively "renounced their desires for revenge, demanded no settling of accounts. There were no purges of the executioners, torturers, jailers, informers, or those close to Franco who had enriched themselves during the dictatorship. By the same token, large numbers of Franco's more moderate and far-sighted supporters forgot their own pasts, some collaborating sincerely in building the democratic consensus, others merely fabricating new autobiographies as *demócratas de toda la vida* (life-long democrats).[1]

Even though it was unwritten, the "pact of forgetfulness" was at least as influential as official agreements governing the democratic transformation. Motivated by the ardent hope that forgetting would be the better way to avoid a future based yet again on a politics of revenge, it seemed to be the right thing at the right time. But certainly given the psychological imperatives addressed by the Nuremberg trials after World War II, it was also an unproved and risky stance. That it was not widely appropriated as a model for most subsequent emerging democracies, whether they were coming out of left-wing or right-wing dictatorships, is evident from the plethora of lustrations, purges, and councils of truth and reconciliation that followed in, for example, the Czech Republic, former East Germany, and postapartheid South Africa. It should be added, parenthetically, that it remains a puzzle that the "pact of forgetfulness" did not in any way seem to cripple Spain when, only a few years later, a similar, albeit far more extreme approach in Argentina—premised on avoiding holding anyone seriously accountable for the past—succeeded in psychologically crippling much of the population. It is also fitting that as the century came to a close it was a Spanish judge who that felt compelled to try Chile's Pinochet—a close colleague of Franco.

In Spain, in a way that was not replicated anywhere else—because of the dynamics of its particular post–civil war period—obliterating the taste for "getting even" actually seemed to energize the country. This phenomenon could be discerned in the governing of the country's museums in the same way that it was in other mainstream activities. Demonstrating their acceptance of the "pact," museums avoided large-scale accusatory, partisan exhibitions. Instead, they embraced the present and looked to the future. On the other hand, and of equal importance, the democratically inclined majority adopted a laissez-faire, proactively indifferent attitude toward the minute percentage of the population that held tenaciously to the most incendiary and regressive attitudes of the old regime. Thus, the aggressively partisan Army Museum in Madrid and the Museum of the Alcázar in Toledo were allowed to exist just as they had before the change in government, when they had been tools of the "victorious right." In an extraordinarily mature way the young Spanish democracy did not think it necessary or even wise to snuff out the ultraconservative narrative promoted in those museums, even though it celebrated the story of those who had fought against the republic every step of the way. In them, Franco's forces were presented and trumpeted as the moral "winners" of the civil war, long after the concept of winners and losers had been discredited. They continued, unimpeded, to address their primary audience, those citizens who needed a place to cultivate nostalgia for the old, extinguished regime.

It would be an oversimplification to assume that continued support for these museums was only about placating the thinning and increasingly demoralized members, both in and out of the service, who still believed in the values the military once epitomized. Their support was due in large measure to the part they played in nurturing and supporting the values of tolerance, even of the extreme right, in the more progressive democratically inclined population. Their significance could be assessed by measuring the degree to which all elements of society were granted their shrines—especially those with whom the new political leadership most profoundly disagreed.

The military museums are also a microcosmic reflection of Spain's willingness to acknowledge even the most troubling aspects of the country's longer history. They are just one more example of the pervasive national attitude that even the most painful histories should not be denied. In other words, no matter how devastating a particular episode might have been to the national welfare, it still needs to be afforded its place in history: Saint Vincent Ferrer still has streets named after him in Toledo even though he was personally implicated in the violence of the Inquisition; statues of Isabella II, the queen who was at least complicit in the Inquisition, are revered in churches by the faithful; kings who brought Spain financial ruin by squandering her wealth and governing poorly are memorialized with bronze equestrian sculptures in the grandest plazas. And Franco, despite having his name dropped from most cities' main avenues and plazas, can still be worshiped by his devotees. They can undertake extravagant pilgrimages to that temple of revenge, the Valley of the Fallen. And they can travel to the Army Museum and to the Museum of the Alcázar, two havens more modest than the Valley of the Fallen, but still indelibly marked by the honor they grant the devastating exploits of the man who once led them to victory.

It is cause for wonder that leaders on the left and center who took charge of Spain had the foresight and courage to allow these military museums to continue without any restriction at all—that they did not require that they at least narrate the "other side of the story." Their one-sidedness, it must have been understood, contributed to the balance between forgetting and remembering that was achieved and maintained throughout the democratization process. Notwithstanding this rationale, it is still surprising to see this tolerance extended to the military, the branch of society that had been so heavily charged with carrying out

Franco's politics of post-civil war revenge. Even later, after Franco's death, ultraright-wing military leaders flaunted their scorn for democracy. And the democratic government, during the planning stages, was fully cognizant that certain members of the military were plotting its downfall. Several coups were planned and aborted at the end of the 1970s. Then, on February 23, 1981, Colonel Antonio Tejero succeeded in storming Parliament, fully expecting to undo the work that had been accomplished up to that point. This last attempted coup failed, but it was nerve-racking proof that the creation of democracy could not be taken for granted. With a confidence that continues to amaze, the democratic leadership took heart from the Spaniards who demonstrated their overwhelming rejection of the values of dictatorship by marching in the streets in solidarity. It became apparent only later that the government had been clever rather than weak by not tampering with Franco's version of history as promulgated in those military museums. There was wisdom in refusing to further inflame extremist sensibilities any more than necessary. It was twenty years after Franco's death before there was the slightest sign that these museums might eventually alter their version of the Spanish civil war.

The Army Museum remained exactly as it had been before, throughout, and immediately after the socialist period. Located in the heart of Madrid, just steps away from the Prado in the former Palacio de Buen Retiro, its origins can be traced to a royal decree issued October 19, 1756, ordering that arsenals with exhibitions and models be established in Barcelona, Zaragoza, Seville, and La Coruña. Madrid's own installation did not take place until 1803 in the Palacio de Monteleón, when it commenced collecting artillery and models of forts and cities. Soon thereafter the Madrid site began receiving a significant annual budget as designated by King Fernando VII. After the Palacio de Monteleón was destroyed a second site was found in the Palacio de Buenavista, following the War of Independence in 1816. The Army Museum, in 1841, now moved to the Palacio de Buen Retiro, began to house not only artifacts, but also a lithography workshop for creating books and plates for pedagogical purposes, a photo laboratory, and a printing press. Succeeding years saw the growth of a passionate constituency that has enabled the museum to get to the point where, today, it has more than 13,000 objects (not counting miniatures) in its collection and almost 30,000 square feet of exhibition space. By 1932, during the first republic, the museum had galleries devoted to artillery, infantry, cavalry, and military engineers. There were separate galleries for memorabilia from the War of Independence, Charles I, Arab warfare, the Medinaceli family, Spanish heroines, and the many souvenirs of empire.[2]

By 1940 the Army Museum was dedicated solely to army history. On the surface it had become a place for the investigation into the intellectual, scientific, and technological aspects of war and its material accouterments, but it had also, by then, taken on a sacred tone. Increasingly, especially after the end of the Spanish civil war, its supporters came to view its contents more as holy relics than as mere artifacts. Tattered flags were not removed for repair because the primary constituency might worry whether they would be replaced. Decomposing, blood-stained uniforms were not cleaned because the blood, which was considered the true relic, might disappear in the attempt to save the uniform. (As in any military culture, including West Point's, the sacralizing of blood and the flag is not unusual.) But such thorny conservation issues were only a part of what prevented the Army Museum from modernizing. The underlying reason was that, just as with the *Enola Gay* exhibition at the Smithsonian, the recency of Spain's civil war made it virtually impossible to attempt a distanced, critical look at the meaning of the institution or to impose a balanced interpretation of it. This reason was greatly exacerbated since the directors of the military museums were retired generals.

The Army Museum took on those sacred overtones once the Spanish civil war was over and it became associated with Franco in the minds of the people. On March 6, 1946, in the midst of doing everything possible to bring his own supporters together to glorify himself and the nationalist cause, Franco decided to preside over the opening of new galleries at the Army Museum in the company of his senior military officers.[3] These included the "Guerra Civil" gallery, "División Azul" gallery, and "Guardia Civil" gallery. They were set aside solely for telling the story of the war, but only from the right's perspective. Paintings of Franco throughout the museum attempted to establish him as one of the "Spanish immortals." In one portrait in front of the "Arabe" gallery he is posed on horseback exactly as Velázquez once posed King Philip IV in a seventeenth-century painting. Additional portraits of Franco were installed in other galleries, including of course the one devoted to the civil war. The "División Azul" gallery commemorates Franco's decision to send a volunteer Spanish force of 18,000 men to Russia, from 1941 to 1944, to aid Germany.

The *Retrato de Franco (Portrait of Franco)* by Agustín Segura. Courtesy of the Museo del Ejército, Area de Cultura. The *Portrait of Franco* belongs to the Museo del Ejército.

Claiming to be fighting communism, Franco sought to extricate additional support from Germany and Italy. The "Guardia Civil" gallery highlights "maximum" heroes of the nationalist cause and offers general tribute to the infamously harsh state police. Yet another gallery commemorates the Sisterhood of the Blue Auxiliary, an organization of women that clandestinely aided Franco's cause in "Red Madrid" during the War of Liberation in 1936–1939. One looks in vain throughout the Army Museum for any intimation that there was a legitimate, alternate republican narrative of the Spanish civil war, soon realizing that this is not the place to seek balance. The Army Museum honors the cause of the victors of the civil war and attempts to turn and maintain their fifty-year-old propaganda into lasting, holy truth.

And who has been the Army Museum's primary audience? Who is it that the democratic government chose not to offend? The Army Museum is a place where those who wish to pay honor to the old right came during and after the dictatorship. They comprised by far the largest audience, which also contained casual visitors and military-history buffs. Sometimes visitors from the old political left visited there too. Occasionally it was possible to hear them angrily commenting on the civil war battle dioramas, furiously rebutting the nationalist representations. They would explain to anyone who wanted to engage them in conversation that these exhibits were "fascist lies, fascist inventions." They were furious that their side of the story is not yet offered in this museum. It is not that this part of the audience balks at the "pact of forgetfulness," rather that they also want their own different stories recalled in one of the country's "sacred sites."

The Museum of the Alcázar is the only military museum more extreme in its ultraright-wing outlook than the Army Museum. The Museum of the Alcázar was and remains the symbol of nationalist resistance to the republican forces. It became a memorial to the republican siege, which gave Franco some of his side's most colorful history and propaganda. Through the 1990s the Museum of the Alcázar was, in its civil war sections, an unrelieved, melodramatic paean—complete with dungeons, written testimonials, dramatic room settings and paraphernalia of all kinds—dedicated to the nationalist cause. It was unabashedly designed to demonize the republican side. There was not the slightest bow to the other side's humanity, much less to any possible nobility that its members might have possessed. It functioned as a museum about winners and losers, good and bad, revenge and vindictiveness. And it was always well attended. Even in the mid-1990s one could observe busloads of elderly women and men arriving in Toledo expressly for the purpose of visiting the Museum of the Alcázar and paying their respects to what they considered to be heroic days when the victors were fighting for the sake of their world. What they would encounter at that museum was a complete affirmation of their own myths of the civil war. As uncomfortable as it must have been, the democratically elected government sensed that these profoundly painful memories needed to have a few museums of their own where such a version of history could go unchallenged.

By 1994 the situation showed signs of change. The Ministry of Defense made a surprising appointment, Leticia Azcue Brea, a civilian and the first woman to be placed in such a high position, as the director of all military museums in Spain. Azcue had been the vice-director of the Museum of the Royal Academy of Fine Arts of San Fernando in Madrid and had accumulated valuable experience working in the Ministry of Culture before that. In an interview in spring 1995 she indicated that one of her challenges would be to "complete the story" by telling the other side.[4] The time, she explained, was finally right to begin that task. To make her point about the timing, she told me that she had just returned from a commemorative ceremony for Spanish volunteers who had fought in World War II under the aegis of Allied countries against the Axis powers. That this ceremony was sponsored by the Ministry of Defense was something that, even in the recent past, would have been inconceivable. Furthermore, having just returned from a trip to study other modern military museums such as the Imperial War Museum in London, Azcue was researching how military history could be related in more neutral, less inflammatory ways—how it might be possible to accommodate multiple perspectives. Azcue, with her keen understanding of the latest museological and educational techniques, wanted to devise methods of teaching visitors how they could discern the attributes of propaganda or demagoguery. Speaking to her and perceiving her clarity of purpose and her immense intelligence, one felt that change was just around the corner and that Spain no longer needed to keep its most prominent military museums from modernization.

Azcue reminded me in that conversation that sensitivities must still be taken into account on all civil war issues. For example, she and her colleagues wanted to exercise extreme care when deciding whether and when to release classified material from civil war archives. Probably, she said, they would wait until the last person who might be affected was dead, because to find out that brother killed brother or that child had turned on parent could, even now, be devastating. In spite of these precautions, change was taking place, but as late as 1996 it remained very much behind the scenes. By then Azcue was reporting directly to the defense minister, which indicates the increased preoccupation of the army with these plans. By March 1998 the Army Museum had a professional director and curator and was expecting an additional four curators, all to improve the museum's professionalism. In quiet but irreversible ways preparations were being made for even the right-wing military museums to enter the democratic era.

There was some subtle progress on the public front as well. The language describing the galleries, for example, had begun to take a distinct turn away from the heat of the old cultural politics. A comparison of museum guides highlights the transformation that was slowly but definitively being wrought.[5] The 1983 guide produced during the transition opened with a quote from the Book of Job, which intoned that man's life on earth is one of perpetual war, and his days are spent as an unhappy traveler. The sacredness of the displays was thus being reinforced by biblical allusion. By 1995, democracy now fully consolidated, the words chosen to introduce the revamped guidebook come, instead, from Baltasar Gracián, a seventeenth-century Spanish writer. Entirely different in tone, Gracián's words allude to the wonder inspired by contemplation of celestial and earthly globes, spheres, astrolabes, cylinders, compasses, mathematics, and artifacts that historically served "noble painting and architecture." This shift to cooler, more rational language prepares the museum visitor to learn in an academic sense, abjuring the glorification of war as divinely ordained and inevitable.

The earlier guides were illustrated not only with photographs of Franco's bronze death mask but also, somewhat ghoulishly, with images of his hands and feet. In describing the "Guerra Civil" gallery the guides pointed out nationalist heroes and ideals. They also directed the spectator to the paintings of Franco and glorified his subordinates and the famous generals who served under him. These were guidebooks that made no pretense to objectivity; they were meant to stir the blood and elevate the emotions, summoning up bitter memories against the red troops. They led the visitor to the "sacred" approach to the museum's relics, writings, and personal belongings by highlighting such items as a letter written by a soon-to-be-executed soldier who had refused to take command of troops of the left and by reproducing a melodramatic poem lauding the right's courage during the siege of the Alcázar. The 1983 guidebook, overwhelmingly committed to the nationalist cause, made only a single nod to reconciliation, when, under a bloody Spanish flag, a few lines by José Luis Hidalgo seemed to accept the universality of the pain of this civil war: "I weep," he wrote, "for those who have fallen because they are of my village. . . ."[6]

A decade later the 1995 guidebook is unambiguously devoted to preparing the ground for the work that Azcue was hired to undertake—redefining the role of the military museum in Spanish society. Beyond Gracián's quotation Gustavo Suárez Pertierra, minister of defense, writes in the new preface that the concept of the military museum is in flux, that it is time for these museums to approach the rest of society, that is the nonmilitary classes.[7] His language is consistently pithy, and the entire guide is devoid of any inflammatory rhetoric. The "Guerra Civil" gallery, which was discussed so flamboyantly in the 1984 guidebook, is practically dismissed in one brief sentence that laconically notes that the gallery contains objects donated by the families of outstanding personages in the war. Similarly short shrift is accorded the "Guardia Civil" and "Division Azul" galleries. The description of the Museum of the Alcázar is equally surprising in its lack of the heated, quasi-religious prose and poetry the Ministry of Defense thought it still merited only ten years before. Based on this revised guide, one would expect the Museum of the Alcázar to be merely a standard museum of historical firearms, coins, costumes, medals, and flags.

Newspapers regularly began floating rumors in the mid-1990s that the Prado would actually take over the Army Museum's site for its much vaunted (and long delayed) expansion and renovation. Rumors were also constantly planted that the Museum of the Alcázar might absorb the Army Museum and that it would be rethought completely. Clearly all of the behind-the-scenes activity, all of the intellectual exchange, and all of the professionalization that was in the works had been careful preparation for a move that would be well expected by the public. Then, whenever the Army Museum does actually relocate (which was being openly discussed as an inevitability by the end of the 1990s), the overhaul of both museums will come as less of a shock to what little remains of the ultraright. In the meantime, many of the twenty-nine other military museums had already been updated. They all began to take on the look of history museums in love with their musketry, ship models, paintings, globes, maps, and compasses. They ceased having even the whiff of propaganda about them.

Recently the Ministry of Defense decided to produce temporary exhibitions in collaboration with nondefense government entities. One example of this was a 1994 exhibition, the *Royal Factories of Sargadelos: The Army and the Navy (Las reales fábricas d Sargadelos, el ejército y las armada)*, held in Madrid.[8] This exhibition was produced in cooperation with civil authorities and partially financed with loans from many nonmilitary organizations such as the National Libraries, city and provincial museums such as those in Pontevedra and Lugo, and the Spanish Red Cross. It was intended to redirect the perception of the historic role of the Spanish military from being one exclusively connected to the battlefield to one of being a developer of local industry and economy, in this case in Galicia— one of the country's poorest regions. *Royal Factories of Sargadelos* was meant to offer additional "proof" that the military no longer wished to be alienated from civil society; it signaled a desire by the military to realign itself with the majority of the population.

The military has thus begun to view museums, one of its few outreach tools, as a means of increasing its reintegration into mainstream society. This is a pragmatic path to follow since Spain, given its citizens' current distaste for the military, has become one of the most pacifist countries in Europe with the largest number of conscientious objectors. Clearly the nation's bent has been fully absorbed by the military, which cannot deny that Spaniards see themselves as peacemakers—hence their pride in their high-profile role in the United Nations as *cascos azules* (blue-helmeted) soldiers.

Exactly how the Army Museum and the Museum of the Alcázar will reinvent themselves was not known in 1999 as this book was being completed. That the two museums will share the same building in Toledo is the expectation; but their missions, future programming, and museological and museographical plans remain a mystery. What *is* completely new is the extent to which their future has entered into the conversation among professionals. The most surprising of all proposals was made in the *Revista de Museología,* Spain's version of the American Association of Museum's magazine *Museum News.* The coauthors, after lamenting the fact that the Army Museum and the Museum of the Alcázar do justify war in the ways they have presented themselves, proposed that when they come together, they should "metamorphose" into institutions advocating peace. They then asked whether or not it would be possible for the museums to radically reverse their mission so as to serve as another kind of sacred site: a site where one would reflect upon and critically analyze the conflicts endured in Spain from its prehistory until the twentieth century. Wouldn't it be a better legacy for our children, they asked, if they are given a museum of peace rather than one of sieges; if they can finally dispose of the notion of conquerors versus those who were conquered?[9]

Although it is unlikely that these two museums will change to that extent, it is already quite clear that they have played a special role, albeit an extremely subtle one, in promoting the peacefulness and stability of Spanish society during the years of its democratic formation. By granting the ultraright wing their corners of space and allowing the time its adherents needed to adjust to their unexpected fate, they contributed to the calm and constructive atmosphere of the transition. Left and center politicians made no moves to prevent this constituency from spinning its own superheated, partisan version of history in the Army Museum and the Museum of the Alcázar. By extension, this openness further demonstrated that a fair and free society, one distinct from the society out of which it emerged, was going to be the norm. Now, with the passage of time, the last bastions of the outdated military culture will finally give way—their power to shape identity in the old way depleted. They will not, however, have "disappeared." Rather, they will have to share their own best public forum—the museum—with versions of history that will differ from their own.

MUSEUMS OF THE CHURCH

The hundreds of religious museums in Spain do not have nearly as aggressive a support system as do the military museums. Consequently, their impact on society is, and may be expected to continue to be, quite modest. These museums were, though, more important in the Franco years than they are now, functioning as vessels for the artifacts and art of the Catholic religion—the faith that presumed to unite the state. In fact, religious museums were among those institutions that helped infuse the state with Franco's notion of spirituality. On a more practical note, the church-related museums were places where the enormous, often threatened artistic legacy of Catholicism could be kept relatively safe, was sometimes conserved, and was somewhat protected from export. Because these museums, both ecclesiastical and diocesanal, were so instrumental in those respects during Franco's day, they had grown to be practically ubiquitous by the end of his regime. It should be noted, however, that even though Franco always identified with the church, several years before Franco's death key elements of the church had distanced themselves from him and from his most destructive and controlling policies. There had always been areas of tension of different sorts between both the Vatican and the Spanish church and state. Indeed, by the end of the regime the church did not consider itself a loyal party to the dictatorship.[10] Rather, "it looked toward restoration of the monarchy under Prince Juan Carlos to direct Spain's path toward peaceful reform and liberalization."[11]

Notwithstanding the church's distance from Franco at the end of his life and the secularized character of Spain today, an awareness of its religious museums is necessary to any full understanding of the country's historical spiritual identity. Even today, to assume that Spain is completely secular would be a mistake, since most Spaniards still choose to marry and be buried with the church's blessings, to baptize their children, and to later arrange for their communions. "Much traditional baggage and some traditional values have been jettisoned, but whether a firm spiritual foundation has been retained, or a new one found, is less certain."[12] Through it all most church museums continue to play their quiet, unappreciated, and usually self-effacing role of reminding, affirming, and underlining by their sheer existence that the primary religion of Spain is, without question, Catholicism. They do this partly through the heft of their inventories: the collections of these museums comprise approximately 70 percent of the national historical patrimony—if one includes the cathedrals, churches, monasteries, and convents.[13] Their importance as vessels for the bulk of the national historic patrimony is further confirmed when one scans any of the guidebooks describing the cultural amenities of any Spanish region. These museums largely came into existence as part of a desperate effort to save religious works from being sold, pillaged, or confiscated. The following account is typical: "In 1939, after the end of the civil war, the archbishop created the Diocesan Museum (Museo Diocesano-Catedralico) to gather, in one place with minimum guarantees for their preservation, religious pieces and objects that, because of changes in the liturgy, had fallen into disuse, as well as those works that were rescued during the war."[14] Sadly, unimaginative and endlessly repetitive displays of reliquaries, ritual and decorative objects, textiles, paintings, and sculptures in distressed and vulnerable condition are the norm. There is usually little professional management, minimal budget (if any), and scarce documentation or modern scholarship to enliven the displays.

Dreary as these museums ordinarily are, there is some comfort in knowing that the greater part of the church's most outstanding works were long ago sent to national and provincial museums where they are being cared for in professionally supervised, secure, and climatically controlled conditions. Thus, in the Museum of Burgos (Museo de Burgos) in the Castilla y Leon region one will find stunning architectural fragments, chancels, capitals, paintings, doors, and other sculptures and decorative arts displayed imaginatively, conserved well, and interpreted in an up-to-date manner. Most of this movement, from church to civic museum, happened in less than felicitous circumstances during the nineteenth century when thousands of artworks belonging to religious institutions were expropriated by the state. Tragically, many extremely valuable works were lost in this process. Nevertheless, among the pieces that do remain in ecclesiastical or diocesan museums, one will frequently come upon masterpieces, more often than not in execrable state. An increasing percentage of them have been cleaned and restored, usually because they were lent to an exhibition where desperately needed conservation was undertaken in exchange for loaning the object. This is the case in the Colegiata, a church-owned building in the town of Osuna, which is the owner of many fine paintings by Jusepe de Ribera. Over the years, given the renewed interest in Ribera's art, these paintings have been requested and restored by such major institutions as the Metropolitan Museum of Art in New York. It should also be noted that the cathedrals, churches, and monasteries—the structures to which these museums are connected— are increasingly accepted as museums themselves and as a part of a larger, more universally valued monumental heritage. They are receiving much-needed attention both from inside and outside of Spain. In 1994 the cathedral in León received advice on the conservation of its great stained glass windows from the Getty Conservation Institute in Los Angeles. Since 1996 the secular authorities of Spain, especially after the victory of the Conservative Party, have more actively been stepping in to help save the greatest of these monuments, such as the cathedral in Burgos, from further deterioration.

Even if the works of art in church-related museums are usually not presented in modern displays or imaginative installations, there are noteworthy exceptions. The Diocesan Museum in Cuenca is an example of such a treasure house where the art objects within have fared brilliantly. Credit for this belongs, however, not to the ecclesiastical bureaucracy but to the dedication of Gustavo Torner, a civically involved artist who was also one of those responsible for the development of the Museum of Abstract Art (Museo de Arte Abstracto Español) in Cuenca. All the art is presented dramatically, meaningfully, and with the refined aesthetic sensibility normally only seen in "high art" exhibitions. The result is lively and inviting, bringing the well-preserved objects into the contemporary world. Works by El Greco and Gerard David and anonymously created treasures are superbly presented in rich and appropriate settings. Red and brown velvets and green silks surround the paintings, dramatically setting them off while carefully reminding the spectator of how they originally functioned in a religious setting. Another institution of this type that has been recently remodeled is the Museo Diocesanal in San Sebastián in the Basque Country. After adapting a 1967 building, which had been intended as a conference center, the result (combined with creative and vital museography) is a fresh and exciting invitation to the contemplation of sacred works. There are a growing number of projects of this type throughout Spain, and one suspects that we are witnessing a small but significant trend.

Occasionally ecclesiastical or diocesan museums have been able to present exhibitions that attempt to infiltrate the modern consciousness and assert certain religious values, even in the antiauthoritarian, materialistic atmosphere of post-Franco Spain. These are exhibitions that signal the church's desire to rekindle whatever might remain of the religious interest of the modern Spaniard—but they have been known to do so in more adventurous ways than one might expect. Utilizing its wealth of artworks in an innovative collaboration with the support of the local autonomous government and the Ministry of Culture, the church leadership in the Castilla y Leon region conceived of a new exhibition form—one described in the Spanish press as a macroexhibition. In order to engage the maximum number of people, *The Ages of Man (Las edades del hombre)* was designed to take place over five years at four cathedrals in the cities of Valladolid, Burgos, León, and Salamanca. In each of these four sites the church elaborated the history and meaning of its patrimony by utilizing the various arts. Producing successive stages of the same exhibition for different audiences in the cities mentioned above, they marketed their "product" in a series of enticing, unexpectedly creative ways. Large and heterogeneous crowds came to see the shows in these distinctive venues, willingly standing in long lines, justifying to both church and region the expensive, expansive, often theatrical, and sometimes high-tech museum techniques they employed. It became apparent that curiosity about the ecclesiastical could be stimulated again, so long as it was presented in a contemporary and pertinent manner.

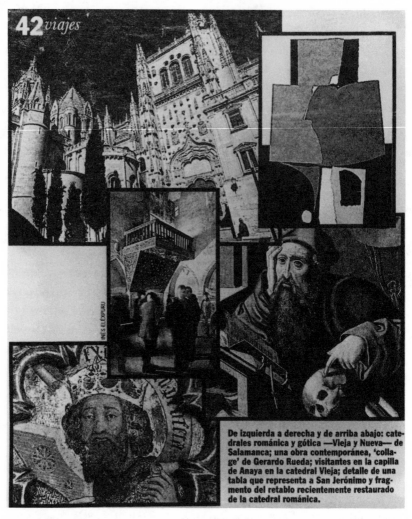

De izquierda a derecha y de arriba abajo: catedrales románica y gótica —Vieja y Nueva— de Salamanca; una obra contemporánea, 'collage' de Gerardo Rueda; visitantes en la capilla de Anaya en la catedral Vieja; detalle de una tabla que representa a San Jerónimo y fragmento del retablo recientemente restaurado de la catedral románica.

Montage photograph in *El País,* by Inés Eléxpuru, to publicize *The Ages of Man* exhibition. Courtesy *El País*

At *The Ages of Man* visitors were able to look at paintings, sculptures, and books while seeming to travel through space and time, all the while enveloped in the sacred music that the church believes has always nurtured the soul. Of course the church used the exhibition to tout its own conservative perspective on family life, daily pleasures, religious duties, and storytelling in a variety of sacred venues. At Salamanca both of the city's cathedrals were drafted into service: an "older" Romanesque cathedral and a "newer" Gothic cathedral. In these two gorgeous stone settings visitors were confronted by unexpected juxtapositions of old and new art as well. Sixteenth-century Spanish polychromatic sculptures were paired with modern abstractions by collagists from Cuenca. Without doubt the effort was highly successful for the church. It touched many people who had been alienated from the church, bringing them together through the arts, history, and contemporaneity. *The Ages of Man* was premised on the possibility of dialogue between modern culture and the ancient faith. Most of the people, often standing in freezing weather, seemed intrigued at this ambitious, innovative attempt by the extremely conservative Catholic church to reintroduce itself to the contemporary Spaniard. This approach to using the inventory of the church museums was so successful that ultimately it was mounted in six (not just the original four) venues, the final one opening in summer 1997 in the cathedral in the charming city of El Burgo de Osma.

The church has, then, shown in a few dramatic instances that it can use its wealth of art and artifacts in an original and compelling way to communicate its message. Throughout the socialist period the Ministry of Culture offered only minimal and grudging support for that message. But with the election of the Conservative Party there have been more substantial efforts to aid these museum and museum-related projects than had been the case in the early years of the democracy. It seems likely that there will be more conservation of permanent ecclesiastical collections, more conservation of important cathedrals, and more collaborations between secular and church authorities such as *The Ages of Man* exhibition as long as the electorate aligns itself with the conservatives and their policies.

It is clear that those in charge of the Catholic church–related museums will have to continue to radically rethink the nature of their work if they wish to reenter the positive consciousness of the majority of Spanish people, who are well aware of the church's excesses, especially those that occurred during the early stages of the dictatorship. Should that happen the museums and the exhibitions that could then be created from Spain's fabulous religious-artistic treasury would once again be part (if radically altered) of the cultural identity of the modern, secular Spaniard. It seems, though, that church museums will thrive only when the identity they are promoting is intended to broaden rather than constrict lives.

With the church's power so diminished since the end of the dictatorship, it will have to continue to constructively reimagine itself if it is to assert and maintain any real influence in a Spain no longer interested in submitting to any authoritarian systems. Certainly one can see glimmers that the church's most creative minds are working hard to meet this challenge.

4
PROGRESSIVE PRIVATE FOUNDATIONS LEGITIMIZED BY THE STATE

While justifiably proud of a long and rich tradition of state and church support for culture, Spain also has a far less-known history of nongovernmental, secular patronage of the arts. Beginning in the mid-nineteenth century, the entrenched and socially responsible bourgeoisie in the Basque Country and Catalonia developed a tradition of patronage that survived, albeit greatly weakened, throughout the Franco years. After the birth of democracy private support for the arts was gradually rejuvenated in the Basque Country and Catalonia, and it began also gaining appeal and credibility beyond those two regions. Almost immediately after Franco's death private foundations recognized by the state became a force to be reckoned with: an effective means of offering sustenance and advocacy for the arts in a variety of visible, often high-profile ways. Taking a share of responsibility for the country's creative expression, a number of foundations took advantage of their legal rights and their considerable capital to operate outside of the government. Their ability to claim outsider status has enabled them to maintain the continuity of their upper administration and pursue their purposes despite changes in government. They offer a telling example of the willingness of the new democracy to incorporate entities into Spanish society that, by their very nature, are able to withstand political pressure—to operate independently of current fashions in order to best perpetuate their missions.

By 1993 there were 785 private foundations listed in the Ministry of Culture's directory.[1] Around 90 percent of Spain's foundations came into being after the dictatorship, and they represent a wide spectrum of perspectives, approaches, and philosophies. It should not be a surprise that some of them have always run counter to the views of the existing government. Many of those listed are also registered in their respective autonomous regions, but all of them are dedicated to furthering some aspect of Spain's cultural life through philanthropy. The larger and richer of the foundations have had an impact far beyond any region they might nominally represent.

In 1994 a long-awaited philanthropy law was passed by the state, giving increased fiscal incentives to the already burgeoning world of foundations.[2] The law was passed in hopes of igniting a more pervasive, more American-type spirit of private giving in Spain, with the full understanding that America's system is based as much on tax relief as on civic generosity. In 1996 the newly elected Conservative Party stated, as one of its basic tenets, that private support for the arts was essential to preserving and enhancing the hard-won freedoms of the Spanish people. Its platform therefore called for citizens to start assuming greater responsibility for their own cultural lives.[3]

The success experienced by cultural foundations during the socialist period, the discussion in the press of the merits and limitations of the 1994 philanthropy law, and the conservative rhetoric demanding "a radical change of mind" leading to "greater social participation in both the fostering and spread of cultural creation" converged in 1996. All three factors convinced a majority of Spaniards that private support for culture was one of the stamps of modernity they should adopt. Furthermore, fears about the economy drove home the sentiment that the health and well-being of the arts depended on diversifying their sources of support. Courses and masters degree programs focusing on the American system of management and fund-raising sprang up in metropolitan centers. Capitalist gurus from the United States were imported and paid extravagant fees to inspire and train young leaders in how to wean themselves from total dependence on government. It would be a mistake to think that Spain ever intended to completely discard the old state-support system. It was, however, interested in absorbing alternative means of financing the arts and sculpting its own hybrid model that would incorporate traditional Spanish patronage patterns.

This chapter relates the stories of two private, progressive foundations registered by the central government and headquartered in Madrid that took great responsibility upon themselves to enhance the democratization of the Spanish sensibility throughout Spain's post-Franco period and beyond by stimulating wide-ranging debate and discussion about culture. (La Caixa, the huge and powerful foundation based in Catalonia, will be discussed in part two of this book.) These two organizations concentrated their resources on educating Spanish citizens so they could better adapt to the demands and opportunities of the global society in which they were finally full participants. Each has proven to be an essential partner in Spain's evolving museum world. Each has expanded the very definition of the word "museum." In fact they were both major contributors to the aura of excitement and celebration that surrounded the highly publicized and enthusiastic reception of contemporary art throughout the late 1970s and 1980s. Exposing the general public to challenging visual-arts experiences was one of the satisfying and highly symbolic ways to affirm and celebrate their country's participation in the world, and they did this regularly and frequently. They were fully committed to the type of art that encouraged the chipping away at the notion of certainty so loved by the dictatorship that had plagued Spanish society for so long. With art as their means these foundations piled one ambiguity on top of another, introducing previously unheard of habits of seeing and thinking to a welcoming Spanish society.[4]

THE JUAN MARCH FOUNDATION

Juan March Ordinas and his eponymous foundation, the Juan March Foundation (Fundación Juan March), epitomize the contradictions and paradoxes that inevitably rise to the surface in any study of twentieth-century Spain. March was one of Franco's early financial supporters, supplying the funds that enabled Franco to play his role in the 1936 coup against the republic. March was, by all accounts, a businessman who aided Franco not necessarily because he believed in him, but more likely because he suspected that it would pay off financially. That being said, it still seems strange: before the Spanish civil war, March had actually been a progressive representative of the republic from Las Palmas and always had a strong interest in the avant-garde. Given the predictably authoritarian, regressive nature of Franco's regime, millionaire March would seem to have been an unlikely participant in the rebellion against the legitimate republican government. In fact, his independent spirit did eventually antagonize Franco to some extent much later in his regime, and later events proved that he had not abandoned his progressive inclinations.

Taking advantage of one of the rare political interludes during which it behooved the Franco government not to appear as if Spaniards were completely closed off from the rest of the world, March, in 1955, created his private foundation in Madrid. Today many credit this organization with having been one of the crucial players in preparing the ground for the successful transition to democracy. March's immensely well-endowed foundation acted discreetly until Franco died, granting generous scholarships to young members of the Spanish elite, enabling them to travel and widen their horizons. Going abroad, many thus obtained educational experiences and fresh views from outside the claustrophobic universe that was their home.[5] One is often told in Spain today that anyone who is anyone now received a Juan March *beca* (fellowship) back then. The *becas* went to scholars, scientists, social planners, and artists, helping to mold a class of people who were thus exposed to and engaged with open societies during their formative years. As March must have hoped, those young people he had helped were among those poised to seize the opportunities that presented themselves once Spain was on the brink of its social transformation. Many became quite influential in that process.

In the realm of the visual arts, the leaders of the Juan March Foundation denied in print as late as 1980 any involvement with politics.[6] Notwithstanding that demur, the foundation did achieve one profoundly political goal: the foundation and its activities made it socially acceptable for the middle and upper levels of society, those people in Spain who were normally inclined to conservatism, to be engaged with the avant-garde. By introducing the scions of Spain's most elite families to material that was by its very nature ambiguous in content and form, challenging to authority, highly individualistic, and determinedly unconventional, the Juan March Foundation diminished the thirst for the absolute in its future leaders—a thirst that is one of the hallmarks of ideological fascism. The importance of the twenty-year trickle of ideas and attitudes that the Juan March Foundation so consistently abetted, attitudes directly contrary to those of the dictatorship, cannot be overstated. Spain's upper classes may have identified with these fascistic attitudes, but their children were given socially acceptable means to rebel against them. By leaving home for awhile they were preparing themselves for future leadership roles in the inexorably changing society.

From 1955 to 1970 the Juan March Foundation devoted itself exclusively to awarding those scholarships. It also began and continued an important art restoration program for the traditional patrimony. But, from 1970 until Franco's death five years later the foundation moved into a new tactical phase. It continued providing scholarships for travel abroad and within Spain, and it began to initiate the organization of exhibitions. In 1973 the Juan March Foundation installed a show of forty-one contemporary Spanish artists, all of whom had previously been granted a scholarship. *Arte 73*, the initial exhibition, traveled around Spain's periphery and Europe until December 1975, when Franco's death finally made it possible to mount it in Madrid. This was also the year the foundation opened its stylish headquarters in an upper-class neighborhood of the capital and began to function as one of its main cultural and scientific centers. Although the Juan March Foundation site in Madrid technically does not call itself a museum, it is, for all intents and purposes, precisely that. Collecting, preserving, and regularly exhibiting artworks in Madrid and in its two other sites in Cuenca and Palma (which do bear the name "museum") eminently qualify it for that status. After 1975 all Juan March Foundation exhibitions were accompanied by an expanded education program featuring conferences, courses, concerts, and publications. By doing this the foundation actually introduced modern museum programming practices to Spain.

When the foundation inaugurated its exhibitions in Madrid, bringing contemporary art to large general audiences that had never seen such work before, it had a profound effect. Audiences saw their first Kokoschka, Giacometti, Dubuffet, Bacon, and DeKooning paintings in its galleries. In 1977 Picasso had his largest exhibition in Madrid since 1936 at the foundation's headquarters. Always free of charge, the Juan March Foundation's exhibitions have been a key means by which the arts of the second half of the century have been made available to the general Spanish population. By 1980, twenty-five years after its inauguration, the Juan March Foundation was counted among the most successful humanities foundations in Europe along with Gulbenkian, Volkswagen, and Krupp— for its resources, range, and intensity of activities. It takes pride in being an

Crowds at the Picasso exhibition, September 1977, at the Juan March Foundation (Fundación Juan March). Courtesy Fundación Juan March.

organization that, because it is private and has economic autonomy, can act with agility, independence, and originality. The Juan March Foundation has had immeasurable impact in all its areas of interest, but the contributions in the realm of the visual arts have been the most publicly known and appreciated.[7]

The foundation continued, throughout and after the transition, to mount international art exhibitions for the rapidly democratizing Spanish public. It became an ever more lively presence on the Spanish art scene, with long lines of visitors always waiting to get into its groundbreaking shows. Eager and intent audiences attended them, and by 1997 well over six million people had attended more than 425 shows. Over the decades the foundation expanded its patronage of living Spanish artists from various regions across the country, accumulating an impressive collection of paintings, prints, and sculptures in the process. It undertook financial responsibility and management of the Collection of Contemporary Spanish Art (Col·lecció March. Art Espanyol Contemporani) in Palma, which was to operate along much the same lines as the foundation's headquarters in Madrid. In 1980 the Juan March Foundation accepted management responsibility for the Museum of Abstract Art (Museo de Arte Abstracto Español) in Cuenca, which had been founded fourteen years earlier by a group of artists. The Museum of Abstract Art is an especially complex element of the paradoxical story of contemporary art in Spain, and it is more than fitting that the Juan March Foundation has played so critical a role in its survival. The balance of this section will examine the history of the museum in Cuenca as yet another extraordinary manifestation of the role of the museum as institution in the construction of the identity of the newly democratic Spanish citizen.

It comes as a surprise, knowing how much abstract art was abhorred in the left-wing Soviet dictatorships, that nonobjective painting and sculpture had a life of its own in Spain's right-wing dictatorship. Abstract art began to slowly surface in Spain after 1953 and received official recognition by its inclusion in the Spanish pavilion at the 1958 Venice Biennial. It soon found an enthusiastic audience and became a part of the national aesthetic fabric. The pavilion featured the country's most well-known pioneers of abstract art, the stars among them being Antoní Tapies from Barcelona, associated with the Dau al Set group, Antonio Saura from Madrid, associated with the El Paso group, and Eduardo Chillida, the internationally acclaimed sculptor from San Sebastián. It remains something of a mystery that this art was not repressed as, by its nature, it brought to the fore thoughts and emotions that should, by all logic, have been considered antifascist. Abstraction, as many of the earliest Spanish practitioners employed it, was a disconcerting projection of disequilibrium and contradiction—a harsh or disquieting representation by artists at home with chaos and at odds with the enforced order of society. And, abstraction in the twentieth century has always been a statement and defense of "art for art's sake." By virtue of its distance from the concrete, its rejection of any inherited norms of truth or beauty, and its use of signals only insiders can understand, abstract art mitigates against outside control of meaning and significance. Totalitarian governments generally deplore such ambiguity and ambivalence. They realize full well the threat this kind of "communication" poses to the monolithic, hegemonic thinking critical to their survival. These are governments that thrive on depictions of conventionally idealized reality meant to aid them in furthering their constructed illusions of unity, absolutist authority, and harmony. They seek, and tend to employ, an imagery that is ultimately utilitarian.

All things considered, one would have expected Spanish abstract art to have been stamped out or, at the very least, forced underground as it was in the former Soviet Union. Neither happened. On the other hand it would be simplistic to suggest that this disconcerting style of art just slipped by Franco, that he did not grasp any of its implications, or that he saw it merely as a harmless venting at one of the early moments of internal dissatisfaction with the regime. Rather, as was Franco's wont, he used it; he co-opted it for the purpose of advancing the society he was in the midst of building and promoting. It probably mattered little to him that the artists were also using him to promote themselves and their own anti-Franco attitudes.

How, then, did Franco "use" the abstract artists of the late 1950s? After World War II until 1953 Spain was ostracized by much of the international community. Intellectual life within the country continued its stiflingly narrow course. Beginning in 1953, when Spain was permitted to enter the United Nations, Franco came to appreciate the advisability of turning an occasionally progressive mien to the outside world. In 1956 there was pressure from the left, especially from within the universities and among the children of the elites, to open up further. By 1957 Spain had, in certain ways, complied: Spain's pioneering abstract art groups were allowed to exhibit their work—with official approval—at the 1958 Venice Biennial. By that time Franco had come to appreciate that there was value in having two faces: one for the outside world and one for the world at home. Apparently, he realized that the Venice Biennial, an immense international art showcase, could lend him the face he needed to present to the world. He thus allowed the El Paso and Dau al Set artists their exposure, making it appear to one and all that he was finally permitting or even encouraging some freedom of creative expression. In fact, Franco was constructing his own version of a Potemkin village. This small part of a larger strategy paid off beautifully in 1959, when President

Dwight Eisenhower, after visiting Franco, wrote that he was "impressed by the fact that there was no discernible mannerism or characteristic that would lead an unknowing visitor to conclude that he was in the presence of a dictator."[8] Franco's long-term satisfaction with his two-faced strategy can be seen in a 1971 comment to his future successor, Juan Carlos I. Juan Carlos I (who had already been designated "crown prince of Spain" by Franco in 1969) had recently returned from a trip to America, where he had discussed the touchy issue of Spanish freedom in public. Franco did not reprimand him for having done this, but approvingly said instead: "There are things which you can and must say outside Spain and things which you must not say inside Spain."[9] One suspects, however, that even the artists, who at the time saw themselves as resisting Franco because of the nature of their art, may have had some difficulty being his official representative during that period. Certainly, the late Antonio Saura, a principal founder of the El Paso group and one of the artists whose abstract work was the most violent, discordant, and passionate, seemed defensive in an unpublished interview in 1988, where he insisted that while he, Tapies, and Chillida had indeed been the official representatives of Franco's regime at the Venice Biennial, that their participation had been strongly anti-Franco. Yet, bowing to the evident ambiguities of their position, Saura admitted that he would not have done it again.[10]

After the Venice Biennial Franco was astute enough to allow the issue of abstract art to fade. He was successful in having allowed the abstract artists official sanction in that it became one of the many ways that some members of the international community could convince themselves that he was not a "real" dictator. Was Franco also clever enough to intuit that this art, especially if he did nothing to prevent its seeping into the general culture, would do him no immediate harm? We have no way of knowing how much he thought this out. We do know, though, that after an initial frisson, abstraction in Spain (as it eventually did elsewhere) lost its edge and devolved into a decorative and "domesticated" style easily imitated by succeeding generations of artists. A wealthy Spanish-Philippine artist, Fernando Zobel, who had befriended a number of the early abstract artists, soon began collecting their works. In 1966 he, along with artist friends Gustavo Torner and Gerardo Rueda, created an abstract art museum in Cuenca—the first of its kind in Spain. The building itself is a piece of abstract sculpture situated in a gorgeous city of cliff-side houses. This museum has, over the years, become a permanent monument to the

Spanish abstract movement. It boasts some of the finest (even iconic) works made by that first daring generation—Antoní Tapies, Antonio Saura, and Eduardo Chillida, along with Rueda's, Torner's, and Zobel's paintings and sculptures and works by other less internationally renowned artists of the movement. As Franco might have suspected, the art it contained—and the other abstract art being created in Spain—did not overtly undermine the regime, and was soon somewhat paradoxically perceived by Spaniards as innocuous: it rapidly seemed to become harmonious and ideally beautiful. Nevertheless, the art did increase society's contact with the outside world. The population of this out-of-the-way museum transformed Cuenca from a poor provincial town into a thriving tourist city, furthering the breakdown of Spain's isolation. Perhaps because abstraction never had to become an underground movement (like that of similar art in the Soviet Union) and also being so far from Madrid, it was met with official indifference.

It is, nevertheless, puzzling to see so many present-day Spanish intellectuals dismissing the Museum of Abstract Art in Cuenca as having been politically insignificant. This is especially unfortunate, since much of the art of that first generation, when evaluated within the context of the time and place of its creation, ranks high for its love of chaos, vigor, and originality. It represented an ideal of free humanity in a disordered universe. The Juan March Foundation, always taking the longer and broader view, recognized what had indeed been accomplished by Spain's abstract artists in closing the gap between their country and ideas from abroad, between fascistic ideas about aesthetics and those of the democratic world. It grasped that only with the passage of time would the Cuencan legacy be properly studied and appraised. With that in mind, not only did the foundation save the Museum of Abstract Art by accepting the obligation to run it, but it complemented the museum's holdings by purchasing a significant body of those artists' works that had been in the collection of Abraham Cahan of New York.

It is intriguing that the complexities of Spain's most daring art movement of the 1950s and 1960s, as preserved in Cuenca, is neither explored nor discussed as such in the museum itself. Unlike other Juan March Foundation exhibitions and installations, rich with didactic materials, including contextualizing panels and labels, lavish catalogs, and illuminating brochures and orientation pamphlets, the works in the Museum of Abstract Art are left to speak for themselves. Evidently the foundation sees it as futile to argue for the integrity of those artists at a time when its audience wants to ignore the details of their past. When sufficient years pass, however, it seems likely that Spanish society will begin to give more credit to those who questioned the values of the regime by creating art essentially antithetical to it—even if Franco did succeed in co-opting them to some extent in the process. Only then will there be more discussion made available to the general public. For now, the works are beautifully hung but mute, with no attempt whatsoever to relate their compellingly ambiguous role in Spain's modern cultural and even political history.

Juan March, his family, and the subsequent leadership of the Juan March Foundation have possessed great foresight. In sum they understood power and influence, took the most expansive possible views, and even during the dictatorship managed to educate members of both the elite and less privileged classes to options beyond the world they inhabited. By doing so, they wrestled with and tamed the legacy of their own modern history. The Juan March Foundation has more than earned its founder's redemption for his early support of Franco. It has been a major player, through its museum-related activities and its many other science and humanities programs, in effecting the transformation of Spain's citizenry after the post-Franco era. The foundation did its work long before it was politically safe to do so, taking full and creative advantage of any windows of opportunity that it could find to promote liberty. Fortunately, it has thrived and can bear witness to the fruits of its labors and to continue its excellent work.

ARCO

Spain's international contemporary art fair, ARCO (Feria Internacional de Arte Contemporáneo), is not merely one more international art bazaar. By the early 1990s ARCO had become one of the top five such fairs worldwide. Inaugurated in 1982 ARCO was intended to be the primary vehicle for stimulating the collecting of contemporary art in Spain at a time when that activity was virtually nonexistent. Until the advent of ARCO, there were no museums where one could come into regular, direct contact with the art of the moment and few galleries dedicated to displaying the avant-garde. It is hard now to believe this, when walking around any major city in Spain today, confronted as one is with a plethora of such sophisticated venues. In 1982, with some notable exceptions such as Miró, Tapies, and Chillida, the only living artists who were generally known in Spain were the by then increasingly out-of-fashion abstract artists of Cuenca. Furthermore, hardly any exhibitions of contemporary art had traveled to Spain from the United States or Europe.

Madrid's long-lost reputation for attracting the most exciting contemporary art can be traced to Spain's Golden Age in the seventeenth century. That reputation had been well earned by royal patrons who sought, purchased, and commissioned fabulous paintings by the most talented and well-known artists: Rubens, Titian, Velázquez, and Zurbarán, the avant-garde in their own times. What they created was seen to be as contemporary as any "Soho trend" was in the 1980s, and the reputation the successive courts earned as patrons of culture was intimately connected to their sense of engagement in the world and their willingness to aggressively purchase the most adventurous art available. ARCO set out to recover this reputation in the earliest days of the democracy—but with a vastly different patronage focus. ARCO's focus was to be on developing the private "impulse" and on creating a much more diverse web of buyers than had ever existed before in Spain's history. A casual, huge, commercial setting, the modern fair was meant to encourage businesses, foundations, museums, and individuals, including those of the middle class, to begin to build their own collections of contemporary art.

Throughout the 1980s and 1990s ARCO was successful in influencing its targeted audiences. It contributed to a rapidly heightening awareness in Spain of the wide range of painting, photography, sculpture, and conceptual and installation art that was sweeping so much of Europe, America, and Japan. The "transvanguardia" and neo-expressionists from Italy invaded the Madrid fair, followed by the Germans, Greeks, Americans, and Latin Americans. Spanish artists were profoundly affected by the exposure they received and by what they themselves saw at ARCO. Especially during the 1980s, ARCO kept artists, curators, and nonprofessionals abreast of the newest thinking in the contemporary art world. ARCO brought foreign experts to Madrid to give lectures and conferences to inspire debate and dialogue. It was also a place where art professionals could be sure they would run into each other, attracting curators from every Spanish museum to this marketplace of trends. In the early years of the democracy many of these art professionals did not have the budgets to travel outside of Spain, and when they did, their frequent lack of ability to speak languages other than Spanish often kept them from getting the information they needed to make the best decisions on purchases and exhibitions. ARCO brought the art and the supporting cast together. By demystifying the art-buying experience in a casual environment it encouraged collectors to spend. By encouraging a broad spectrum of prices, some surprisingly reasonable, ARCO succeeded in redefining collecting as something even young people and those of modest means could participate in. In the process, ARCO took steps that transformed it from just another "art fair" into what can only be termed an "ephemeral museum."

In 1987 ARCO created its own foundation. The ARCO Foundation became responsible for the systematic collecting, preserving, and exhibiting of international and Spanish examples of contemporary art. The foundation's work indelibly imprinted ARCO with meaning beyond what the marketplace alone could endow and decisively demonstrated the seriousness of ARCO's connection to Spain's art scene. The collection, decidedly eclectic, included revered Spanish contemporary artists and classic international stars. It also had acquired less well-known artists from Cuba, Costa Rica, Canada, and Holland, so as to introduce iconoclastic perspectives. In 1996, when the holdings had grown to be significant in number, the foundation contracted with the Galician Contemporary Art Center (Centro Gallego Arte Contempóraneo) in Santiago de Compostela to display the collection well into the twenty-first century, profoundly enriching the inventory of this out-of-the way institution. ARCO's collection was without doubt ranked museum quality within six years.

By the late 1990s ARCO exhibitions had attracted more than one million visitors. ARCO's yearly bashes in Madrid, the most eagerly anticipated gathering of Spanish art-world professionals, students, and enthusiasts, continue to be one of the liveliest and influential events in the country. Usually praised but sometimes also criticized (as behooves an institution that tends to the avant-garde and then is sometimes not credited for being sufficiently avant-garde), ARCO has definitely become an inclusive forum for the presentation of controversial ideas and a meeting ground where many levels of society can rub shoulders, in a way that most museums can only dream about. Far more than a junket for museum professionals or potential collectors, it also belongs to the public.

Protected by IFEMA (Institución Feria Madrid), Madrid's commerce consortium, ARCO was directed, until 1985, by its energetic founder, the contemporary art dealer Juana de Aizpuru. Within a few years and throughout the end of the century ARCO's ongoing expansion and ded-

Visitors at ARCO (Feria Internacional de Arte Contemporáno). Courtesy of
Rosina Gómez-Baeza.

ication to quality must, however, be credited to the leadership of Rosina
Gómez-Baeza. But it was the passionate commitment and financial protection offered by Adrian Piera, president of Madrid's chamber of commerce and of IFEMA (until 1998) that played the most critical part in its
longevity. Gómez-Baeza's untiring efforts to make ARCO preeminent in
Spain and a driving force throughout Europe and the Americas were
always sustained by the economic support Piera was able to garner
throughout good and bad economic times. Piera was responsible for getting Madrid's chamber of commerce to guarantee ARCO's existence
through the year 2000 whether or not it was profitable. Piera's macroview
and his proactive stance that the private sector must support Spain's vigorous, humanistic connection to modern ideas kept ARCO alive through
changes of artistic taste, elections, political control, and economic crises.

Considered by many Madrileños to be one of the city's leaders and
healers during that period when the country was moving away from fascist values toward freedom and reconciliation, Piera simultaneously
strove to maintain a sense of community and continuity, while also fostering innovation. (Thus, it is not out of character that Piera was also one of
the driving forces behind the completion of Madrid's Roman Catholic

cathedral, a project that had been languishing for decades.) Further-more, because Piera recognized that there would never again be a body—state or church—that would have the will or the resources to com-mission great contemporary art for the Spanish, he was a proponent of tax relief legislation to stimulate the purchase of art and its eventual placement in Spain's museums. Piera's long-term dream for ARCO, a cor-ollary to encouraging the "collecting habit," was to provide a forum for cre-ativity and critical thinking about creativity, two qualities that he believed were crucial to the perpetuation and nurturing of a democratic society.

Piera's dream has been fulfilled because ARCO is more than the usual international art fair. In 1999 232 galleries from thirty countries partici-pated. Almost 200,000 people attended over its six-day run. The crowds always appear not merely dutiful but buoyant, energetic, and engaged. People chat with friends and strangers about the works of art they encounter. All the while they eat, drink, smoke, and express opinions on the significance of what confronts them. There is an absence of the pre-ciousness and intimidation one so often associates with such events in the United States and the rest of the world. ARCO, over the almost two decades of its existence, has annually imbued an interested community with a high level of comfort about the discomforts intrinsic to so much of contemporary art. It complemented and provided an alternative to the formal, more daunting museums—those relatively lofty "treasure houses" where art is often validated by unapproachable, incontrovertible, and anonymous art-world professionals.

ARCO's offering of an alternative way for the Spanish public to enter the world of art is from the perspective of an American, no small accom-plishment. The United States, in the 1980s and 1990s, suffered a growing alienation between the general public and the visual arts. Writer Steven Schiff mused that Americans "seem to have lost all comprehension of the uses of art: in the universities, it is widely viewed as the pallid reflection of the power structures that have produced it; in the mouths of political can-didates, it becomes a purveyor of evil and a corrupter of children; even in the eyes of some critics, every new work is a message-bearing unit, to be scrutinized for its politics and its morality and judged accordingly."[11] ARCO invites the Spanish public to see for itself and to make personal judgments without the mediation of absolutist higher authority. The newspapers present widely divergent opinions about what is and is not on display, praising and criticizing the selection process—giving freedom to the public to disagree among themselves and with the art professionals. ARCO provides an annual reminder of the infinite number of ways artists see, interpret, imagine, and represent the world. By extension, it is about the infinite number of ways available to the general public to make sense of the world.

ARCO has taken on many obligations other than its original purpose of expanding Spain's contemporary art market. It is now a forum for education about art and the nature of art collecting. ARCO supports individual museums by giving them space to present themselves and to test their most creative projects. Museums offer previews of their programs and get ideas for new ones. For example, the Guggenheim Museum Bilbao, when it was still the most controversial museum in Spain, announced its long-awaited art acquisition policy at ARCO 1997, confronting rumors about those policies that had been in the air for months before. ARCO has also devoted special gallery sections to single countries, such as Belgium, Germany, the United States, France, and Portugal, or whole continents, such as Latin America. This has brought, in unprecedented numbers, dozens of non-Spanish galleries and visitors to Spain. Outside the fair's grounds, every year there is a series of seminars, prizes, and conferences guided by a variety of scholars and critics. It even runs courses for art dealers, to teach them how to sell certain types of art. In 1998 ARCO collaborated with the ministries of education and culture, as it does in other aspects of its work as well, to deliver a three-part seminar on various aspects of selling photography.

To better accomplish its multiplying goals, the ARCO Foundation began working side by side with a private support group called the Friends of ARCO (Amigos de ARCO) in 1987. Another example of private citizens taking charge of their cultural lives, the friends' group has aided the foundation enormously. Their projects at the fair itself include funding a photographic documentation program, which resulted in an exhibition of work by young photographers that traveled throughout Spain and raised the status of photography as art in Spain. The Friends of ARCO also organizes art-appreciation courses with non-ARCO institutions such as the Fine Arts Circle in Madrid (Círculo de Bellas Artes) and IVAM (Instituto Valenciano Arte Moderno). The Friends of ARCO has taken an important role in defining ARCO for the 1990s, including developing CD-ROMs of the fair beginning in 1995. They have also assumed the responsibility for ARCO's extremely valuable scholarly projects,

ARCODATA ESPAÑA and *ARCODATA LATINOAMERICA* (through a unique public-private partnership including the Valencian regional government and Madrid's Carlos/III University), dedicated to locating and describing Spanish and Latin American contemporary artists. The friends group has also initiated a system of scholarships for art-related studies in the United States. Furthermore, it supports the exhibition of those artworks purchased by the ARCO Foundation in the Galician Contemporary Art Center in Santiago de Compostela.

ARCO has by no means abandoned its business-oriented goals: providing an outlet for the purchase of contemporary art to fill the walls of museums, corporations, private homes, and foundations. Depending on the country's economy in any given year, this purpose has been achieved. And, notwithstanding the health of the economy, there has not been a diminishment in ARCO's long-term commitment. As a result, it can be categorically stated that contemporary collections of all types in Spain have swollen because of that commitment. Any number of Spanish museums (state and regional), foundations, local governments, and corporations do make large annual purchases at the fair because ARCO gives their representatives and their curators a sure grasp on what is happening, both in their own country and worldwide. For ARCO, business is still the bottom line. But it has never been the only line.

ARCO wanted to imbue the private sector in Spanish society with the belief that all of the effort, expense, and risk related to the production of an art fair constituted a meaningful contribution to the emergence of a more aware and more thoughtful citizenry. It wanted to nourish a synergy between the international and local in hopes of turning Spain into a full participant in the contemporary art world once again. And it wanted to promote the belief that being a full participant in the art world would redound to society's benefit in general. These goals have been met. The lasting impression both foreigners and Spaniards alike take away from ARCO is that Spain is a place where vibrant dialogue about art and creativity is rampant, and that it is a place where everybody can have an opinion—the more iconoclastic the better. ARCO is everyone's soapbox; it is a wide-open channel. It has truly become a communal event, characterized, unlike "real" museums, by its antihierarchical, nonjudgmental juxtapositions of "high" and "low" art. By now ARCO is a full partner in the establishment, mostly upheld by the private impulse but supported by public institutions as well. Its true power transcends the art market: it lies in the ritual, annual, flamboyant affirmation of democratic values *through* art in the city where power used to be dedicated to the suppression of those values. ARCO has become an integral part of the country's post-Franco identity. It has earned a place of honor among the more conventional brick-and-mortar museum institutions that will always be the more proper, but not necessarily the more exciting or liberating, sites for encountering and wrestling with the art and ideas of our time.

2 THE POWER OF THE REGIONS

Regional art museums, as they have developed since the advent of democracy in Spain, constitute a stunning phenomenon within the universe of that country's cultural life. The Spanish state museums, especially those located in Madrid, as described in part one of this book, demonstrate the strength and vitality of the idea of Spain by impressing citizens and foreigners alike with the quality and richness of the state's collections. Their underlying mission is, and always has been, to support and enhance the idea of "Spanishness." Some of these state museums have received more support than others and have been, therefore, more or less successful in achieving their goals. Regional museums scattered throughout the country are, conversely, charged by their own regional legislation and, significantly, by the state itself with advancing and enlivening local identity formation.

Regional museums' missions powerfully attest to the existence and value of the diverse populations within Spain. They bear witness to populations whose identities are in some part traditionally Spanish, but are in other parts representative of meanings that were not so very long ago seen as sowing the seeds of separatism—existing in competition with dominant Spanish ideology. Ironically, Franco's desire to strip the country of such distinctions resulted in ever more emphatic autonomic aspirations in the Basque Country and Catalonia after the Spanish civil war. Franco's ideology also encouraged inchoate nationalisms in regions that had not historically been overly tendentious. Paradoxically, during the dictatorship, regional folklore museums were widespread. But these were museums actually dedicated to the promotion of Francoism, which meant celebrating the collective identity of the regions within the unitary state. They did not allow highly individualistic expression by artists setting themselves against any notion of aggregate identity. They did not promote the recalcitrance essential to individualism. Today regional museums proudly proclaim their own varied legacies and any number of individualistic, and often recalcitrant, cultural positions in the face, not only of "Spanishness" but also of those related to a growing European and American presence. In fact, these museums are now the mirrors of Spain's political reality, which has fully reinvented itself as it reversed the crushing centralism of the Franco years.

The rise of regionalism could have aroused crippling tensions throughout Spain had the full panoply of cultural institutions not worked to harness and channel the energies behind those tensions. Generally they were successful, allowing for not only the release of tensions but also for the transformation of those energies for the civic good. As democracy has matured, they have actually fostered the persistence of the nation-state by presenting individual citizens with indisputable evidence that they could, in contemporary Spain, "patriotically" possess conflicting, affirming, negating, and even overlapping and shifting state and regional identities. These museums, each with its own mission, are usually recognized as the voices of the people they "represent." They are proof that the regions can be their own best agents, and that Madrid, in the redistribution of power that made all of this possible, would present no obstacles to the construction of local identities, even those opposed to what was being promoted by the capital. Notwithstanding this constructive environment, museums have occasionally sorely tested center/periphery relationships.

Traveling throughout Spain, one cannot help but be surprised by the quantity, liveliness, and sophistication of the regional museums. After visiting a number of them it becomes clear that, even within their own typology, they convey a wide range of messages about who their own constituencies are and how these constituencies should relate to Spain, Europe, and the Americas. As in the museums of the center, each one of these messages is shaped by many things: the choices, interpretations, and juxtapositions of artworks and artifacts in the galleries; the blatant or subtle employment of resonant architectural forms in specific urban settings; the exhibition program; and the choice and order of language or languages that appear on the wall labels and publications. Part two of this book is dedicated to discussing case studies of these regional museums (new museums and those that have been totally reformed) touching on several of the roles they play in the construction and recognition of the manifold identities that make up the new, democratic citizen in today's Spain.

5 SEEKING BALANCE WITH THE CENTER

MEIAC, or the Extremaduran and Ibero-American Museum of Contemporary Art (Museo Extremeño e Iberoamericano de Arte Contemporáneo), in Badajoz, the Fine Arts Museum of Asturias (Museo de Bellas Artes de Asturias) in Oviedo, and IVAM, or the Valencian Institute of Modern Art (Instituto Valenciano de Arte Moderno), are models of museological clarity and focus. Each reflects a regional desire to strike the correct balance, through a powerful cultural symbol, between the identity needs of its own geographical area and the needs of Spain as a nation-state. They share a fundamental obligation to showcase regional art as a means of advancing the construction of the identities of their local citizenry in the interests of enhancing cultural confidence. There is little else that would link any one of these three museums to the other two—or to any other museum in Spain. They can never be assessed as functioning merely as formulaic elements within a static and predictable political situation. To do so would be to miss the nature of their symbiotic relationships to that kaleidoscopic concept of the Spanish nation-state invented in the last twenty years. Studying the evolving roles of these museums in the construction of a changed social identity permits us to understand that these museums are much more than institutions for the collection, protection, and exhibition of art. As in the United States and other democratic societies these museums have emerged as testing grounds for ideas that challenge entrenched prejudices and constructively reexamine repressed memories. They have proved to be open and critical arenas for some the most daring ideas and some of the best and most idealistic hopes of Spain's now eminently civil society.[1]

MEIAC

Usually dismissed as devoid of cultural interest, Extremadura is not on the itineraries of most Spanish, European, or American travelers. It is sometimes sentimentally recalled as a place abandoned by such explorers as Balboa and Pizarro who crossed the sea to what would become New Spain. Having lived in poverty, they sought riches, glory, and honor. Extremadura, a desolate, poverty-stricken landscape, has throughout the centuries proved nearly impossible to cultivate and is often described as a remnant of Old Spain at its least compelling. There is a great deal, however, that might attract one to Extremadura. The hot and dry southwestern United States mirrors the severity and hardness of Extremadura, so that region might seem romantic to anyone bred on American myths and history.

To unduly romanticize Extremadura, though, would be to overlook the debilitating sense of marginalization that the region has suffered for centuries. Even if we are thinking of its main urban locations—Badajoz, Trujillo, Cáceres, or Mérida—merely being in Extremadura placed those cities, not only physically and materially, but spiritually, culturally, and intellectually, outside the Spanish mainstream. It is only in the twenty years since Franco died and democracy was reborn that there has been an attempt to refigure a new picture of Extremadura so that its people might attain a civic pride that would permit them to define their own centrality. This was done first in the city of Mérida by construction of an imposing state museum celebrating Extremadura's ancient past. It is there we find Spain's National Museum of Roman Art (designed by Rafael Moneo), a fabulous, evocative contemporary structure built among classical ruins. This museum was a powerful confirmation of the magnitude of the region's history in relation to the underappreciated Spanish-Roman period and Extremadura's remarkable presence in it. A redefinition of Spain was also accomplished outside the desolate town of Malpartida in

The principal nave of the National Museum of Roman Art
(Museo Nacional de Arte Romano) in Mérida. Courtesy
Museo Nacional de Arte Romano de Mérida. Archivo M. N. A.
R., Barrera. No. negativo: R-480-32.

Cáceres by the late artist Wolf Vostell. Vostell built his own totally unexpected and absolutely eccentric Museum Vostell Malpartida (Museo Vostell Malpartida) to celebrate not only his accomplishments but those of other artists who participated in Fluxus, the movement best known for its "happenings" and the conceptual art that followed the 1960s.

In order to understand the moral force of the Extremaduran and Ibero-American Museum of Contemporary Art (MEIAC), one must first learn what happened in Badajoz on August 15, 1936. That was the day the Badajoz bullring became the site of one of the first massacres in the Spanish civil war. Franco's forces, the nationalists, took the city, which had sided with the legitimate government of the Spanish republic. In order to take revenge against those who had supported the republic the nationalists rounded up large numbers of men and women and massacred them before the eyes of an already shattered populace. Some eye-witnesses counted 1,800 dead; later, others counted only 400. Recently Paul Preston, in his respected 1994 biography of Franco, wrote: "After the heat of battle had cooled, two thousand prisoners were rounded up and herded to the bull-ring, and any with the bruise of a rifle recoil on their shoulders were shot. The shootings went on for weeks thereafter."[2] James Michener, who wrote *Iberia* thirty years after the event, tried to talk to the townspeople about it and reported, "I have never spoken to a man who would admit that he had been in the bullring that day, but once at a café in Sevilla I was shown a man who admitted to having been there. I asked if I could speak with him, and friends approached him, but he stared at me across the tables and shook his head no. Men in the bar said, 'He told us it was the worst thing a man could see on earth.'"[3]

MEIAC, as the museum came to be formally called, opened in 1994. It is located in what was previously the city's "preventive and correctional" prison, constructed during the early part of the dictatorship. Like the Valley of the Fallen, Franco's monument to himself, the former prison was built by republican inmates. Located near the infamous bullring, MEIAC has become one of the most emotional and eccentric of the regional museums in Spain. To build the city's museum in the former prison was a farsighted decision, a recognition by a civic leadership of the necessity to strike a balance between a society's need to remember and its wish to forget the unspeakable.[4] Planners and politicians were confident that such a balance could be achieved and a launching pad established for a renewed future. MEIAC was able to be such a vehicle because its physical presence made it unavoidable. Whether or not the people of Badajoz passed through the museum's doors, they would all be confronted by its looming figure over the cityscape. A clear reminder of one the most tragic events of the civil war and the oppression that followed, MEIAC would finally become both memorial and clarion call to reconciliation.

MEIAC's founders wanted to transform Extremadura, not by continuing to make reference to old and outmoded nostalgia surrounding the explorations of the Americas but rather by cultivating present-day culture and by encouraging Extremadura's sense of its own creativity.[5] With these guideposts, the founders decided to employ a design that incorporated the shared history while symbolizing their hopes for the future. Unlike so many modern museums, they would not tolerate yet another pseudo-universalist allusion of the Pompidou in Paris (no "Sofidu" for Badajoz).

Nor did they want to import someone else's artistic legacy, as in the Basque Country where they imported an American architect, an American collection, and an American directorial vision for the Guggenheim Museum Bilbao. And, the last thing they wished was to build a museum that would suggest an intimate relationship with Madrid.

Extremadurans wanted the new museum to somehow come to grips with and reverse entrenched historical associations that had always been crippling for them: emigration, isolation, and marginalization. It was also envisioned that the museum would honor Extremadura's special transnational allegiances to Portugal and Latin America. Planners and politicians were optimistic that MEIAC would contribute to a progressive, inner-city renewal in the run-down neighborhood near the prison. The more idealistic among them wanted to use the museum to motivate all of Extremadura, not only residents of Badajoz, to reconceptualize the ideas of exploration (whether it be cultural or economic) as one based on self-confidence, creativity, and success instead of the poverty and its concomitant humiliations that forced Balboa, Pizarro, and anonymous thousands of other emigrants to abandon their homes in search of betterment over so many centuries.

Normally a museum begins with its art collections. MEIAC is unusual in that it began with the building, which had been reborn from Badajoz's ugly and abandoned Franco-era prison. Construction of the prison began in 1942, and it was formally inaugurated in 1958 "within the framework of a civic-religious ceremony, profusely adorned with the symbols and emblems of the old [fascist] regime."[6] The architecture, its highly allusive decorative regalia and the ostentatiously public and ritualistic manner in which it was inaugurated, all undoubtedly reminded the citizens of Badajoz who the victors were, who the vanquished had been, and who was in charge. The prison is the exact other side of Franco's two-faced policy: he had this forbidding, totalitarian structure erected at approximately the same time that he authorized the abstract artists to show at the Venice Biennial—at the same time that he was working so hard to convince President Eisenhower that the dictatorship was not unreasonably oppressive.

Inspired by the panopticon of Jeremy Bentham, the prison was based on the notion of the all-seeing eye of central inspection: "An abstract and eloquent paradigm, it is an authentic machine for guarding and watching over, an ad hoc apparatus for the custodianship and punishment of prisoners. . . . In this way the omnipresent eye of power would produce the

Prison interior before renovation for Extremaduran and Ibero-American Museum of Contemporary Art (Museo Extremeño e Iberoamerican de Arte Contemporáneo). Courtesy MEIAC.

dread and respect necessary to assure the inmate's proper behavior."[7] The purpose of Franco's prison, however, was not only to exercise its powers of inspection over the prisoners within its walls; it was also intended to make an unnerving impression on passersby. A perversion of the ubiquitous Spanish medieval castle, the prison on the hill dominated Badajoz. With its blank eyehole windows it would seem that the whole city was under constant surveillance. Although Bentham's ideas were held in great esteem in nineteenth-century Spain, the reality of its explicit function, its implicit one, and its progressive deterioration and abandonment, made Badajoz (already unattractive from decades of indiscriminate expansion) yet more unattractive.[8] It was an institution that echoed the Franco regime in its most unsightly and repressive aspects. No doubt, its continued presence after Franco had been dead for twenty years was, at the very least, a depressing reminder of bygone days that had been shrouded in pain and denial.

Given Badajoz's past it is remarkable that city planners wanted the Francoist prison as the core structure of their new museum. They also made it a requirement that the penitentiary tower be retained, making their chief visual reference the very form that might trigger the worst memories. Optimistic as it may have seemed it was their hope that this ominous form would be transformed into a building that would become the city's most prominent, forward-looking representation of its aspirations. José Antonio Galea, the Extremaduran architect in charge of the project, found the challenge to his liking. In his intensive research into nineteenth-century museums he discovered that elements necessary for a functioning museum could be adapted from the existing prison. He was also able to justify disposing of nonessential elements of the old building, such as the radial naves. The core goals being achievable, it was then no problem adding a service annex, a huge subbasement to hang the collections that would not fit in the tower, and elaborate gardens and terraces. The result is a splendid and haunting vision of the potential for liberation.

It is proclaimed in MEIAC's thoughtful and beautiful first catalog that

to create a new museum in the location where a prison previously existed is to bring to completion an act of social transformation. . . . The space for punishment is transformed thus into a space of freedom. Even if art and delinquency are two parallel forms of transgression and for many, the avant-garde is an authentic crime against good taste, nevertheless such an act of transformation is to oppose the repulsive with the beauty of aesthetic creation, to make both acts, the artistic and the delinquent, antithetical concepts.[9]

Still, as optimistic as the MEIAC creators might have been, their project should also be considered as a civic warning. By retaining the control tower as the dominant formal device, neither the visitor nor the passerby can forget that there is always potential for the most utopian of ideas to turn sour, and that the museum itself holds within it the potential of becoming oppressive and repressive. Indeed, to retain its conceptual validity the new museum must question and honor the concept of place that controls the museum. It must remain committed to dialogue and to encouraging the inclusion of art that actually enters into discourse with all of the issues raised by the architecture and the historic and symbolic memories of the city of Badajoz.[10]

What art was meant to fill this poetic space? MEIAC's fundamental acquisition policy was to recover and preserve that modern art of Extremadura that was still salvageable. Most of that region's art was lost or destroyed due to the constancy of exile, migration, poverty, neglect, or war. The collection dates from the first third of the twentieth century and focuses on local artists noted for their affinities to significant trends of

Gallery at the Extremaduran and Ibero-American Museum of Contemporary Art.
Courtesy MEIAC.

Spanish modern art. The next goal was to acquire the paintings and
sculpture of contemporary Extremaduran artists. Then, the collection
was meant to encourage and pay homage to the region's relationship
with Portugal—a complex one that has long been characterized by both
affection and condescension. Portugal is the natural neighbor of Extremadura and many residents claim to be closer in spirit to the Portuguese
than the rest of Spain. (Consequentially, all publications and wall labels
are in both Spanish and Portuguese.) Additionally, the museum will
actively acquire Latin American art. Throughout Spain there is a reawak-
ened sense of affinity with Latin America, and no other Spanish region's
sense of this is as strong as Extremadura's. Some of the museum's first
purchases were, therefore, significant works of Latin American art. The
educational programming will include serious dialogue that admits to
the painful and the positive impacts the various cultures have had on
each other. Hard questions about colonialism and postcolonialism will be
posed. Finally, MEIAC hopes to expand and enrich Extremadura's relationship within Spain by collecting contemporary Spanish art. It speaks
well for the politicians who are supporting the museum and the professionals who guide them in their efforts that the art in the collections is of

high quality, suits the stated goals, and that the budget was sufficient to launch MEIAC so that it could begin the work to fulfill its challenging mission.

MEIAC is a spectacular regional museum that frankly admits to being in the business of identity construction. It is one of the most effective tools of the region for educating the "ideal" democratic Extremaduran in the postmodern age. Visitors to the museum (Extremaduran or not) learn not only to tolerate but to enjoy and share pride in Extremadura's active role in the competing discourses that characterize today's and tomorrow's Spain. That the postmodern world recognizes the existence of many centers and that Badajoz is Extremadura's center is a critical one for a region long accustomed to considering itself in the margins. At the end of the twentieth century, the average citizens of what may still be the poorest, most provincial area of Spain have become infinitely more prosperous and hopeful about their ability to make positive contributions outside of the region. MEIAC, transformed as it has been from a symbol of oppression into one of freedom, confirms the power of art and architecture to validate and expand the best and most ambitious dreams of a democratic and pluralistic society.

FINE ARTS MUSEUM OF ASTURIAS

Often referred to as "Green Spain," Asturias possesses landscapes of intense beauty, the kind that appear in children's storybooks with mythical heroes. Dramatic mountains are backdrop to breathtaking vistas comprised of dizzying heights and lush valleys. Hillsides and meadows soak up the ever-present dampness and in the occasional but brilliant sunshine sparkle in the clear air. White farmhouses clamber up mountains or nestle in the dales. Hydrangeas clump around the ancient porches of pre-Romanesque and Romanesque churches found throughout the countryside and in almost all Asturian villages and cities. It is, however, a paradise where the weather can turn cruel. A winter or spring tempest on the Cantabrian coast will test the mettle of any visitor.

Asturias is not known for its high culture. With the exception of a minority of prosperous people, Asturias is made up of hardworking sheepherders, miners, steelworkers, farmers, and fishermen. Life was especially onerous for them during the long dictatorship, when Franco was hostile to striking workers and the encouragement of labor unrest.

Throughout that period Asturians saw themselves as defiant, and this characteristic has deep historical roots: the Asturians were the first of the Spanish kingdoms to expel the Moors. Although the Asturians do speak Spanish, they also have their own dialect—language would be too strong a word—which is employed from time to time to enhance their sense of individualism. But Asturians also are proud of their fast developing modern cultural life. The region's two principal cities, Gijón and Oviedo, have taken advantage of democracy to create a number of excellent cultural institutions. Nevertheless, Asturias is still normally visited for its scenery and its superb, hearty food, not for the several fine art museums, art galleries, and public art installations. But travelers are missing something if they do not take advantage of the artistic riches of the region, because one of the most successful museums in all of Spain has taken root in Oviedo, the capital of Asturias.

The Fine Arts Museum of Asturias (Museo de Bellas Artes de Asturias), is one of the early fruits of the first democratic elections in Spain held after the adoption of the 1978 constitution. It is an institution brimming with regional pride, yet, because of the sophistication of the professionals who run it, devoid of provincialism. The founders of the museum were conscious that they were undertaking a significant role in the identity construction of post-Franco Asturians. They knew they were working in a region that most Spaniards (including the Asturians themselves) seldom take seriously for its cultural contributions. Their purpose was to change that perception. And so the museum program was developed in 1979: first and foremost it would display Asturias's own artistic patrimony. It would also display works from Spain and Europe insofar as it related to Asturias. Wise political leaders saw the importance of highlighting local artists, in a nonpatronizing manner, to immediately enlist the support of their own citizens. Paintings with recognizable images of nature, husbandry, industry, and even of the political upheavals Asturians had suffered would be displayed to make the museum relevant and non-threatening to the average visitor. At the same time the curators exhibited less accessible, unknown, or unappreciated Asturian art from Spain's Golden Age to the present day. The challenge for this museum from the start was to elevate the self-image and self-confidence of its Asturian visitors by making them aware that they had never been as one-dimensional as the rest of Spain (and they themselves) assumed. It was hoped that non-Asturian visitors would absorb a similar message about a region that had for so long been stereotyped as merely agricultural, industrial, or politically plagued.

Energy, elegance, intelligence, connoisseurship, and clarity of purpose are the hallmarks of the Fine Arts Museum of Asturias as it appears today. One would like to attribute these qualities only to professional acumen, but without Spain's change from a dictatorship to a participatory democracy, it is unlikely that this museum would ever have come into being. Any museum-related activities during Franco's regime were sporadic and diffuse. It was only with the challenges, attitude shifts, and opportunities accompanying the transition to home rule that it became possible for responsible, proactive citizens to create their own museum.

By all accounts the history of the Fine Arts Museum of Asturias began by royal decree on June 13, 1844.[11] According to that decree, all the provinces of Spain were required to protect their cultural monuments. Although too little and too late, coming after many of the convents and monasteries, which had owned uncountable numbers of paintings and sculptures, had fallen into ruin or been dismantled, that order was nevertheless the first directive that the provinces should care for their own cultural patrimony. Unfortunately only fifteen paintings were gathered in 1844 as a result of that decree. Ten of those still could be accounted for (although in a lamentable state) in 1980. They were supplemented by other old master works that had been discovered since the royal order. These were found in museums in Madrid, Oviedo, and smaller museums in Asturias. Paintings by the finest of Asturias's twentieth-century artists were gathered together piece by piece. The core collection consisted of only seventy-eight works of art (seventy-three paintings and five sculptures) on May 19, 1980, the day the Fine Arts Museum of Asturias was inaugurated. So much had been lost or destroyed that it was no wonder the region had a sense of cultural inferiority.

In 1973 the Palacio de Velarde in the center of Oviedo was purchased to house the Fine Arts Museum of Asturias. Located in the historical downtown, an area both picturesque and filled with businesses, it was expected that the museum could be easily integrated into the region's capital. The Palacio de Velarde was built in 1767 by the Asturian architect Manuel Reguera González, a disciple of the locally renowned Ventura Rodríguez. Another native son, Florencio Muñiz Uribe, immediately began renovating the palace as a museum after the purchase. Uribe was considerably hampered for the next three years by a weak plan that did

The Palacio de Velarde, home to the Fine Arts Museum of
Asturias (Museo de Bellas Artes de Asturias). Courtesy Museo
de Bellas Artes de Asturias.

not account for conservation laboratories, storage, and study spaces. In
the years immediately before and after Franco died there was no sustained political will to develop a well-thought-out scheme for a serious
regional institution of fine arts. Not until 1979, when local elections put
new leadership in charge, did the Asturian Ministry of Culture aggressively support the planning and construction of the museum. By 1980 the
museum opened its doors.

The winners of the 1979 national election, the Center/Conservative
Party (Union de Centro Democrático), or UCD, were the first to act on
the urgent need to begin building a powerful sense of Asturian identity.
These public servants were willing to work toward creating a fine arts

Reception area of the Fine Arts Museum of Asturias. Courtesy Museo de Bellas Artes de Asturias.

museum in the hope that their constituency would show their appreciation at the polls. If the project was successful it would reflect on the party that created it. The museum was designated as one of the UCD's flagship projects. Old ideas were scrapped; fresh goals were set; the museum was supported and protected by an enthusiastic political will.[12]

The plan called for galleries on the main floor to be dedicated to temporary exhibitions of contemporary Asturian art and nineteenth-century Asturian art. The second floor would exhibit Spanish and European Renaissance and Mannerist works. Additional galleries were to be reserved for the most accomplished and established Asturian artists. Great care was taken in remodeling the Palacio de Velarde for lighting, security, and storage. Time and money were lavished on conservation of the artworks, which were quite deteriorated. Funds were supplied for education programs; generous moneys were also set aside to buy exceptional works of art, which allowed the collection to grow quickly. Donations were encouraged. Scholarly libraries were purchased. Publications, both academic and popular, were produced. While most of the language was Spanish, occasionally the Asturian dialect was used in some brochures. Collections management met the highest standards. Conferences, meetings, lectures, and concerts explored region- and culture-related issues.

In 1982 two visionaries, codirectors of the museum, Emilio Marcos Vallaure and José A. Fernández-Castañón, spearheaded the purchase of another building adjacent to the Palacio de Velarde called the Casa de Oviedo-Portal. The renovation of the Casa de Oviedo-Portal, supervised by architect Fernando Nanclares, is as beautiful as the Palacio de Velarde's, making the joining of both buildings metaphors for the marriage of past and present. The overall effect is dynamic, imposing, and inviting.

The Fine Arts Museum of Asturias has had a long and positive association with the Prado and is one of the beneficiaries of the *Prado disperso*. As long ago as 1900, by royal decree, the Prado started sending art from its storage vaults on long-term loan to Oviedo. Although many works were lost or ruined during the years preceding the opening of the museum, some of the paintings were recently rediscovered, restored, and are now hanging in the museum's galleries. This is one of the best examples of the *Prado disperso* being put to work in an exemplary fashion. The loans have enabled the Fine Arts Museum of Asturias to fill gaps in its collection and, sotto voce, to demonstrate that constructive cultural linkages with the state government are possible. The loans create a positive presence in a regional setting. The spirit of cooperation extended by the state is further fostered behind the scenes by the conservation work Asturias has had done on its paintings by the National Conservation Center (Centro de Resaturación) in Madrid. For a region that, during so much of its modern history, suffered a highly adversarial and often painful relationship with Madrid, the Fine Arts Museum of Asturias has become a new kind of paradigm. It is an example of the positive results to be gained through a collaboration between a museum far out on the periphery and one at dead center. More significantly, the museum is additional proof to Asturian citizens of the concrete civic benefits associated with the complex new identity they have accepted and adopted throughout the first two decades of democracy.

The Fine Arts Museum of Asturias has provided a venue for the region's citizens to become comfortable in the Spanish cultural landscape and in the larger world as well. This is accomplished by the thoughtful and imaginative exhibitions the museum mounts displaying Asturias's own artistic present and past. The permanent collection exhibits a great portrait by Juan Carreño de Miranda, a first-rank Spanish court painter from Asturias, of King Carlos II and a number of other oustanding native sons. At the same time, traveling exhibitions help to educate the rest of the region about its unknown patrimony. The museum maintains modest loan and exchange programs with other similar museums in France, Germany, and the United States, knowing that it is not wise to spend all of its time, as codirector Emilio Marcos Vallaure says, "looking at our own navels."[13] The Fine Arts Museum of Asturias has encouraged thousands of citizens of the region to shed their old sense of isolation and to enhance their understanding of their heritage and creative potential. It has been one of the varied and effective means of enriching and complicating the local sense of identity and of integrating it with today's Spain.

IVAM

Valencia is often described as a *huerta* (garden). The capital city of the province, also called Valencia, has in its downtown a splendid farmer's market, where one can find a wide variety of fruits, vegetables, flowers, hams and sausages, fish, breads, and cheeses. The city also has beautiful ancient ruins, Renaissance and Baroque churches, and some fine contemporary architecture. Grand avenues, expansive parks, and a bustling commercial life make it one of Spain's liveliest cities. The region of Valencia, with over seventy museums, is one of the most culturally endowed in Spain. There are several types of museums including archaeological, ecclesiastical, maritime, fine art, natural science, ethnology, history, military, medical, agricultural, and museums dedicated to single artists. All contribute to the identity of the Valencian citizen. In the post-Franco period both city and region wanted to keep intact their own already well-established identity and advance it into the emerging modern times. Proud of its autonomy Valencia's main cultural concern was maintaining equilibrium between local and global, and old and new. The museums that have emerged or been reformed since Franco's death have tried to find that balance. So much political and cultural faith has been put into the idea of museums as vessels of identity in Valencia that it sometimes seems to visitors that there are more museums than could possibly be digested. Even the former director general of the cultural patrimony of Valencia, the official in charge of museums, Evangelina Rodriguez Cuadros, wrote in 1991 that this growth could be described as a "veritable museological bulimia."[14]

Interior of original IVAM (Instituto Valenciano de Arte Moderno) building.
Courtesy IVAM and Dirección General de Promoción Cultural, Museos y Bellas
Artes.

There is, among the great variety of Valencian museums, one that
emerged during the socialist period as the embodiment of the best aspirations of the postdictatorship years—the Valencian Institute of Modern
Art (IVAM). A serious contemporary museum, it was at the same time
daring enough to highlight the multilayered and contradictory meanings
implicit and explicit in the new Spain. When the Reina Sofía was in crisis
in 1995 the state looked to IVAM as a model for solving the problem.
Using a regional museum for operational and philosophical clues is an
indication of how fine an institution this museum is. It is also a barometer
of how much attitudes have changed since the days when Madrid alone
set standards for the nation's cultural institutions.

IVAM employed every means at its disposal to position itself as the
leading museum of the region. Beginning with its architecture, it elected
to have not one but two buildings and two distinct sites for its museum
complex. These buildings immediately announced IVAM's goal of medi-
ating between the past and present, the local and international. The original building was housed in an elegant seven-hundred-year-old convent—
the Centre del Carmé—one of the most evocative buildings in the old
quarter of the city Valencia. The Carmé, as it is called, was one of the first

monasteries to be erected in the city. Its parish activities and the Gothic cloister still continue to function today. It was remodeled only once before in the seventeenth century. IVAM is composed of three adjacent areas within the convent: the Renaissance cloister, which dates from the first half of the sixteenth century; the old refectory and the chapter room, now called the Gallery of Ambassador Vich; and the "Ala Goerlich" gallery, which was built in the early years of the twentieth century to complement the installations in the Royal Academy of Fine Arts (Real Academia de Bellas Artes) of San Carlos, which was located here from 1838 to 1946. The Carmé is now the site of IVAM's changing exhibitions. The building is considered one of the most striking examples of adaptive architecture in Europe.[15]

The new IVAM structure is located across a narrow street and down from the Carmé. Designed and built by a team of Valencian architects, Emilio Jiménez, Joaquim Sanchis, José Murcia, Vicent Martínez, and Carlos Salvadores Navarro, in 1989, it is named the Centre Julio González for the Catalan *modernista* master and creator of the iron sculptures that form IVAM's core collection. The building is in the international modern style.

Lobby of the new IVAM building. Courtesy IVAM and Dirección General de Promoción Cultural, Museos y Bellas Artes.

Its location is along the perimeter of the old city walls, which were torn down in 1865. Of the building's over 161,000 square feet about 51,000 square feet is dedicated to exhibitions and the balance to offices, reception, storage, restoration, security, and the education department. There are nine classically designed galleries for painting and sculpture. Not accidentally, the last of the nine galleries occupies the subbasement to dramatically reveal the remains of Valencia's ancient wall. An exhibition of local medieval ceramics in that gallery reminds visitors that, as avant-garde as the museum might appear, it is deeply embedded in the past.

IVAM's founder and first director, Tomás Llorens, insisted that in order for this museum to have lasting impact and weight within the museum world it needed a permanent collection of painting and sculpture that encapsulated the meaning of the project. The museum therefore immediately acquired a major collection of works by Julio González and purchased paintings, prints, and sculpture of other modern Spanish masters. The permanent collection also consists of art from Spain's first and second avant-garde periods, modernist artists from Valencia, and contemporary international art from the 1960s to the present. Artists from the second avant-garde period in the collection include Antonio Saura, Manuel Millares, Eduardo Chillida, and Antoní Tapies. Abstract works from the 1930s include art by Joaquim Torres García, Jean Arp, Laszlo Moholy-Nagy, and Kurt Schwitters. Some of the contemporary Valencian artists represented in the permanent collection are Miquel Navarro, Carmen Calvo, Joaquim Michavila, Grupo Parpallo, Andreu Alfaro, Joaquim Armengol, and the Equipo 57, an important local "team" of artists. Many of these local artists also have strong reputations in Europe, and IVAM provides an important bridge for them to other parts of the world. Successive directors, Carmen Alborch (who went on to become Spain's minister of culture) and J. F. Yvars continued the direction set by Llorens after he was recruited to direct the Reina Sofía in Madrid.

IVAM's temporary exhibitions paid tribute to international artists in the museum's much heralded early years. The museum, for example, installed the following exhibitions: Cildo Mireiles from Brazil; Henri Michaux from France; Markus Raetz from Switzerland; Andy Warhol, Josef Albers, Mark di Suvero, and James Lee Byars from the United States; and Sigmar Polke from Germany. The staff, under the guidance of a succession of gifted directors and, until 1996, with the artistic guidance of chief curator Vicente Todoli, made certain that there was open dialogue between the international avant-garde community and the city of Valencia and that works by Valencian artists were purchased and exhibited frequently. IVAM, because of its prestige, has also been able to circulate a number of the exhibitions it has organized throughout the world and has raised awareness of local artists—just as it has contextualized them in an international frame.

Not content with just presenting objects IVAM initiated sophisticated public education and outreach programs to better communicate its vision. To a degree uncommon in Spain at the time, IVAM developed a large audience due not only to its acquisition and exhibition policy but also to innovative public activities and events. Interactive workshops and projects brought children and adults close to the creative process. IVAM also became a magnet for intellectual and general cultural debate that was of interest to both its local and its international audiences. It produced both scholarly and popular publications. Labels and didactic materials are always presented in Spanish and Valencian. Audiovisual and bibliographical material are made available to schools, and a library and documentation center is available for scholars. IVAM has organized valuable conferences and symposia, and it has even offered training courses for museum professionals. It has lived up to its name as an institute for research, as a modern art museum, and as a vehicle for the construction of a richer and broader international sense of itself for its already profoundly rooted and confident citizens.

Valencian citizens, with IVAM as one of the high-profile symbols of the region, have created for themselves an effervescent mix of internationalism, nationalism, regionalism, and municipal pride. Other fine institutions, such as the Museum of Fine Arts (Museo de Bellas Artes), the National Museum of Ceramics and the Sumptuary Arts (Museo Nacional de Cerámica y de las Artes Suntuarias), and a variety of other elegant exhibition spaces adapted from historically resonant buildings, lend enormous depth to this mix of identities. The forces behind IVAM have always clearly understood that to continue to be supported by its populace the museum must not neglect its roots. But the politicians of the early 1980s, along with the citizens who elected them, also realized that it was contemporary art that had emerged as one of the most effective rallying cries of international engagement. IVAM therefore is Valencia's unequivocal, celebratory statement that its citizens are full participants in the modern world.

One would think that because of its success IVAM might have been free of the threat of political evisceration that haunts so many of the museums at election time in Spain. But that has not been the case. Even though founding director Llorens did managed to establish IVAM with more autonomy than any other public museum in Spain at the time, the directorship was seen as a political reward after the 1995 elections, when the region of Valencia swung to the right, followed a year later by the rest of the country. IVAM's director of several years, J. F. Yvars, was forced to resign in 1995 simply because he was not a member of the victorious party.[16] In spite of strong preelection rhetoric proclaiming IVAM to be an unqualified success under Yvars, Conservative Party candidate Eduardo Zaplana still found it expedient to change IVAM's management once he had been elected head of the Valencian government.[17] There was no serious consideration given by the local conservative party to retaining the incumbent based on acknowledged past achievements, and this led to a public controversy over the naming of the new director. It was not until the national Conservative Party in Madrid stepped in that the situation was resolved.

Taking advice from art world professionals, national Conservative Party leaders and museum intellectuals engaged in a constructive and open dialogue such as had seldom been seen in similar situations in Spain's museums. Because Tomás Llorens had taken precautions to safeguard IVAM somewhat from the political process, the institution was not completely subject to political manipulation. As a result of the ensuing debate a decision was reached and the directorship of IVAM was awarded to conservative art critic Juan Manuel Bonet. The job of promoting Valencian arts in general, a post with great (and growing) influence, was created expressly for Consuelo Ciscar Casabán. This was an important compromise allowing both politics and art to each win a little. Bonet, although he did reduce IVAM's sense of adventurousness and internationalism, did not destroy the institution as had been feared by the socialists. He merely brought it more into line with the prevailing conservative taste. Ciscar Casabán, on the other hand, has performed brilliantly. She developed a lively program that brought Valencian art and artists to the widest possible international audience, and through generous sponsorship of performances and exhibitions inside and outside Spain she has nurtured many artistic reputations. The solution of adding the position to promote Valencian artists and to separate that from the management of IVAM proved to be a genuine victory for the democratic process and a model for positive change in Spain. It showed that a change of party does not have to be a rout, but rather can be a route to unexpectedly positive change. It was also a signal to the rest of Spain that the country's politicians needed to be more careful than they ever had before with regional high-profile cultural institutions. It was apparent that the whole country was watching and that museums had now become an extremely visible means of testing democratic values. This was not a role they had ever had to play during the Franco years.

6

Spain's Basque Country boasts splendid beaches, gorgeous resort cities, breathtaking mountain scenery, exquisite fishing villages, fascinating architecture, vital financial institutions, intriguing archaeology, and a significant agricultural economy that produces everything from superb wines to succulent fruits and vegetables. All of this, plus a cuisine that is considered by many to be among the best in Europe, are only some of the qualities that distinguish this northernmost region from the rest of Spain. Inhabitants of the Basque Country will, if asked, quickly tell you that they are members of a distinct ethnic group that crosses political boundaries, extending into France on the one hand and Navarra, a neighboring Spanish region, on the other. A few will also point out that their blood type is different from most other Spaniards. Then there is Euskera, the mysterious, ancestral language of the region, which bears no relation to Spanish or, for that matter, to any other Romance or Indo-European language. It is Euskera that has become the essential differentiating factor in any description of Basque ethnicity.[1]

Notwithstanding pride in their uniqueness (and to the chagrin of the small population of vocal extremists), there is no doubt that the Basque Country is a region, however autonomous, within the Spanish nation-state. And, for the most part, Basque inhabitants share two overriding values with the majority of today's Spaniards: they treasure their democracy and they wish to participate fully in a global environment. This desire for participation in the world, however, has not always been the majority view, and debate over the "true nature" of the Basque has inspired a variety of models for "ideal" identities since that subject itself became an obsession a century ago. Basque museums have been, along with other cultural manifestations, in the forefront of this debate at critical junctures throughout the twentieth century.

Since the region's culture is of paramount importance to Spain's stability, and since the constitution requires that it be financially supported by every branch of government, the people of the Basque Country have had a remarkable opportunity to reinvent themselves. This reinvention in the name of modernizing Spain actually epitomizes postmodern thinking in that it is polycentric and polyvalent. In democratic Spain, Basques can freely project themselves as Basques first, if they so wish, and then, in varying degrees, as Spaniards, Europeans, or citizens of the world. This nonlinear, variable, manifold, and at times overlapping sense of self is life sustaining for the citizens of the modern Basque Country. Their postmodern defiance of a single "center" is the antithesis of the unitary, ideal nation-state with Madrid at the core, which had been enforced by Franco (and had been probably most harshly directed at them) throughout his long regime.

Most inhabitants of the Basque Country continue to keep a watchful eye on the Spanish nation-state. They are suspicious of creeping state hegemony and see it as their duty to push for the highest possible degree of independence in political, fiscal, and cultural matters, knowing that autonomy will never be absolute. Basque suspicion stems from the long, if intermittent, history of suffering under excessive controls emanating from the central government—a force to be simultaneously endured and held at bay. If not watched vigilantly, they agree that the state would inevitably attempt to homogenize and chip away at their uniqueness. In democratic Spain the majority of Basques are reasonably satisfied with the degree of independence they currently enjoy. That majority believes it can retain its "Basqueness" and also be a part of the larger Spanish society. Even so, one cannot deny that there still was, throughout the whole transition to democracy up until the late 1990s, a dangerous minority of Basques undermining the hard-won democratic structure in order to further its own antidemocratic, separatist agenda. Nevertheless, every time there was a killing, kidnaping, or bus burning, this minute group further marginalized itself from the general society. Given the progress that has been made in its unique identity construction, it is probably safe to assert that the Basque Country, having been a part of Spain for many centuries, will remain so in the foreseeable future. It is equally safe to say that, given the Basque obsession with its identity, there is in this part of the Iberian Peninsula an extraordinary consciousness of the power and influence of their cultural institutions. This consciousness is not something to be taken for granted and its public expression is most definitely a product of the democracy. It is no accident that in the Franco era the official cultural institutions were significantly less appreciated—even depreciated—by ordinary people because they were seen as a reflection of the hated center rather than a product of their own creativity.[2]

The greatest cultural achievement of the first generation living under the new democracy was to bring Euskera back to life as the region's official language—one that could be spoken in the classroom and in public gatherings. Because Euskera was a language that had existed for a long time in many dialects without standardization, and was primarily used by the peasant classes, it required enormous financial, political, and intellectual resources to be brought to a viable state. It is now a living language used by intellectuals, businessmen, and peasants alike—it is also a scientific and literary language for the first time. In fact, the generations of children born since the end of the 1970s all speak both Spanish and Euskera. Many Basques are also encouraged to learn a third language, often English. Language for the Basque people thus fulfills several functions: Euskera fosters regional identity; Spanish reinforces that there is a national identity; and a third language enables participation in the global environment.

Another of the notable achievements was in the world of museums. There was concern in the 1980s over the lack of museums of all kinds in the Basque Country. To remedy that dearth (the opposite of Valencia's plethora of museums) plans were discussed for museums of natural science, labor movement, agriculture, and timber.[3] When it actually came time to allocate money, however, there seemed little support and none of these museums materialized. Rather, because the visual arts are especially valued in the Basque Country, the bulk of funds for these institutions went to the support of art museums specifically. The policies that enabled this phenomenon and the history that make the policies seem inevitable provide a revealing narrative that complements but is not equivalent to the Basque obsession with Euskera.

Although, historically, the Basque Country lagged behind the rest of Spain in realizing the potential of art museums as aids in the construction of civic identity, by the end of the nineteenth century the city of Bilbao had begun to think along those lines. Bilbao's leaders created their first great public art museum, the Bilbao Museum of Fine Arts (Museo de Bellas Artes de Bilbao) in 1908. It opened officially in 1914, at the very time when a great number of citizens desired giving shape to and nurturing what was still only a latent sense of "peoplehood." In its earliest years the museum was extremely progressive, contemporary, and inclusive of local, national, and international trends. During the Spanish civil war and Franco's dictatorship, it adapted to the tastes of the regime, collecting well, especially old master paintings. But it was no longer progressive, contemporary, or international; the Bilbao Museum of Fine arts, along with the rest of society's institutions, became cloistered.

The Fine Arts Museum of Alava (Museo de Bellas Artes de Alava) in Vitoria, the capital city of the Basque Country, did not open until 1941. Although less influential than Bilbao's museum it was still important in the region. Since it actually was inaugurated during the dictatorship, it did nothing at first to challenge inward-looking views. The museum's collection focused on religious art, genre artists of the region, and, above all, artists without any dangerous avant-garde tendencies. Practically the moment that Franco died, the Fine Arts Museum of Alava began to buy the type of art unavailable to it in the past—it was one of the first museums in Spain to buy a Miró. Its curators rushed to ARCO to absorb all of the latest trends, and they built a diverse collection of regional and national artists that to this day is one of the finest in the country.

Democracy infused vigor throughout the Basque Country into many old museums and created an environment that nurtured the building of new museums and art centers. In turn, these institutions encouraged openness and discussion. They became visible and occasionally controversial symbols of the never-ending Basque debate about civic identity. A number of Basque museums are worthy of their own chapters. Bilbao's museums, however, presently form a particularly sensitive ecological group of institutions that are, by all accounts, significant players in the current Basque narrative of self. That this happened once before at the beginning of the twentieth century makes it worthy of an extended discussion.

Bilbao was the locus of the earliest organized artistic efforts, setting the stage for all subsequent art efforts in the Basque Country. By the end of the nineteenth century Bilbao was becoming an extremely prosperous industrial city. Not unlike Chicago and Pittsburgh, certain influential members of Bilbao's haute bourgeoisie came to the conclusion that if the Basque Country was to be perceived as a developed society and if it was to be respected not only in Spain but in the larger world, it needed to be associated with something more than its increasingly rich resources and markets in iron and steel. Joined by artists and intellectuals they moved ahead with their plans. Some of these were Basque nationalist activists latching onto an opportunity to further their political aims. These "nationalists" believed that the very dearth of a cosmopolitan fine arts tradition in the Basque Country in 1876 provided a vacuum that they could fill by creating and promoting an inward spirit of ethnicity. They envisioned an art that would be essentially folkloric. Paintbrushes were seen as weapons to be wielded in the formation of local identity. They rejected influence from Spain as domination by the state itself and universalistic ideas as a kind of contamination that would weaken the Basque's particular identity that they saw as their life's duty to foster. On the other hand there were some implicated in the effort who were aggressively internationalist in their beliefs. The latter group was convinced that turning inward was not the road to enhancement of civic pride; nor did they see the provincial art that would emerge from a so-called pure and unspoiled approach as appropriate. It was their belief that the proper first step was to cultivate artistic contact with the larger world. Hence they promoted artistic pilgrimages to London and then to Paris and Rome, where the highly experimental and influential currents of creativity that would mark the next one hundred years were fomenting. They imported art from abroad and the rest of Spain and by the turn of the twentieth century had succeeded in attracting important exhibitions to Bilbao. As a result Basque artists, along with the general public, were exposed to art from outside, and the forces of European modernism entered their consciousness even as visual ideas of ethnic identity were formulated in the region.

In the 1900s a third perspective, one that offered an effective balance to localism and internationalism, entered the conversation through *Hermes,* an influential art journal. The journal published articles that proclaimed an openness to both the international and regional spirits. *Hermes* had, overall, a cautiously anticentralist bias against Spain. Now a variety of journals and magazines began disseminating ideas about art and its relationship to Basque high culture throughout Spain. By 1914 Bilbao had succeeded in gaining a spirited artistic life largely due to the growing acceptance of the legitimacy and currency of this essential discussion about identity that had captured the educated population. Although final conclusions about the true nature of Basque ethnicity have never been reached, the number and quality of possibilities have definitely appreciated as a result of that critical, vital, and polemical period from 1875 to 1914.[4]

In 1914 World War I brought prosperity to the Basque Country. Both the region's steel and agriculture became valuable and profitable resources for neutral Spain. As a result there was now real money to spend on art. The war, despite all of the agony it brought the rest of Europe, brought the Basques an animated and increasingly civil society. Most sophisticated Basques had by this time chosen the moderate road, demonstrating a greater sense of confidence in their Basque identity within the world at large. Art had become a force for the public good and the bourgeoisie wanted to integrate it into civic life. This combination of factors led to the decision to found the Bilbao Museum of Fine Arts.

BILBAO MUSEUM OF FINE ARTS

The Bilbao Museum of Fine arts was unlike most other major Spanish museums (except those in Catalonia) in that it was not an inherited royal collection, a legacy of the Catholic church, a creation of the government, nor a gift of a single aristocratic individual. Its birth and its continued existence was an act of will by a self-confident, cultivated, and generous public in concert with the region's artists. The museum's dynamic links outside of Spain and at home were made immediately apparent by the nature of the collections. The first works purchased included paintings by famous international artists like Gauguin, Mary Cassatt, and Paul Sérusier as well as Basque contemporary artists.[5] Clearly, if one of the museum's goals was to integrate the city and the region into what were then considered by Europe to be the most advanced ideas about art, it was equally committed to supporting Basque art, Spanish art, and historical master works. It was immensely successful in reaching that dual goal of promoting the ethnic and more outward-looking identities. The museum became an essential part of the fabric of the city, part of Bilbao's euphoric cultural self-awareness, and connectedness. Certainly the cultural elite, but also citizens who might never actually visit the Bilbao Museum of Fine Arts, grew to comprehend how it signified that Bilbao valued beauty in a way that was, in Spain, second only to Madrid. They took enormous pride in knowing that they were citizens of a cultivated city. Unfortunately the economic depression that hit immediately after World War I brought an end to the art-buying spree. Nevertheless, the collection of the Bilbao Museum of Fine arts was well enough established by then to make it a cornerstone in the development of the city's cultural life.

During the Franco dictatorship, the museum was not perceived as a threat to the state. Its collection strategy was folded into the government's mandated views and reflected a unified relationship to Spain, and most of the additions to the collection were of a conservative nature. The museum, in effect, rode out the storm.

Once democracy was reestablished, the museum's purchases and exhibitions included daring contemporary art from European and American artists Joel-Peter Witkin, Cy Twombly, David Hockney, Matta, Jim Dine, Henri Cartier-Bresson, Henry Moore, as well as from many local artists. Exhibitions included the sculpture and painting of the most renowned Spaniards, Chillida, Miró, Picasso, Dalí, Oteiza, Ibarrola, and dozens of others from the international art scene. The museum was proudly supported by the Basque Country regional cultural counselor, Joseba Arregui, who in a 1987 interview in the *New York Times,* discussing the great rebirth of Basque culture, said: "Our objective is to recapture our cultural heritage . . . there is a lot of activity, and the Government's role is to help organize and support it."[6] The Bilbao Museum of Fine Arts saw itself and the region as reborn and profited by the energy that democracy was sparking. It was such a positive time that the institution surpassed its original mission of collecting, preserving, and exhibiting art. In 1986 the Bilbao Museum of Fine Arts was among the first of Spain's museums to organize a truly modern education and outreach department. It seemed to have a bright future, reclaiming as it was its contemporary sensibility and its centrality in the city's life.

This optimism was not to last as the role of the Bilbao Museum of Fine Arts was about to change once again. Very soon the Bilbao Museum of Fine Arts was informed, in no uncertain terms, that it would have to yield any plans to be the flagship of modern and contemporary art to another institution that did not yet exist. This new museum, it was further informed, was going to exert a major force in the contemporary art world.

Furthermore, the venerable institution was going to have to surrender the role it had once played and was hoping to resume to a newcomer: the Guggenheim Museum Bilbao (Museo Guggenheim Bilbao). Having survived the dictatorship intact, it had become apparent that the Bilbao Museum of Fine Arts was about to play a much different role than it had anticipated in leading the city into the next century. Politicians had once again grasped that culture was a formidable tool that, if manipulated pragmatically and strategically, could be of great assistance in the fulfillment of their dearest ambitions.

By 1988 passionate discussions about a museum dedicated to contemporary art had already begun filling the airwaves and the pages of local newspapers. The debate about the essential "Basque spirit" was reignited by the mayor of Bilbao, José María Gorodo, and the country's most outspoken artist, humanist, architect, and thinker, Jorge Oteiza. According to Oteiza, until the "Basque spirit" was defined, the idea of universalizing the spirit of the region would be premature; the journey toward the universal could not start without a set of predetermined essentialist principles. Since, by the end of the 1980s Basques had more freedom to think critically and express their ideas than during the Franco era. Oteiza wanted to create a huge center of creative investigation that would include a library, meeting area, and section for cultural experimentation—a major element of which would be a contemporary Basque art museum. It was to be housed in an old building in the center of town known as the Alhóndiga and would open in 1990. Basque architects would build it, and there would be no international involvement at all in the project. Oteiza's plan sparked intellectual controversy from 1987 through 1989. Local and national newspapers covered the roller-coaster ride of approvals, changes, and finally cancellation. Arguments about identity covered the range of possibilities. The message of lasting importance that emerged from the project was complex: the Basques in Bilbao did not want to be branded as an essentialist people. That, while most Basque citizens do enjoy being grounded in their own uniqueness, especially in their own autonomy of Madrid, they also like to visualize themselves as operating in a wider sphere. On the other hand, if they were to be linked to the international, it must not appear as if they were being totally subjected to it.[7] Therefore, it seemed then that for any major cultural enterprise to go forward in Bilbao, an extremely tricky balance would have to be achieved—one reflecting the majority (but not unanimous) agreement that Basque identity was a peculiar blend of ethnicity, internationalism, and anti-Spanish statism.

The failure of the Oteiza project prompted the elected politicians in the years immediately following the debacle to rethink their cultural strategy in two ways: first, they responded to the message they believed they had gotten about the electorate's thirst for internationalization, and second, they decided to move whatever project they might undertake as quickly as possible to minimize the debate that had effectively killed the Alhóndiga. By December 1991 Joseba Arregui must have no longer believed that developing Basque culture was crucial, because he was extremely busy inspiring his fellow politicians to sign a contract for completing an art museum that would lie at the opposite end of that identity spectrum.[8]

GUGGENHEIM MUSEUM BILBAO

The opportunity to build a Guggenheim museum in Bilbao was thrilling for the city's politicians. The New York museum making available its collections of great modern art in the Basque Country did appear to be the perfect proclamation of the growing taste for global engagement—it provided a high-profile alternative to the aggressive nationalism that still had appeal in the region and, through occasional terrorist acts, was the biggest threat to the population's well-being.[9] It did not take long, however, for many of the artists and intellectuals, even those who had originally welcomed the idea of a Guggenheim Museum Bilbao, to start feeling uneasy about the project. They suspected that local politicians were being propelled by insecurities about being provincial, on the one hand, and by the opportunism of the Guggenheim on the other. Thus, once plans to have a Guggenheim museum in Bilbao became public questions arose in the local press, in Bilbao's artistic community, and throughout Spain. According to Ramón Zallo, writing in the daily newspaper *El Mundo*, the Basque intellectual community was asking why their region was being treated like a "banana republic" subject to the direction of yet another capital city and why such an immense and expensive project had been pushed through without any articulated cultural policy to support it.[10] The project began to be referred to throughout the art world as "McGuggenheim" and "VascoDisney." Constant complaint was heard that there had never been any significant or sustained community debate about the project—only the constant marketing and placating of various constituencies.

It quickly became apparent to the Basque politicians that their project would survive only if they learned another lesson: they had to prove to the public that there was no intention whatsoever of snuffing out the particular Basque creative and cultural voice in the process of opening the region to the world. They needed to make the prospect of the new museum attractive so enough Basques, moderate nationalists and internationalists alike, would not feel as if they had been sold out. Furthermore, they had to accomplish this without completely abandoning the Guggenheim's much vaunted slogans of "excellence" and "quality." These were the Guggenheim's code words, it soon became evident to Basque watchdogs, for not catering to "local taste"—to avoid filling the Guggenheim Museum Bilbao's galleries with the work of local artists. The project's survival called for a strategy that met all of these conflicting goals.

Now that the politicians realized what they were confronting, they expanded their marketing strategy for winning over the intellectual and artistic elites. They did this by arranging for the creation of a few small but fine avant-garde museums and museum-like institutions in Bilbao and the vicinity. This high-stakes approach minimized the dissension that was starting to emanate from those communities because they were distracted by their chance to see more contemporary and modern art exhibitions than they ever had before. Unfortunately, in order to accomplish this the politicians had to wrest funds from the Bilbao Museum of Fine Arts, effectively pushing it from the center to the sidelines of Bilbao's cultural map. But, this strategy succeeded in, to a large extent, wooing a class of art professionals and art lovers who could be expected to articulately advance (or at least not impede) the politicians' aspiration for a Guggenheim in Bilbao. The revised configuration of institutions that resulted would play an indispensable role in the new marketing plan for the Guggenheim Museum Bilbao. It would enable the civic leaders, with the assistance of a small group of advocates, to convince enough of the elite population of the city that rejection of the Guggenheim Museum Bilbao would be tantamount to scuttling any chance for Bilbao to assume a modern identity or protect the regional identity. These new institutions were meant to prove that the intent of the politicians to support internationalism would not preclude their aggressive support for Basque cultural identity reinforcement.

The first institution to play that role for the Guggenheim Museum Bilbao was modestly called the Sala Rekalde, named after the street where it was located. Funded initially by both the local and the Basque governments, Rekalde took the initial high-profile step toward the displacement of the Bilbao Museum of Fine Arts as the city's principal contemporary art institution. By appointing the respected art historian and museum professional Javier González de Durana as director, the Sala Rekalde gained immediate respectability. The politicians, at the same time, gained a superb advocate for the new Guggenheim museum even though Durana always denied being a spokesman for the project. Still, Sala Rekalde's most important achievement at this time was to create an expectation and hunger for the continuous showing of great international art. During its first six years, Sala Rekalde mounted exhibitions of works by Andy Warhol, Sol LeWitt, Tony Smith, Robert Rauschenberg, Josef Albers, Julian Schnabel, and Philip Guston. By no means coincidentally, in November 1993 Sala Rekalde opened *Masterpieces from the Guggenheim Collection, 1909–1957* to much fanfare with its display of extraordinary paintings from the New York Guggenheim to build an appetite for the project. Nevertheless, complaints remained loud although not ubiquitous. It was still muttered among artists and intellectuals that Sala Rekalde was, indeed, being used for promotion of the Guggenheim Bilbao Museum. Durana found himself being attacked in the press by Oteiza, for example, for his perceived role as a "parasite adviser" to the Basque government as it planned the Guggenheim Museum Bilbao.[11] Generally, however, people were thrilled and enchanted by the exhibitions he offered at Sala Rekalde, and they were tantalized by the promises of more great art from the Guggenheim once it was able to settle permanently in the Basque Country. Ultimately, Sala Rekalde, through its exhibition schedule, became quite adept at demonstrating that the government was committed to established and emerging local artists as well as to the international stars by featuring them side by side in the exhibition schedule. The institution's hip newspaper, *REKarte*, further confirmed its balanced engagement with the regional and with the global by means of language parity: it published its reviews and articles of Basque, Spanish, European, and American art in both Euskera and Spanish.

The Rekalde was an expensive exhibition venue to finance. By 1994 it had a budget almost four times the size of the Bilbao Museum of Fine Arts. As had been hoped, the Bilbao Museum of Fine Arts was becoming accustomed to operating on a much reduced funding base. No longer the city's preeminent museum presence, it was seen as the reliable, but

The Guggenheim Museum Bilbao under construction. Courtesy La Sociedad "Immobiliaria Museo de Arte Moderno y Contemporáneo de Bilbao, S.L."

necessary, dowdy older-sister institution that would, when called upon, serve as the dispensable "handmaiden" to the new museum. This reached a humiliating low point when the New York Guggenheim's 1993 exhibition *Picasso and the Age of Iron* was scheduled at the Bilbao Museum of Fine Arts. The Picasso show would have put the Bilbao Museum of Fine Arts in the unattractive position of promoting its usurper. That was uncomfortable enough, but then, unexpectedly and humiliatingly and without concern for the museum's programming, it was canceled. This kind of high-handed dismissiveness occurred on more than one occasion, always diminishing further the profile and prestige of the old museum.

With the Guggenheim Museum Bilbao skeleton beginning to reshape the city skyline Durana asked for and was given permission to build

Rekalde 2. Rekalde 2, a second "kunsthalle" for young and less established artists that only existed for a year, was envisioned as another means
of defusing some of the tension that persisted in the artistic community.
It should be said that Durana firmly and sincerely believed that Bilbao
needed to have a more richly textured art presence than the Guggenheim Museum Bilbao or even the original Sala Rekalde could provide if it
was to be a success in macroeconomic terms. The more enriched and
better marketed the art network of Bilbao was, he insisted, the more
cultural tourism there would be. This would translate into millions of
dollars annually because people would stay longer and visit other
museums than if the only sites were those already in place. Durana was
already making his argument for the continued existence of Sala Rekalde
as a gallery for Spanish and Basque artists after the Guggenheim Museum
Bilbao opened. With the lengthening of the visitors' stay in mind and with
the economic revitalization of the Basque Country at stake, Durana also
encouraged the opening of other art institutions in Bilbao: the Urazurrutia Art Center (Centro Artes de Urazurrutia), a workshop for local artists
and work space for visiting artists from the Guggenheim Museum Bilbao;
the Museum of Reproductions (Museo de Reproducciones Artísticas),
which collected and exhibited photography and other modern "arts of
reproduction"; yet another huge exhibition space for young artists in the
Alhóndiga, the Diocesan Museum of Sacred Art (Museo Diocesanal de
Arte Sacro); and the Bullfighting Museum (Museo Taurino de Bilbao).
These projects were all intended to underline regional identity and
enliven Bilbao's museological map—to create the kind of "art scene" that
would complement the Guggenheim Museum Bilbao.[12] Durana's job was
to convince the public that "Basqueness" was not going to be neglected in
the internationalization of Bilbao. The Guggenheim Museum Bilbao was
an essential element of a comprehensive plan, *Bilbao 2000,* to attract capital by transforming Bilbao's civic personality. The new museum had to
be a success for the whole plan to work. And the politicians were learning
their lessons quickly and well.

Bilbao 2000 had many projects beyond the Guggenheim. One of its
aims was the improvement of the communication and transportation infrastructure. Thus Bilbao built a subway system designed by the well-known
British architect Norman Foster and hired the Spanish architect Santiago
Calatrava to redesign the airport and the Puente Uribitarte, a major foot-

The Guggenheim Bilbao Museum. Courtesy La Sociedad "Immobiliaria Museo de Arte Moderno y Contemporáneo de Bilbao, S.L." Archival photograph by Erika Barahona Ede.

bridge entryway into Bilbao. American/Argentinian architect Cesar Pelli was hired to redevelop the waterfront. Education and culture were targeted to receive serious attention and resources. Building their contemporary art museum, however, was considered the most visible and compelling element of the *Bilbao 2000* strategy. A stunning museum, one as daring as the Pompidou Centre had been when it was erected in Paris twenty years earlier, was envisioned. According to *Bilbao 2000,* this museum would be not only a required tourist stop, but also a sign to global investors of the Basque Country's transformation into a politically stable, sophisticated, and outward-looking city. The feasibility study for the Guggenheim Museum Bilbao is explicit: "The actual and symbolic presence of the Guggenheim Museum Bilbao as a major institution of European and international culture would emphasize the progressive outlook of the Basque sensibility."[13]

Thomas Krens, director of the Guggenheim Museum in New York and the force behind all of the Guggenheim's expansions, promised the Basques a building so spectacular and emblematic of Bilbao that it would rival Australia's Sydney Opera House. With a budget of $250 million for design and construction, the museum far exceeded everyone's expectations. The Guggenheim Museum Bilbao will undoubtedly be remembered as one the most beautiful, original, and influential museum buildings at the end of the twentieth century. American architect Frank Gehry's compelling structure was considered a design landmark, welcoming in the twenty-first century from the minute it opened its doors. Gehry was selected from a small international group of architects, which appears to have deliberately excluded Spanish or Basque participants. Gehry's building, a masterpiece of titanium, glass, stone, and steel, swooping curves, spectacular planes, splendid interior spaces, and stunning use of water, succeeded in becoming an attraction that far surpassed its contents, and that became a pilgrimage site for art lovers who might never otherwise have visited Spain.

It was, it should be noted, quite surprising when Basque politicians donned an American face with an American-run museum and American leadership and architecture to achieve their civic goals. Given Spain's European Union ties and the growing prestige of the union itself Basque disposition was originally toward Europe, a more likely point of reference for identity construction for this Spanish outpost, which, more than anything, wanted to negate any supplicant or subsidiary role to Madrid. This predilection changed when word of the Guggenheim Museum's plans to expand in Europe reached Bilbao. Attracted by the idea of a privately supported museum similar (at least superficially) to older Basque traditions of private support for the arts; its politicians felt comfortable with American management and fund-raising practices and were, of course, impressed by the reputation of the Guggenheim collections. An extraordinary financial deal was made with Krens that included an initial $20 million rental fee for use of the collection, participation in New York–originated exhibitions, and the commitment of an extensive budget for future purchases. As part of the deal the Basques had ceded the lion's share of artistic control to New York.[14]

It soon emerged that the Guggenheim Museum Bilbao's art acquisitions policy would be to purchase mostly works of international reputation—"excellent" and of the "highest quality." This did not sit well with Basque artists or art dealers who recognized the code words and who had no problem voicing their opinions. It became immediately clear that neither Basque nor Spanish artists were going to play a significant role in the museum's collections. This prompted a new burst of outrage. Once again there was a response and the museum shifted its policy and began acquiring works by some of the best-known artists from Spain and the Basque Country. This relatively modest commitment did mollify some of the more vocal local artists and gallery owners, but it never eradicated concern that the art shown at the Guggenheim Museum Bilbao would by and large feature those same artists whose work could be encountered in any other museum in the Western world. Some Basques recognize that a steep price was paid in ceding so much artistic control. As early as 1992 Ernst Lluch, culture critic for *El Mundo,* wrote that the money spent on renting the historical, modern collection from New York (plus the funds dedicated to the development of the permanent collection) could have gone toward the purchase of a large and original body of contemporary art. Lluch also brought to the attention of his readers that the project was infused with the obsequious attitudes of the colonized toward the colonizer, and that Basque institutions were surrendering their right to intervene in the future life of the museum.[15]

Lluch was right about the loss of creative control. However, the Guggenheim Museum Bilbao has been enormously beneficial to the city even if by denying Madrid's influence Bilbao has subjected itself to another, more powerful center. Thomas Krens, the head of the project, delivered everything the Basque government could ever have dreamed of. Of course, as he said in 1995 everything he has done for Bilbao has been driven by New York's financial needs.[16] First, he pointed out that the Guggenheim Museum received the large rental fee from the Guggenheim Museum Bilbao. Second, in the longer range, the Guggenheim Museum Bilbao will share the expenses and risks associated with the organization of major traveling exhibitions. Furthermore, Krens acknowledged that, though the Guggenheim's permanent collection is important to the history of modern art, it will never again have blockbuster status in New York City. In Bilbao, on the other hand, the display of the collection is elevated to a blockbuster event and, simultaneously, its dollar value continues to be enhanced for the mother institution. As far as Bilbao's economic interests are concerned, Krens considers art and culture to be a cheap investment with incredible returns for any ambitious city, when comparing, for example, the cost of building a museum to the cost of adding a single mile of highway. He had promised that Bilbao would get the best museum in the world: one and a half times taller than the original Guggenheim, 50 percent taller than the Pompidou; that it would get the American-style management and expertise it desired; it would not be held hostage to typical Spanish politics, as was exemplified by the unwarrented or capricious dismissal of directors that the Prado and even IVAM had suffered so often. One could happily infer after a conversation with Krens that the museum would not be involved in anything like the sort of seesaw approval and disapproval involving the *La Dama de Elche* that had marred the local celebration because of a conflict between regionalist and statist needs. This interference and lack of continuity, he insisted, was the bane of Spain's museums, and he would be pleased to have a role in eliminating it.[17]

Intriguingly, it was not long before Krens himself encouraged interference in Spanish museum politics by requesting the removal of Picasso's *Guernica* from the Reina Sofía in Madrid to the Guggenheim Museum in Bilbao for the museum's opening festivities. Knowing that the *Guernica* had raised the Reina Sofía's attendance immensely, it was reasonable to assume that it would work to bring in crowds in Bilbao as well, though this was not the real reason for wanting the painting there. Krens fully knew that by fighting to display the *Guernica* in Bilbao, sixty years after the fatal bombing of the nearby Basque town of Guernica, the Guggenheim Museum Bilbao would appear less of an arm of New York City and more an integral part of the region. What Krens did not to take into account, either through ignorance or by chance, was what the painting symbolized not only to Basques but to all of Spain. Housing the *Guernica* in Madrid clearly claimed that it belonged to the Spanish people as a whole; moving it to the Basque Country could only exacerbate tensions that had been somewhat smoothed by the "pacts of oblivion," which had allowed Basques to reconcile themselves to being a part of Spain after democracy had taken hold. In Madrid it was seen as a key symbol of the country's ability to move forward toward a consolidated liberal democracy. Requesting the transfer was a very aggressive political action.

The Reina Sofía refused to loan the *Guernica* on the basis of technical reports that deemed it unfit to travel. Krens neither accepted this report, nor did he discourage Basque politicians and government officials from trying to override it. He was, it appears, not averse to rekindling old divisive nationalist emotions so as to better market the museum. The central state government, however, stayed firm. Its leadership in Madrid, aware of the symbolism of having the *Guernica* in Madrid, did not respond to this American brand of meddling in Spanish politics. "History can be used in efforts to counsel restraint, but it can also be used to reawaken old hatreds, to rekindle old passions; it can be used to justify either appeals for national reconciliation or calls for revenge." Those who had suffered most under Franco understood, after his death, that "the creation of a stable democracy was vastly more important than revenge or the narrow pursuit of partisan interests."[18] With historical memory intact, the government of Spain refused the loan.

Two days before the Guggenheim Museum Bilbao's inauguration, with the issue of the loan of the *Guernica* still raw, a guard, while investigating a suspicious looking truck that was indeed carrying garden pots filled with explosives intended to be detonated on the opening night, was murdered by an ETA gunman. Had the attack succeeded many people, including possibly the king and queen, would have been killed. It was never determined what exactly provoked the attempted attack—anger at Madrid's declining to lend the *Guernica* or rage at the museum's excessively internationalist identity. But, it was undeniably an extreme and tragic reminder that in the Basque Country, art and art museums are not and never have been politically neutral issues. The attack also demonstrated that rhetoric in the Basque Country needs always to be handled with extreme care and with the full awareness of its implications. Inflaming local tensions as a way of showing solidarity with the region is not an appropriate marketing tool. Krens tried, surely in good faith, to please two masters—to be both international and local simultaneously. ETA, looking for any reason to act violently, exploited the museum's strategies for its own ends.

About a year after the Guggenheim Museum Bilbao opened ETA publicly renounced violence, a promising pledge at a hopeful time. Without suggesting that the Guggenheim had anything directly to do with that renunciation, it cannot have been detrimental that, just as the eyes of the world were on Bilbao, so too were Bilbao's extremists feeling especially scrutinized by the world. They also knew that mimicking the peace efforts being made in Ireland and the Middle East would be rewarded with greater than normal attention. Reconsidering their means if not their ends, they made a peace pact of their own. One cannot now calculate the museum's significance in the political arena, but it must be at least considered one of the principal elements contributing to events as they unfolded, if only because a forgotten city at Spain's northern margins had gained a place on center stage.

Remarkable as the Guggenheim Museum Bilbao history has been, it would be unfair to leave the reader with the impression that the venerable Bilbao Museum of Fine Arts was destroyed. That stalwart survivor of days gone by, despite the early attempts to neutralize it, regrouped and flourished. Under the leadership of a young and dynamic director, Míguel Zugaza, it has raised its own money, drawn large audiences, and restored true Basque philanthropic support of the arts. Rather than being a spoiler, Zugaza has increased the self-financing of the museum from 2 percent to 30 percent and has added to the cultural fabric of Bilbao immeasurably. Living up to its potential again, the old institution has figured out how to take advantage of the Guggenheim's ambitions—without rancor and without the benefit of any largesse to speak of. It is now attracting large and enthusiastic audiences again. This itself is a grand and serendipitous achievement.

Indeed, two years after its inauguration, the Guggenheim Museum literally rejuvenated and redefined the city. People who could barely pronounce "Bilbao" are flocking to visit. Whether they consider that they are traveling to Spain itself or have accepted the Basque Country's dream of negating Spain as its center, the region's identity has been irreversibly altered and resituated. It has truly earned its own centrality—even as it remains located at the nation's periphery. The preeminence of the Guggenheim Museum Bilbao as, at the minimum, a site of architectural pilgrimage has ineluctably added another ring to the many circles of regional significance that constitute today's Spain.

In the end, the Guggenheim Museum Bilbao must be judged a supremely democratic institution simply because it could never have been imagined during Franco's dictatorship. The fruit of ambitious elected officials who responded to the people even as they indulged their admittedly inflamed dreams. Problematic as the process of its realization was, it was characterized by ambiguities and conflicts attendant to a free people searching for a potent definition of selfhood. It was a rejection of what was understood as centralist Spain. But it was a simultaneous submission to the centrality of New York. Nevertheless, the decision about which master to accept was made by Basques *not* Madrid. The Guggenheim Museum Bilbao's full history is not yet written, and one might also confidently suggest that the history of which centers are to be negated is not yet complete either. The Basques may yet wish to claim the museum as wholly of the Basque Country—as a reflection of a deeper confidence in their own true, unique, changing, but enduring selfhood.

7 A NATION WITHIN A NATION: CATALONIA

The Spanish region of Catalonia has a long history of asserting its own separate identity. The political leadership in Barcelona, the region's grandest city, has always exercised economic and political clout. Catalonia exerts powerful influence on the Spanish ruling parties in Madrid through its political parties' ability to garner votes for the party, either socialist or conservative, that offers the best deal. It has achieved these political goals with pride and confidence. Catalonia's leaders constantly work to enhance this empowering sense of regional and global identity in their population.

Catalonians have built their identity on their distinguished history of literary, artistic, scientific, and economic achievement. Their own official language, Catalan, restored and in full flower, they see no need to turn to outsiders for validation. So strong is their sense of self, it is inconceivable that Catalonian politicians would have ever succumbed to the siren song of the Guggenheim in New York as did the Basques. When Catalonia decided to strengthen its own network of museums, it either invented new institutions or strengthened its older ones, always meeting and engaging the world on Catalonian terms. It is beyond imagining that they would court and then import an American museum structure to adopt an international identity as the Basques did when they bought a Guggenheim franchise. Catalonia's regional pride in its own creativity, along with its much touted business sense, would never have permitted it to earmark so much money, which, it could be plainly seen, was going to shore up the budget of an institution in New York City while costing the Catalans a fortune in pesetas and in pride.

Barcelona was considered the most European and modern of Spain's cities during the Franco era. Afterward Barcelona recognized that bowing to or imitating Madrid, Paris, New York, or any other cultural mecca would be not a mark of sophistication but rather an indication of provincialism. Barcelona has labored instead to offer the world another center, one that travelers would flock to for a special cultural experience in and of itself. Although this confidence is much admired, sometimes this push for separateness has gone too far for some Spaniards. There was, for example, fury in Madrid when Barcelona took out full-page ads in U.S. newspapers during the 1994 Olympics inviting the world to "two countries": Catalonia and Spain. The fact that Catalan is favored over Spanish in the schools also causes much criticism. Notwithstanding such developments, Catalonia has accepted some restraints in its quest for even more autonomy in exchange for an acceptable return on its share of tax dollars and a more than acceptable quota of political influence. Hence they can also claim to be proponents of Spanish stability even as they are asserting their independence.

Franco could not forget that Barcelona had been the last holdout during the civil war and, as much as he tried, he was never able to eradicate its independent spirit. Nor was he able to completely control the Catalonia region; there always seemed to be more freedom in Barcelona than there was in the capital. Some said it was because it was so close to the French border and its uncensored books, movies, and libraries. Or, Barcelona's relative liberty is attributed to the disproportionate number of visitors to Barcelona and travelers from Barcelona to Europe and America during those years. All of those reasons are probably true. But it needs to be stressed that just as dictatorships are unevenly efficient over time (Franco's regime was much more repressive in the first twenty years than it was in the last twenty) so, too, can they be unevenly efficient over space. The long arm of the center did not reach as efficiently out to Barcelona as it did to other places. And Franco's failure also must be attributed to the idiosyncratic organization of a deeply rooted civil society, which had been in place in Catalonia long before the dictatorship and which Franco could never totally eradicate.

Unlike other regions Catalan society never developed a high degree of dependence on the government for its social and cultural well-being. During the industrial revolution, the leaders of Catalonia's banks developed a financial scheme that would generate funds from the workers' own savings to pay for retirement, health, and education benefits. Leaving aside their motives (which were, no doubt, at least partially self-serving) these business leaders were able to form nonprofit, privately run institutions that put local people in charge of savings and loans, hospitals, opera houses, libraries, and museums. There were no royal collections or aristocracies to endow these institutions, so they were built by civic associations, local administrations, and private collectors. The Catalonian population adopted the deep belief that it could only depend on itself, taking care of its needs through a complex network of private institutions, associations, and foundations. And it took pride in doing so. The Franco regime must have sensed that it could never totally destroy that sense of pride; thus, it did not try to obliterate it entirely—knowing that any such effort would have only resulted in embarrassment and failure.

Catalonia, especially Barcelona, began dividing itself into official and unofficial cultures as early as the 1950s. The official Francoist culture was ubiquitous and reeked of historicism, revivalist values, unreal harmony, and vapid idealism. Unofficial culture was driven, not surprisingly, by artists and was less easy to find. Discreetly, though, it began to emerge and was characterized by its abstraction and surrealism, its praise of ambiguity, its emphasis on the disorder of the unconscious, and complete disregard for harmony or idealism. Antoní Tapies led the movement, and his group, Dau al Set (along with Madrid's El Paso artists), went public at the Venice Biennial in 1958. By 1960 abstract art was the dominant style in Barcelona. Soon, other examples of art, architecture, literature, and theater began to surface that did not reflect authoritarian culture. As Franco lay dying in 1975 it became quite evident that the ground had been prepared well. Society was ready for democracy, and in that same year with the unofficial opening of a museum for artist Joan Miró in Barcelona, it celebrated its readiness for an active role in the full transition that was to come.

JOAN MIRÓ FOUNDATION MUSEUM

The Joan Miró Foundation Museum (Fundación Joan Miró) was the most inspirational art museum to open near the end of the dictatorship, rapidly becoming a civic institution symbolic of resistance to Franco. Further, it represented three things to Barcelona: a contemporary face during the critical transition period; a home to one of the century's most influential artists; and private support that goes to the heart of Catalan identity. Joan Miró had been making plans during Franco's regime to donate a body of work to a Barcelona museum for several years. When the museum opened six months before the dictator died it immediately made an enormous impact throughout Spain because of its blatant commitment to outspoken contemporary art. According to its founding director (who has guided the museum since) Rosa María Malet, the political atmosphere in the late 1970s was certainly not one in which free expression could yet be taken for granted.[1] (It had only been one year since the bishop of Bilbao, Monsignor Antonio Añoveros, had been threatened with expulsion from Spain for allowing the publication of tracts in defense of ethnic minorities and, closer to home, a Catalan anarchist, Salvador Puig Antích, had been executed by garrote—a gruesome form of strangulation—despite an international outcry. In 1975, despite the all pervasive "sense of the regime crumbling," there were several attacks on radical lawyers, clergymen, and bookshops by right-wing terror squads.[2]) The founders of the Joan Miró Foundation Museum were fully aware of the museum's activist role as an art institution dedicated to unfettered expression and experimentation during the rebirth of democracy. In those days no such place existed in Catalonia, and Miró in particular wanted one. Furthermore Miró was adamant in not wanting the museum to display only his paintings and sculpture, but rather to be a venue for contemporary art in general. He also believed in the necessity of exposing Barcelona's citizens to the work of the young and unestablished. In Catalonia this was an unprecedented gesture and the positive response to it was enormous.

In 1968, in celebration of Miró's seventy-fifth birthday, the mayor of Barcelona had organized the first public retrospective exhibition of the artist's work in Spain. Discussions began at that time about a future museum. Miró donated part of his oeuvre to the city, and in response, a glorious site on Montjuic, a mountain within and overlooking the city, was promised, with the government agreeing to bear approximately half the museum building's construction cost. Miró's many good friends, including artists, art dealers, and architects, became involved in the project, making generous individual donations. Although the museum

Entrance to the Joan Miró Foundation Museum (Fundación Joan Miró). Courtesy Fundación Joan Miró.

received support from the city of Barcelona and the regional government the governance of the museum was structured as a private foundation. The Joan Miró Foundation Museum made it a point not to receive *all* of its support from public entities. This, according to Malet, allows it to operate with significantly more autonomy and flexibility than if it is 100 percent dependent on the government. It also forces her to be more resourceful and creative. Malet also takes pride in being the first Spanish museum to have significant fund-raising and serious volunteer programs. The Joan Miró Foundation Museum depends on its audiences for support; the museum tries to be very responsive to that audience. A friends' association, a private fund-raising group, play a significant role here—as this type of group does more and more throughout Spain with citizens taking on ever larger responsibilities for their cultural lives.

The Joan Miró Foundation Museum's building is an imposing structure that, although radical when first built because of its brutally simple, windowless facade of unadorned cement, was immediately appreciated for its "strange beauty." It was designed by Catalan architect Josep Lluis

Sert, a longtime friend of Joan Miró. Their friendship began in 1937 when they worked together on the Republican Pavilion for the Universal Exposition in Paris, the famous pavilion that housed Picasso's *Guernica,* Alexander Calder's *Mercury Fountain,* and other landmark modernist works. Before designing the Joan Miró Foundation Museum, Sert had designed the Maeght Foundation museum in St. Paul de Vence, France, and the Museum of Contemporary Art (El Museo de Arte Contemporáno) in Majorca. The interior of the Joan Miró Foundation Museum is filled with natural light and promotes the art not the building. Arranged around a central patio with vaults and half vaults reminiscent of Roman architecture, the building instills a sense of history in spite of the exterior starkness. Sert's design also allows for the range of museum services—library, conference rooms, performance areas, and a restaurant—desired by Miró. When it outgrew the original space, the building was sympathetically expanded in 1987 by architect Jaume Freixa.

By the mid-1970s Miró had donated 10,000 works: 217 paintings, 153 sculptures, 9 textiles, his complete graphic work, and 5,000 drawings, sketches, and notations. Many other works were donated by art-world luminaries. On the day of the museum's official opening in June 1976 (one year after the unofficial opening and six months after Franco was buried), it received several important gifts including Alexander Calder's personal donation of the *Mercury Fountain.* Other artists in the collection include Marcel Duchamp, Max Ernst, Julio González, Henri Matisse, Henry Moore, Eduardo Chillida, Phillip Guston, Robert Rauschenberg, Saura, and Richard Serra.

The Joan Miró Foundation Museum also functions as a forum for scholarship, granting fellowships to students interested in Miró who wish to study at the museum. There have been fine temporary exhibitions of Miró's drawings, graphic work, paintings, sculpture, ceramics, tapestries, theatrical designs, and books. Other artists have had temporary exhibitions at the museum, including Antoní Tapies, Wolf Vostell, Paul Klee, Henry Moore, Kurt Schwitters, Marcel Duchamp, Joseph Cornell, Anthony Caro, Eduardo Chillida, Alberto Giacometti, Joseph Beuys, Donald Judd, and Alvaar Aalto; theme shows devoted to Tantric art, New York trends, electronic art, Czech art, and many other genres have been displayed as well. A special space is always reserved for young artists, especially those who work in an experimental manner and who are exploring and investigating untested genres. In accordance with Miró's wishes, conferences, seminars, lectures, concerts, avant-garde films, theatrical presentations, performance pieces, and contemporary dance performances are regularly featured.

MUSEUMS OF MEMORY

Franco's death brought a wave of government support for the creation of dozens of new museums in the areas around Barcelona. However, the Antoní Tapies Foundation Museum (Fundación Antoní Tapies), also inspired by an artist, was the only other contemporary art museum to open in Barcelona between 1970 and 1990. Rather than the art of the moment Catalan society seemed determined to perpetuate the memory of pre-Franco Catalonia—thereby to rebuild a collective self-image of the independent people whose societies and associations had made them so strong before the advent of fascism. Called "museums of memory" these institutions were meant to commemorate those characteristics that had been repressed during the dictatorship.[3] Throughout the 1980s they were able to successfully display those Catalonian cultural contributions, many of the museums they supported grew beyond institutions of memory and actively linking the past and present with the future. Soon an official network of hundreds of provincial museums flourished throughout Catalonia. In villages as small as Orgnac-l'Aven, population 320, a Museum of Prehistory (Museo de la Prehistoria) was built to display the area's archaeological finds; in Capellades a Paper Mill Museum (Museu Molí Paperer) was established in a closed-down seventeenth-century mill; and in Montseny an ethnology museum opened to exhibit the cultural heritage of the surrounding Valley of Arbúcies.

A particularly dynamic provincial museum, the Museum of Gavà (Museu de Gavà), opened in 1978 to serve a population of a half million people that had no other museum in its vicinity and had a need for a better integration of older and newer inhabitants.[4] Franco had encouraged the displacement of huge numbers of people from around the country, ostensibly enabling them to find work. This policy also resulted in the dilution of Spain's intrinsic regionalisms as diverse groups had to adapt to their new surroundings. Andalusians in Barcelona, for example, lost some of their southern ways and, by the same token, affected the characteristics of Catalan residents. This dilution served Franco's political interests to the extent that it promoted his ideology of a unified Spain and a homogenous population. The Museum of Gavà was seen as an opportunity to foster Catalan identity where it was not yet fully or profoundly formed and to instruct the largely unaware population about the rich archaeological, ecological, and anthropological aspects of their relatively new environment. The plan was to give more recent arrivals and their children something to make them feel more deeply rooted, and more acculturated—more Catalan.

The Museum of Gavà was successful, attracting so many visitors that it needed to be expanded in 1991. It employed the most current technologies to create an interactive experience for its visitors and their natural surroundings. By animating local history, dramatizing the effects of recent industrialization, and positing ways that citizens could participate in shaping their own future, the museum has also significantly broadened its mission. It went so far as to reopen the area's prehistoric mines as an archaeological park, quite a popular attraction. The Museum of Gavà also collaborates with neighboring universities on academic projects, archaeological research, and investigations. Its mission has thus grown from one of simple identity construction for an immigrant population to one of empowerment for the whole population. It now seeks to participate in the transformation of a once manipulated group of people to a citizenry far more aware of their responsibilities for their own well-being in their complex environment.

By 1990 almost 200 museums and collections were open to the public in the province of Barcelona. In 1930 there had been only eight. But, with all of their impressive successes, by the end of the 1980s these institutions were on the brink of losing their funding. The tide had turned as it became apparent to politicians and professionals alike that the high cost of funding so many small museums was preventing the development of major institutions such as the often-discussed Museum of Catalan Art (Museu National d'art de Catalan). It was now admitted that older museums with extremely valuable collections were being ignored. Objects, most of them far more irreplaceable than those in the newer museums, were deteriorating. Their infrastructures had been neglected, and there were concerns that the buildings were becoming fire hazards. A lack of trained curators, restorers, and education professionals was a problem that could only get worse as time went on. The patrimony was in danger of being destroyed by that neglect and indifference. By 1990 many opinion makers now considered additional provincial museum expansion to be a political indulgence. There was also concern within the middle class that while the government had been pouring money into local museums of memory, they had unanticipatedly sucked some of the soul out of the Catalan social enterprise, which had been based on private support. With the realization of the contradiction that had emerged, more private citizens began to encourage civic responsibility: once again museum friends groups began to thrive as the region began to convince individuals of the importance of self-reliance.[5] An active umbrella organization, Friends of the Catalan Museums, took on the task of training museum professionals, organizing conferences, and communication among museum professionals and donors. Finally Catalonia began to resemble pre-Franco times in this way—ironically, because government support had become too prevalent in the smaller local enterprises.

On October 17, 1990, the Catalonia Parliament passed a law that shifted the region's museum budget and priorities from local or provincial museum to "national" museums (i.e. the museums of the region as a whole). The law was also meant to codify responsibilities to protect the historical and cultural heritage, which had already been granted to the region by the Spanish state in the Catalan Statute of Autonomy. The Catalonia Parliament, called the *Generalitat,* provided a legal framework for Catalonian management and programming of its own museums.[6] Although Spain's constitution states that the central government (in Madrid) has sole responsibility for the protection of Spain's cultural and artistic heritage against exportation and destruction, the Catalan government has been granted exclusive responsibility for all other aspects of the "cultural, artistic, monumental, architectural, and scientific heritage"— that would include the creation of museums and their collections, exhibitions, and preservation policies. The 1990 law called for the creation of a museums board in Barcelona to minimize the politicization of policy and administration, the core problem of museums throughout Spain. It also established the Museum Assistance Services to aid all museums, provincial and national, by providing a centrally based source of technical resources for reducing inefficiency and duplication. The 1990 law made it apparent that those in power had decided to cement, to whatever extent possible, the perception of Catalonia as a "nation" separate from the Spanish mainstream. This idea of nationhood, it was agreed, needed to be better communicated to Catalonian citizens and to the world. Local museums were still considered relevant, but the cultural policy of the

1980s, which favored them, had ended definitively in the 1990s. A general shift in societal priorities had occurred, and "national" (also known as regional) museums would now play the lead roles.

Though the 1990 museum law was aimed at larger institutions, by 1996 it was clear that it had helped all Catalan museums. After the first few years, a balance was struck between the diverse needs of the various institutions. Professionalization increased everywhere; standards were rising generally by virtue of the training courses that were being provided. Catalonia's smaller museums had learned (as others learned the world over) how to make the most of their reduced budgets and be more resourceful and innovative. It has not been a smooth journey for any of them, but they adapted and greatly improved their services.

BARCELONA AND THE 1992 OLYMPICS

This shift from "memory museums" to "national institutions" was precipitated and made possible by Barcelona's hosting of the 1992 Olympics. The games brought abundant funds from Madrid into Barcelona, and long-standing tensions were raised between the capital and the region's smaller cities as distinct notions of the regional identity clashed. Catalonia wanted funding to honor the "nation's" dominant rural identity, while Barcelona was determined to celebrate the capital's international sophistication. Since the Socialist Party controlled Spain's central government at the time, the internationalist aspirations of socialist-run Barcelona (in contrast to conservative-run Catalonia) won out and funds poured into the city, with goodly sums going into art and museum-related activities.

Most of the approximately $6 billion that came into Barcelona for the 1992 Olympics went to road construction, renewal of the decrepit port area, and building the athletic venues. The city was reshaped, modernized, and beautified, and the project for a "museum without walls," a collection of outdoor sculpture scattered throughout Barcelona, was given a new life. This Barcelona public art project is a fine example of the aesthetic sensibility that lies at the heart of the city's public artistic vision. It was an idea that had been born, although on a much smaller scale, in 1980, but it received its greatest impetus with the planning for the 1992 Olympics. Other than the "Eixample" (the expansion of the city) of 1859 and the International Exposition of 1929, only the 1992 Olympics has made such a lasting contribution to Barcelona's urban fabric.[7] The Public

Art Project was Barcelona's statement that it intended to become a serious player in the contemporary art world. It ultimately became the most ambitious project of its kind in the West.

As early as 1979, when it was first thought Barcelona might host the 1992 Olympics, sculptor Xavier Corberó, Narcís Serra (the first elected mayor of Barcelona after the dictatorship), urban theorist Oriol Bohigas, and New York City art dealer Joseph Helman had begun to encourage the creation of a great sculpture project, an outdoor museum scattered throughout Barcelona. Later Pasqual Maragall, the second elected mayor of Barcelona in the post-Franco era, elected in 1982, was persuaded by the head of urban projects, Josep Acebillo, to commission about seventy large outdoor sculptures for the Olympic celebration. An expansive mind-set, neither chauvinistic nor slavishly international, governed the choice of artists. Half of the commissioned sculptors were Catalan or Spanish, but the rest were British, Austrian, Colombian, French, Dutch, and American. The governing principle was to involve the residents of each neighborhood in the process—a visionary idea since this was still a time when public art was dropped into a neighborhood (plop art) with little concern for the communities' desires or concepts.

The Olympics, as much as they were about the moment and the future, were also used to recall and honor pre-Franco Spain. For example, the sculpture of the mayor of Barcelona, Bartolomeu Robert i Yarzábal, who took office in 1899 (the base of which was created by Antonio Gaudí and the figures by Josep Llimona), was remounted and displayed. It was reclaimed after having been taken apart and put in storage during Franco's regime for being politically incorrect, that is too Catalanist. Indeed the sculpture was a powerful symbol of anti-Madrid and anti-centrist values, and its restoration was a significant, if not loaded gesture that could have backfired if it had been perceived as unnecessarily condescending to those who, although they had won the civil war, had lost the peace once democracy was restored. As we have seen in previous chapters, one of the foundations of Spain's new democracy was the tacit acceptance of "pacts" that, among other things, discouraged flaunting the notion of victors and vanquished, a notion that lay at the heart of Franco's ideology. The reinstallation of the Yarzábal sculpture, which was a clarion call to Catalan identity, was thus quite daring—even slightly transgressive of those pacts. That it caused no problems whatsoever was another indication of the health of the young democracy. Although clearly promoting the spirit of the region, it ignited no outbursts. By 1992 the time for walking so gingerly had apparently passed. Other works were more explicit metaphor for the freedom of post-Franco life.

The Barcelona public art project showed that the city and, by extension, the region, were able to nurture and promote a local identity through art, while contextualizing it within a national, international, and historical framework. It also established Barcelona's willingness to take risks with art and to experiment with current ideas. The pieces varied in quality; some were puzzling, some witty, some fabulous, but it was unimaginable that the majority of them could have been created during the dictatorship. A large Miró sculpture, for example, could not have been "less authoritarian: a lunar, massive torso with a horned cylinder of a head, ponderous but also silly in its dignity, a moon calf dropped from Brobdingnag."[8] Though not all the sculptures will go down in the annals of art history or were beloved (or even maintained) by everyone in the neighborhoods, the project invigorated Barcelona in a manner that was gracious, mature, and self-confident. Most pointedly, with their lack of a single, harmonious unifying perspective, the sculptures proclaimed that public art can be polyphonic, antiauthoritarian, and antifascist in its aesthetic. The tone they set contributed to Barcelona's assured sense of self and of the change they had lived through.

The change that had overtaken Spain can be measured by comparing the Barcelona public art project with Franco's Valley of the Fallen memorial. All the fascist symbolism of the Valley of the Fallen was subverted in the 1992 Olympics's sculpture park. Whereas the Valley of the Fallen (which was the largest public art memorial in the West when it was built) represented monolithic, centralized power, the "museum without walls" in Barcelona brilliantly represented decentralization. Franco's monument was imposed from above; the Barcelona project came from artists working in cooperation with average citizens. The Valley of the Fallen was built largely by forced labor—including political prisoners working off their jail terms; the Barcelona Public Art Project did not use prisoners of any kind. The Franco memorial was a pharaonic tomb; the Barcelona project was ultimately a playground. The Valley of the Fallen epitomized the politics of revenge: at the opening on April 1, 1959, Franco "gloated over the enemy that had been obliged 'to bite the dust of defeat' and showed not the slightest trace of desire to see reconciliation between Spaniards."[9] The Barcelona Public Sculpture Project was the result of a

Grand entrance hall to the Catalan Museum of Art (Museu Nacional d'Art de Catalunya). Courtesy MNAC Photographic Service (J. Calveras/J. Sagrista).

reconciliation among Spaniards, and presented an honest face to the outside world. Spain's democracy had become real, and Barcelona was a good place to witness it in action.

NATIONAL MUSEUM OF CATALAN ART

The revolution in cultural policy that began with the 1990 museum law and the 1992 Olympics became unstoppable when several of Barcelona's medium-sized and small museums consolidated under the National Museum of Catalan Art (Museu National d'art de Catalan), also known as MNAC. This was an extremely ambitious endeavor intended to showcase the uniqueness and greatness of the Catalan culture. The "revolution" joined together the National Museum of Catalan Art, the Prints and Drawings Collection (El Gabinete de Dibujos y Grabados), the Museum of Modern Art (El Museo de Arte Moderno), the Numismatics Collection (El Gabinete Numismatico de Cataluña), the General Library of the History of Art (La Biblioteca General de Historia del Arte), and the Center for Restoration (Centro de Restauración). Plans for the consolidation of these mini-institutions under one giant umbrella had provoked debates about control, and the consolidation itself did not resolve the squabbling over whether the city or the *Generalitat* would be in charge of MNAC. The 1990 museum law settled the governance issues by putting most of the key national Catalan institutions under the control of *Generalitat*.[10] The institution now had the strongest possible regional backing to rectify any perceived identity problem that might be related to art and culture. According to the president of MNAC's board of trustees

Catalonia has, since the advent of democracy and under the auspices of the Statute of Autonomy, gone a long way toward finding its own political personality. It has, furthermore, built up an effective economy that has allowed it to play an active part in the development of the new Europe. In the cultural realm, on the other hand, I believe we have failed to present ourselves and our artistic heritage as effectively as we should have. We have not provided an adequate image either for our own people or for those from abroad, of the extraordinary spirit of the history and peoples of Catalonia.[11]

The president went on to say that with MNAC it had finally become feasible to ensure that Catalonia's cultural life could match the advances made by the political and economic milieus.

Like the Pinakotheks of Germany, the Louvre of France, and the national galleries in England, Canada, and the United States, Catalonia wanted MNAC to be a museum that symbolized a country, that country being in this case a region within a nation-state. The objective was thus intrinsically political. In order to accomplish this, MNAC needed to participate in transforming how Spain and Catalonia would be conceptualized: how the center/periphery relationship would be interpreted and mythologized in a museum setting. In this context MNAC is an expensive and expansive affirmation of the marriage of museums and politics. The spectacular quality of its core collections, along with its intriguing site and architectural presence, make it a compelling affirmation of Catalonia and its creative spirit.

MNAC is housed in the imposing Palau National, which was built in 1929 for the International Exposition of Barcelona. Located on Montjuic (not far from the Joan Miró Foundation Museum) the Palau National provides one of the venerable images of the city. It is sometimes called the living room of Barcelona, the Palau's Great Hall having been an indoor plaza where many private and public functions have taken place. Italian architect Gae Aulenti (the architect of the controversial Musée D'Orsay renovation in Paris) was commissioned in 1985 to adapt the building for use as a museum; unfortunately, her interior alterations, although consid-

Romanesque apses of the Catalan Museum of Art. Courtesy MNAC Photographic Service (J. Calveras/J. Sagrista).

ered totally functional, have reduced that grand interior space to the semblance of a moderately chic department store. On the other hand, the exterior appears unchanged, except for numerous positive improvements with, for example, respect to accessibility from the center of the city.

MNAC has the most unforgettable display of frescoed Romanesque apses from the eleventh to thirteenth centuries in all the world. They were rescued from small churches in the Pyrenees in the early part of the twentieth century at a time when the frescoes, along with other works of art and architecture, were being avidly purchased by Americans for their museums or, like William Randolph Hearst, for their personal mansions. Elders of the region, inflamed by the depletion of their artistic legacy, intervened and took it upon themselves to buy great quantities of these works for the Catalan community.[12] Because these frescoes were painted by humble, anonymous artists, they escaped the attention of restorers and have never been repainted as were more esteemed and famous masterpieces. They are (through this neglect) perfect examples of the convergence of international Gothic with Catalan and Flemish styles. MNAC's holdings reveal how Catalan art assimilated these influences and then invented something of its own. They are some of Western civilization's most prized cultural relics from the Romanesque period. Displayed to mimic their presentation in the churches in their own reconstructed apses, they astonish and enlighten both art historians and museum visitors. They instill pride in Catalan visitors since they represent a unique moment, showing Catalonia to be distinct in its artistic legacy from Spain, but closely linked to Europe.

Begun in the 1880s, the Numismatics Collection component of MNAC is one of the world's most complete collections and research libraries dedicated to rare and unique coins. The Prints and Drawings Collection component consists of 36,000 drawings, 50,000 prints, 15,000 books, and about 20,000 posters. This collection is only second in Spain to that of the National Library in Madrid. Another department of MNAC is the Center for Restoration, which was instituted in 1906 for the purpose of conserving Catalonian art. Currently, not only does the Center for Restoration perform its conservation duties, but it also mounts exhibitions that present a behind-the-scenes look at the role of restoration in art.

MNAC's Museum of Modern Art, the final department of the mega-museum, demonstrates that Catalan art had a strong international presence at the end of the nineteenth and beginning of the twentieth century. The heart of the museum's permanent collection consists of Spanish art-nouveau (*noucentisme* and *modernisme* in Barcelona) works. There are untold numbers of examples by Antonio Gaudí, probably the country's most well-known art-nouveau artist and architect. The president of MNAC's board of trustees wrote that *modernisme* "became an exaltation of the artist at his most powerful and most liberated. . . . In this way it has a particular message for those who feel the need to neutralize the creeping standardization and depersonalization that are unfortunately becoming more common in modern society."[13] Without implying that an exhibition could accomplish such a lofty goal on its own, the president did suggest that as part of a total societal vision, the effective exhibition of pivotal works of art from a moment of cultural prominence could contribute to the resurrection of Catalan identity. His words are reminders that the last thing Franco wanted was to encourage any single component of the citizenry to function at its "most powerful and most liberated." To make its political and cultural goals unambiguous, the Museum of Modern Art does not display history beyond 1936 — the exact year the republic died.

The Barcelona Museum of Contemporary Art (Museu d'Art Contemporani de Barcelona). Courtesy Museu d'Art de Barcelona.

BARCELONA MUSEUM OF CONTEMPORARY ART

In 1995 the Barcelona Museum of Contemporary Art (Museu d'art Contemporani de Barcelona) opened its doors to the public. A contemporary art museum is special in that it needs nurturing from the kind of environment that only an open society can provide. In order to thrive it requires a society that welcomes heterogeneous and fragmented thinking, just the kind of thinking that Franco needed to suppress. Thus, although an earlier attempt had been made (in 1959) to start a contemporary art museum, it could not be made to work, and Barcelonans had to wait until the last decade of the twentieth century for a major contemporary art museum to be a reality.

The Barcelona Museum of Contemporary Art (MACBA) was designed by American architect Richard Meier, also the architect for the High Museum of Art in Atlanta, the extension to the Decorative Arts Museum in Frankfurt, and the Getty Center in Los Angeles. The MACBA building, not uncharacteristically, is a white, crystalline jewelry-box-shaped structure and a tribute to light rather than to any work that might be placed inside. Meier said of his building, "I know that the museum will have to

house sculptures and paintings, big and small, prints and photographs. . . .
I do not conceive of the museum as a container of works of art, but rather
a work of art in its own right."[14] The building does not work, and Meier's
admission is the saddest and most personal explanation of why. Its pre-
dominantly glass walls allow little control over the sunlight that streams
in, there is insufficient wall space for displaying art, and poorly planned
storage facilities make it difficult to move art to the galleries. Although
the Meier building has received harsh criticism, the museum remains an
important part of its historically rich but somewhat deteriorated neighborhood, the Raval, with its libraries, university facilities, research institutions, art school, and theaters. MACBA will no doubt continue to be a
key piece in its urban renewal and succeeded despite it deficiences in
welcoming over 225,000 visitors in its first year of operation.

MACBA was criticized though, not just for its building, but also for not
having a great art collection when it began operations. It did, though, possess a number of works by international artists ranging from Robert Rauschenberg, Lucio Fontana, Christian Boltanski, Anselm Kiefer, and Paul
Klee to Spanish and Catalan artists including Tapies, Barceló, and Miguel
Navarro. The museum soon acquired works by Marcel Broodthaers, Joan
Brossa, James Lee Byars, Oteiza, Carmen Calvo, and many others.[15] That it
did not have a complete or satisfactory collection may have garnered it
more attack than it deserved, given that many museums both in Spain and
the United States (the Museum of Contemporary Art in Los Angeles, the
Museum of Contemporary Art in Chicago, and the High Museum of Art
in Atlanta, as examples) built in the 1980s had similar beginnings.[16] The
lack of a fine collection can actually bring a community together as it tries
to acquire one and to make its mark in the city and on a larger front as
well. Unfortunately a limited and unfocused initial collection was just one
of MACBA's problems, the most grave being a lack of clear governance
and leadership.

When MACBA opened in 1995 confusion over governance and leadership agendas made running the museum nearly impossible. City, *Generalitat,* and the private board struggled over issues of funding and even over
the meaning of the museum. Finally after making the professional lives of
two directors impossible, the board of trustees in 1998 selected Manuel
Borja-Villel, the former director of the Tapies Foundation, as director.
Borja-Villel came in with a strong mandate. He made a cinvincing case for
two policies: that MACBA only purchase art that represented the frag-

mented history and contemporaneity of Catalonia; and that it stop collecting minor or irrelevant examples of international art just so MACBA could claim to have star names in its inventory. By collecting in this manner, he insisted, MACBA would soon have the material to relate the region's history in a dynamic and daring manner. Borja-Villel said that the institution needed to find a way to narrate the living, inflected, nonlinear, and nonmythologized development of artistic ideas that have found their home in Catalonia. Unlike the directors before him, Borja-Villel hoped to build bridges between the art, the artists, and the community. He also hoped to engage in dialogue with Europe and North and South America so as to further contextualize the discourse and dialogue about Catalan art. Borja-Villel wanted to invite artists to make installations that work well within a difficult building, rather than endlessly complain about Meier's structure. The director hoped to use it aggressively and constructively by means of these artistic interventions. To Borja-Villel, every museum is a political instrument. He intended to take full advantage of Spain's maturing democracy by pursuing art and developing programs that will help Catalonians better understand themselves and the creative potential of their region.[17] In 1998 there was every indication that the board would allow him to pursue his program and to implement his clear vision. If he is given the authority and resources to lead, there is reason to believe he will be successful. And, if his success is measured in other ways than only fund-raising or attendance, he may have a chance where his predecessors had none. MACBA is important to Barcelona in that it punctures cultural myths. If it thrives it can and will be a factor in complicating contemporary culture there and enlivening the Catalan idea of self and nation.

MUSEUM OF THE HISTORY OF CATALONIA

In February 1996 the Museum of the History of Catalonia (Museu d' Història de Catalunya) was added to the network of museums in Barcelona. This museum is concerned, as its pamphlets proclaim, with *"la historia i la memoria del nostre pais"* (the history and the memory of our country), but the creation of "Catalanness" seems to be the museum's single mission. (To the point that, when the museum opened, every sign and label was in Catalan, thus preventing many visitors from having any idea of what the museum was about.) The museum presents significant events from prehistoric times to the present, recounting achievements and disasters in a linear manner. Above all, it goes to great pains to establish Catalonians as a supremely gifted people always fighting for their integrity and their singular identity.

The Museum of the History of Catalonia was inspired by a visit that Jordi Pujol, power and head of the Catalonian regional government, took to the Diaspora Museum in Tel Aviv. Pujol decided that Catalonia must have a similar museum of its own so that his people could absorb all of the history, values, and significance that lead to a defining sense of social identity. This is a history museum with only a few original works of art. Unfortunately it does not wrestle with ideas or allow for the nuances and contradictions and multiple perceptions of any real history. Because of this, most educated Catalans do not accept the validity of its simplistic message. As Luis Monreal, director general of the La Caixa Foundation, noted, it is a museum meant to mold an identity that is already firmly in place. Unlike Israel, he said, whose people experienced a diaspora-related condition, the Holocaust, followed by an ingathering of people from the world over, and a concomitant need to completely revive the Hebrew language, Catalonia has not had such a degree of alienating experiences.[18] Others argue that the huge influx of non-Catalans to Barcelona and the repression of the language during the Franco era did create a need to reinforce that identity. And Pujol saw that need as intense. He had no interest whatsoever in encouraging dialogue about the complexities of identity and its consequent fragmentation or about nonlinear historical narrative. He has used the museum as an expensive reminder to the Catalans of who they are supposed to be and what they should be in the future. Didactic and sophisticated in its use of museography, the Museum of the History of Catalonia is one of the few museums in Spain that so extravagantly raises the banner of regionalism by means of a provincial, introverted, and defensive perspective. Oddly, it seems to function as an antidote to the sophisticated complexity that MACBA offers. It caters to another constituency, one looking for a monolithic answer to the question of what constitutes a Catalan citizen. By answering that question as it does, it adds yet another frame to the kaleidoscopic nature of our larger discussion.

LA CAIXA FOUNDATION

Based in Barcelona and in existence many decades before the dictatorship, the La Caixa Foundation (Fundació la Caixa) profited enormously by the general milieu of liberalization when the Socialist Party came to power in 1981 and self-governance devolved to the regions. The most ambitious of the Spanish foundations, it was in a position to assume a much more elaborate responsibility in the humanities, education, health care, sciences, and arts than ever before, and it took full advantage of the moment. Its support of art and exhibition venues throughout Spain qualify it as the most active, and some would say consequential, of all such similar endeavors. Every year the La Caixa Foundation develops many original art projects, reaching hundreds of thousands of people. The foundation also frequently teams up with public and private museums and art centers inside and outside Spain. By the mid-1990s the foundation had built up a superb collection of paintings and artworks of over five hundred pivotal pieces, more than two thirds of them created by Spanish artists during the second half of the twentieth century. The La Caixa Foundation, like the Juan March and ARCO foundations, has become a de facto museum, performing throughout the 1990s all of a museum's duties, but without the limitations of permanent walls. In 1999 it announced plans to adapt the Casaramona factory, one of the icons of Barcelona's modernist movement, as a museum space where it would be able to display its collections regularly and frequently.

The foundation seems, on the surface, to reflect American-style values more than it does Mediterranean, emerging as it has from the private rather than the governmental impulse. Over one hundred years ago the La Caixa Savings and Pension Bank initiated social security programs for its workers at a time when the government was not providing such benefits. Leaders of the bank also built hospitals throughout Catalonia and later considered it a worthy social investment to fund libraries, schools, and a science museum and to support lectures, concerts, seminars, and exhibitions throughout Spain. Without doubt La Caixa has woven a deep respect for fresh thinking, debate, and dialogue into the fabric of Spanish society by means of its inordinately enlightened activities.

In 1991 the La Caixa Foundation absorbed the Fundació Caixa de Pensions, another major Catalonian savings bank. Required by law to donate 50 percent of its profits to public works, the foundation was now the most generous foundation in Spain. In 1994 it carried out 1,867 activities in 489 cities and towns in Spain. Over six million people, almost 10 percent of the country's population, took advantage of these activities. Of its $73 million 1994 budget for public works, over $20 million was committed to the arts and humanities, with the arts receiving the lion's share.[19] La Caixa, during the democratic period, is identified with inno-vation and risk taking. Through the arts and sciences it had attempted to influence Spanish citizens to think innovatively and to welcome rather than abhor change. And, through contemporary art, it did this in a grand way, seeing it as a visible means of proclaiming freedom and engagement with the world. The La Caixa Foundation president, José Vilarasau, real-izing there was a dearth in Spain of significant collections of contempo-rary art, suggested forming an international advisory board, and the La Caixa Foundation began collecting contemporary Catalan art in 1983 and international art in 1987. Their purchases quickly attracted the attention and respect of the art community. María de Corral, director of the acquisitions program during most of its existence, is widely credited with giving the foundation's collection its sophisticated direction.[20]

La Caixa mounted major temporary exhibitions, including shows of Kandinsky, Mondrian, and a range of artists who forged new forms of artistic expression in this century. It also exhibited long-neglected Span-ish artists such as Jorge Oteiza. But it will be especially remembered for developing great thematically based exhibitions. In 1995, in tribute to the fiftieth anniversary of the end of World War II, the foundation orga-nized the huge and impressive *Post–World War II Europe: Art after the Deluge (Europa de postguerra, 1945–1965: art després del diluvi)*. In the "spirit of historical review and serene commemoration," as its posters and public-ity proclaimed, this exhibition showed how a whole continent was able to recover its creative forces and reconstitute its cultural makeup. Orga-nized by Thomas Messer, former director of the Guggenheim Museum in New York City, and four other specialists, it contained over 450 works and was spread over several venues. The exhibition's paintings, sculpture, architecture, and photography demonstrated how recovery had come about through open-mindedness and resourcefulness and how the conti-nent's powers of regeneration and diversity became the source of Europe's strength. Thus, it tacitly posited that another renewal of that diversity would be the way to reawaken still another renaissance as present-day Europe once more faces waves of change and redefinition. La Caixa's exhibitions travel widely throughout Europe.

Publishing its enormous range of materials in Catalan, Spanish, and English is a sign of the La Caixa Foundation's and Catalonia's confidence, prosperity, and progressiveness. It shows Catalonia to be a cultural leader and positions Spain as a leader in a partnership. With the advent of the

Poster from the La Caixa Foundation (Fundació La Caixa) exhibition *Europa de postguerra, 1945–1965: Art després del diluvi (Postwar Europe: Art after the Deluge)*. Permission to reproduce photograph granted by Luis Monreal, Fundació La Caixa.

unification of Europe, the La Caixa Foundation helps by continuing to project the image of Spain as democratic and modern. Furthermore, the foundation awards important prizes in Europe that contribute to mutual knowledge and understanding through culture. The success of the La Caixa Foundation demonstrates that Catalonia *in* Spain can be local and global, free and open, and these are qualities the region must have if it is to thrive and strengthen its own nationhood as time goes on.

CATALONIAN MUSEUM AS SOCIETY'S MIRROR

Catalonian museums decidedly mirror Spanish society today in the way they accommodate an extremely wide range of missions and meanings.

The region's cultural policy has been, as democracy developed, for the most part, flexible, thoughtful, and creative. Private initative has played a large role. And associations of friends' groups have helped all of the museums—public and private. Some museum professionals, ironically, would still prefer that their governing bodies "plan priorities and projects in the long term and make investments in the museums of Catalonia in an ordered process that leads to equilibrium and a sustained development in the museums and their surroundings."[21] But the fluid response to unforeseen political and economic circumstances can also be understood as reflecting the dynamism of a youthful system that possesses the right and ability to remold itself as events and a heterogeneous citizenry require. As one of Spain's strongest regional voices, Catalonia, a nation within a nation, has demonstrated a wisdom that precludes cultural policies from having too much equilibrium and too much order. Excessive equilibrium and order are not, after all, the defining characteristics of a free and creative society.

8 VISIONS AND REVISIONS IN ANDALUSIA

Andalusia is one of the most economically distressed regions of Spain. It is also a region that evokes images of the country's most romantic and flamboyant soul. Andalusia is home to the gypsy caves, the Arabic architecture of the Alhambra, the Jewish intellectual history of Córdoba, the spiritual frenzy of Catholic Holy Week in Seville, flamenco dancing, bullfights, and bull breeding. It provides the essential emotion-inspiring clichés of typical Old Spain. But there is another side to Andalusia, that of astute and rational policy making. This chapter describes a major cultural project in Andalusia that began with high hopes and great optimism but quickly ran into difficulties that seemed insurmountable. And it is about how this region with few financial resources, but rich in imagination and political determination, summoned up the will to meet those unforeseen obstacles in a creative and effective way.

Through the transition to democracy Andalusia's leaders were quick to capitalize on their cultural legacy. Andalusia was already one of the most visited regions in the country, and it was agreed that cultural tourism was the critical factor in positioning the region for a prosperous and meaningful future for the general population. During the 1980s, its artistic and archaeological patrimony was considered an enormously valuable asset that could be leveraged with Madrid to receive a generous allocation of resources for infrastructural needs. Madrid, understanding that so much of the country's tourism was generated from Andalusia, was alert to local needs. It was also discerned that culture was important in building up the confidence of Andalusia's citizens and that such confidence was essential to a creative and productive citizenry. The region's cultural institutions had suffered greatly during the Franco dictatorship because of poverty and internal emigration to regions far from Andalusia. Museums had become dreary, alienating places. Art, music, dance, poetry, architecture, and archaeology were neglected. As the population had become demoralized, regional manifestation of that culture, such as bullfighting and flamenco, had lost their prestige and had become somewhat kitsch. The Andalusian leaders quickly understood the relationship between a vital culture and a successful economy and immediately began to plan for their convergence.

GENERAL PLAN FOR CULTURAL PROPERTIES

Andalusia's 1985 *General Plan for Cultural Properties (Plan general de bienes culturales de Andalucía)* was the first document of its kind published in Spain. It states that the Spanish cultural patrimony is the "principal witness to Spain's historical contribution to world civilization and to its contemporary creative capacities. Protecting and enriching the properties that reflect this historical contribution constitute fundamental obligations that are binding upon the public powers, according to the mandate directed to them in article 46 of the Constitution."[1] The plan quotes in its prologue the 1985 Law of Historical Spanish Patrimony, interpreting it as a directive to the autonomic regions to transmit their cultural patrimony actively and creatively to all citizens because, along with economic well-being, that patrimony is the chief component of a dignified quality of life to which all are entitled. The plan then focuses on its ambitious main agenda—Andalusia's particular collective patrimony, much of which, it expressly feared, had already been forgotten. The plan repeatedly refers to the scarcity of resources available to recover it. Concern is also expressed about the pressing obligation to apply new conservation, restoration, and interpretation technologies, about the lack of consciousness in the general population about the value of that work, and about the absence of trained professionals who could do the required work and impart said consciousness. The plan itself is an extension of Andalusia's

1981 Statute of Autonomy, which made it a legal requirement to raise the consciousness of Andalusian identity in all its depth and variety from its then low state to a much higher plane.[2]

According to the plan, museums needed to change their public image of those institutions as static warehouses for objects, as mausoleums devoid of communal activity, to one of vital centers for the dispersal of culture, scholarly research, and education.[3] The plan approved of the trend toward adapting historic buildings for museums, while warning that this trend, if it were to continue, must do so, not in the emergency mode by which it was then operating, but correctly—by using the highest museological standards. The plan also urged increased publication of original exhibition catalogs based on scholarly research and above all better access to the cultural heritage for all. There was praise for local museums that were already affirming and confirming long repressed identities, such as the house of Spanish poet Federico García Lorca, which had opened as a museum in March 1985. (Lorca had been murdered by the Franquistas, and an official museum dedicated to him had thus been impossible during the dictatorship.) "Identity museums" such as the Lorca house were given high priority in the plan. It was communicated clearly that once the majority of Andalusians gained the "consciousness" of the scope of their own local and regional historical and cultural influence, they would better accept and honor the larger Spanish patrimony. The plan's overall tone and objective was, therefore, one of balance with the center, with Madrid. The plan was especially effective and led to the passage of the Andalusian Law of Historical Patrimony in 1991.

THE MONASTERY OF LA CARTUJA

The renovation of the Monastery of La Cartuja (El Conjunto Monumental del Monasterio de La Cartuja de Santa María de las Cuevas) is described in the plan as a visionary enterprise meant to harmonize a number of conflicting histories that intersect in Seville, the capital of Andalusia. This compound comprises several important historic structures built for a variety of purposes over five hundred years. Fueled by Seville's Universal Exposition of 1992, a generous budget, and the fact that the original Monastery of La Cartuja had figured in Columbus's expeditions to the Americas, the project was put on a fast track. The renovated monastery was imagined as a nontraditional museum that would include but a bare minimum of old master artworks. It was to function as an archive, the regional painting and sculpture restoration center, a museological library, a conference center, a historical architectural complex and garden, and an exhibition space. The goal was to give the region an architectual complex where the history of Seville, Andalusia, and Spain could be meshed with the identity of the new Spaniard.[4]

Renovating the precinct of La Cartuja, as it is usually referred to, would have to be delicate and thoughtful if it was to function as planned; it was, in the end to be a somewhat radical alternative to the conventional museum. Hoping to introduce archaeology and history in a novel way, the La Cartuja experience was to be visceral and challenging intellectually. This history was to be presented without the normal categorical or chronological demarcations, without extended linear, text-based narratives, and, most unusually, with the mere evocation, rather than the physical reality of a significant trove of objects. Indeed, La Cartuja possessed only a few good pieces of sculpture and some fragments of objects retrieved from recent archaeological excavations. But it was the monastery itself and its precincts that were the most inspiring aspects of the museum. It did not seem to be an impossible dream. As novelist Umberto Eco wrote, when musing on alternative possibilities for museums, a museum could exist with only a single painting or sculpture. However, he continued, the viewer would have to have experienced a series of expository moments that revealed the philosophical, artistic, or economic structures that engendered the piece; to have experienced the political, intellectual, or moral value systems that were at its foundation.[4]

La Cartuja attempted to be something like the alternative history described by Eco. The monastery's entrance invites the visitor to travel a path both literal and metaphysical. Each stop on that path is choreographed to yield a small epiphany, which might be triggered by an architectural fragment, a piece of sixteenth- or seventeenth-century sculpture, or a shard of nineteenth-century ceramics. The path itself was intended to stimulate thoughts about the nature of time and change, the spaces between events, or the contradictions and layerings of art, the economy, war, and religion. The visitor could choose to meander in any number of directions rather than down only one or two prescribed courses. La Cartuja thus revealed its secrets by indirection, metaphor, simile, and analogy, not by labeling and text panels. It reveled in leaving slippery

Mid-eighteenth-century print of the La Cartuja Monastery (Monasterio de la Cartuja). Courtesy Archivos del Centro Andaluz de Arte Contemporáneo y Juan Carlos Cazalla.

implications. Unlike most traditional museums La Cartuja was about history's intricacy and resistance to a single perspective. When it opened in 1992 massive crowds visited La Cartuja. It seemed to be a great success, especially in the context of the exciting expo in which it played so integral a part.

Spread over a large area including a number of buildings surrounded by extensive gardens and orchards, La Cartuja was originally founded in 1410 as a cloistered community, which went on to be transformed in surprising ways. In the early nineteenth century it became the quarters for Napoleonic troops during the French invasion of Spain. In 1836, during the *desamortización* (expropriation of church lands), La Cartuja lost its legal religious status forever, as did many other communities of monks and nuns throughout Spain. It was stripped of almost all its sacred possessions, irretrievably dispersing its superb collection of European paintings, sculptures, and decorative arts throughout the world. La Cartuja's holdings had included works by Albrecht Dürer and Francisco de Zurbarán and commissioned portraits by ranking Spanish and international artists. Some of these works can now be viewed in public museums in Andalusia, some are undoubtedly in private collections throughout Spain and France, and some have disappeared without a trace. Contrary to what one might expect, La Cartuja will never reclaim these lost pieces, even those located in Andalusia's own museums. The museum's founding director, Bartoloméo Ruiz González notes: "one simply cannot and should not reverse the course of history."[5] Nevertheless, the spatial configurations and vast walls of the monastery poignantly suggest the ghosts of the hundreds of artworks that were made and purchased specifically for that site. At last count seven pieces of seventeenth- and eighteenth-century polychromatic wooden sculpture, an elegantly carved choir stall, some minor paintings, a marble altarpiece, and miscellaneous archaeological fragments were the only major original pieces displayed in the monastery although others were in off-site storage. After its ignominious use as a military headquarters, La Cartuja was transformed into the Pickman Ceramic and porcelain factory. At that time some of the buildings were fitted with oversized ovens, chimneys, and other pieces of equipment for the manufacturing process. The site was later abandoned. In 1986, due to the interest stimulated by the *General Plan for Cultural Properties,* a team of archaeologists excavated the area. Their findings and subsequent proposals led to an agreement between the state, the Autonomic Region of Andalusia, and the Bank of Spain to restore La Cartuja by 1992.

It was Bartoloméo Ruiz, the director of the monastery in the 1990s, who was intent on achieving far more than a mere restoration of La Cartuja. He was intent on utilizing the complex to represent Spanish culture in a new way. He was never interested in the linear approach to history that in the late 1980s was still the dominant fashion in museology. Ruiz wanted to convey instead the kaleidoscopic nature of La Cartuja's history to show how past, present, and future intertwined inseparably. He arranged for five commissions to be awarded to five different architects, each responsible for interpreting and building a separate area. These architects were given extraordinary creative freedom. Ruiz's aim, by using more than one architect, was to keep the end result from having an artificially monolithic appearance and to preserve the monastery's fluidity and, indeed, multiple influences.

As part of the first generation of democratic leadership in the arts, Ruiz was thereby committed to rejecting even the appearance of unified and prescribed thinking. Ruiz saw La Cartuja as a great opportunity to promote an entirely different approach to memorializing the past than had had currency during the dictatorship. He was less concerned with the concept of monuments as "messages" or "statements" than he was with them as living places of creation and articulation—as places where the subject continues to struggle for meaning. Ruiz hoped that visitors to the Monastery of the La Cartuja would leave having learned better how to actively acknowledge and be comfortable in a world where all inhabitants and events exist in a chain of shifting meanings.[6]

Still, even without a strong conventional narrative, a central meaning could be found in La Cartuja if that was what one was seeking. One of the architects, the sculptor and painter José Ramón Sierra Delgado, believed unwaveringly in the possibility and value of unearthing such core meanings. He wrote that the "absence of an overriding program, which can cause so much consternation and discomfort due to the legacy of modernism, offered nevertheless, a strange and fascinating opportunity: the possibility of listening freely to the monastery's dispersed and mutilated remains, and then with a very fine sensibility to capture its precise shouts and sighs and to transform them into a fundamental premise for the project."[7] Ramón Sierra Delgado was responsible for renovating the cloister, but he also was challenged to create a sculpture on one of its exterior walls. He integrated the two tasks by manipulating pieces of ceramic and wood, which had been excavated on the site, in such a way as to coax from them what he was convinced were their ancient meanings while still convincingly making the case for their contemporaneity. He also included water in his sculpture, an allusion to the floods that regularly threatened to destroy La Cartuja. Those floods became Ramón Sierra Delgado's central metaphor for the cycles of devastation and renewal that the monastery has endured over the centuries. With his sculpture and his architectural renovation, he was able to communicate what he felt was La Cartuja's spiritual essence.

Architects Fernando Mendoza and Roberto Luna were commissioned to renovate the Chapel of Saint Mary of the Caves (Capella de Santa Maria de las Cuevas), the House of Meat, and the Refectory. The chapel, naturally, was meant for worship; the House of Meat and the two-story refectory were for feeding the needy. When La Cartuja became a porcelain factory, these spaces had been converted for manufacturing purposes. Mendoza and Luna were responsible for making those sections into the Royal Pavilion for Seville's Universal Exposition and for insuring that they would later, after the expo closed, be adaptable for conferences, exhibitions, and orientation, press, and education centers. They were

The La Cartuja Monastery after restoration in 1992. Courtesy Archivos del Centro Andaluz de Arte Contemporáneo y Juan Carlos Cazalla.

able to reconstruct a stunning, historically accurate entryway and adapt existing patios and rooms for new functions. Ancient echoes from La Cartuja'a several incarnations coexist with the contemporary without either seeming to dominate the other.

The renovation of the Clausura de Legos was put in the hands of Guillermo Vásquez Consuegra. Its silo-shaped buildings were the part of the complex that the monks had used as living quarters. After 1841 it was used as warehouses and granaries. This area was in quite bad condition and was both hybrid and discontinuous in character. Vásquez Consuegra, exercising absolute integrity, decided to save only that architecture that had aesthetic value or was adaptable to new purposes. This part of the compound was, after the renovations, the least aesthetically pleasing and the least reminiscent of the past, but it was perfectly suitable for workshops, laboratories, administrative offices, and exhibitions.

The South Garden was restored by Luís Marin de Teran, Aurelio del Pozo Serrano, and Emilio Yanes Bustamente. This section had been littered with some undistinguished constructions built for the pottery factory, and none were deemed by the architects to have aesthetic value. Still, all three architects agreed that this garden contained the half monastery–half industrial park feel of the compound in latter days. Thus they decided to create a pedestrian walk that linked the disparate parts and to retain a few of the buildings—just enough to show respect for their existence, while their interiors were remodeled for contemporary functions.

Francisco Torres Martínez was the architect commissioned to renovate La Cartuja's pavilion and the remainder of the gardens. He believed that the monks' solitary existences had been mitigated by certain critical encounters within the compound, and that those encounters were essential to the success of their monastic lives. That is, even though the buildings were all configured in isolation from each other, the gardens, pavilions, and chapels provided contrapuntal possibilities for recreation, for extending the spiritual and psychological boundaries they had taken on their own.[8] The gardens, the architect believed, had been positioned to fight off loneliness. During the days of the porcelain factory, the gardens had been closed off. Torres Martínez's restoration of the gardens allow the contemporary visitor to grasp the original layout and to imagine how it affected those monks living in La Cartuja. Fortunately enough of the plants and documentation remained to guide the reconstruction of the landscape to some measure of its former beauty and productivity.

At first La Cartuja seemed to thrive. Neither neutral nor objective, the reconstruction seemed to function as a work of art itself and a spur to the imagination in a way that few museums ever achieved. It almost succeeded in being the kind of alternative museum described by Eco. However, the monastery was far more circumspect and subtle, far less didactic than Eco was suggesting. It was an example of how history can be re-presented, re-categorized, and de-categorized, but it remained too poetic to be understood easily by the general public. La Cartuja does not, unlike the traditional archaeology or history museum, capture specific periods in concrete terms. Visitors should have left La Cartuja sensing what this part of Seville had been witness to and how it was a participant in a tangled past. They should have also sensed how that past was affected by and how it affected in turn the world around it. Furthermore, the monastery's designers hoped visitors would gain, if only indirectly, a sense of permission for taking charge of the representation of their own personal and collective past, and an awareness of how the narratives they thought were fixed were actually indeterminate. La Cartuja was intended to open up avenues to rethink the cultural patrimony without resorting to authoritarian, kitsch, nostalgic, or folkloric histories.

But the goals were never achieved. By 1995 La Cartuja was not attracting audiences sufficient to justify its continuation. In 1994 and into 1995 there was political change as Spain shifted from a socialist to a conservative government. For the monastery, this party shift resulted in paralysis. After the Universal Exposition in 1992 La Cartuja had run out of money. Also, even though it was across the river from Seville, only a few minutes away by car, access was difficult after public transportation became unavailable. Ultimately, there was criticism from people who did not find La Cartuja a satisfying cultural experience. Without works of art to contemplate, without clear direction, and without an exciting spectacle like the expo to complement it the monastery was simply not a commanding enough museum experience to bring in the crowds. Yet because it was a major artistic achievement for the region, no one wanted to let the restored monument just decay along with the other expo edifices that had been intended for temporary use only. La Cartuja had already proven its ability to survive over a five-hundred-year period. It was only a matter of once again finding a role for it in contemporary Spanish society.

The socialists hoped that huge numbers of people would visit museums if they adopted missions with democratic goals. Citizens were to be made to feel they "owned" their patrimony in a way they could not have during Franco's dictatorship. This is an attractive enough idea, but there was also a troubling side to the kind of cultural politics that measures results largely by "the capacity to attract massive numbers of people."[10] Democracy can have a devastating effect on projects that emerge from a purely intellectual approach to a problem, on projects dedicated to slowly, subtly challenging entrenched sensibilities, and to projects that have nothing to do with entertainment. The Monastery of the La Cartuja was such a project, born of the excitement of the expo, dying in its aftermath. Without the overwhelming impact of the Alhambra in Granada, the Mezquita in Córdoba, or even the Sephardic Museum in Toledo, this relatively minor monument could not survive. With the failure to bring in masses of people, the government deemed that because "people prefer order to disorder; grasp at formulas rather than actuality; prefer the guidebook to the confusion before them."[11] La Cartuja was simply too elitist to continue to exist for the general public.

In May 1995 Bartoloméo Ruiz reported to me that he was planning a new reincarnation for La Cartuja.[12] Now he wanted to create a more conventional museum that communicated the history of Andalusia through eloquent but not necessarily great statues, paintings, and pottery from around the region. Ruiz insisted that the monastery would be straight forward as a means of identity construction, but would not be as ideological as Barcelona's Museum of the History of Catalonia, which had opened only months before. There would still be room for multiple voices and perspectives. It would not be exclusionary or nationalistic but would offer a history of Andalusia as an integral part of Spain. As it turned out, these plans never came to fruition. They were, though, the next step along the way to an appropriate present-day use for La Cartuja.

ANDALUSIAN CENTER FOR CONTEMPORARY ART

In 1997 the Monastery of the La Cartuja became the Andalusian Center for Contemporary Art (Centro Andaluz de Arte Contemporáneo). As a contemporary art museum the Andalusian Center for Contemporary Art (CAAC) is promoting the cultural patrimony as stipulated in the original cultural plan, but it is charged with communicating that patrimony to as many people in the most efficient and economic manner possible.[13] An updated plan stressed throughout that museums must remove obstacles to their development as centers of communication and interpretation of knowledge. It also insisted that they "reinforce the normal functions of museums as vehicles of interpretation and proliferation of ideas that will permit the citizen to know and identify culturally with their own cultural patrimony," and, furthermore, that they must strive to attract large audiences, improve the patrimony, and raise the quality of the experience for the user.[14] The purpose of the museum, in other words, must be to communicate to as many people as possible in concrete, apprehensible ways the nature of the region's contemporary art scene.

By the year 2000 CAAC will absorb two other inchoate institutions in Seville that had hoped to be the contemporary art museums of the city. Its acquisitions policy, with a generous budget to support it, will focus on Andalusian art but will easily include Spanish and international art from the late 1970s to the present. It will be a site of center and peripheral comfort, unlike that communicated in some Basque Country or Catalonian museums. Aside from being a traditional art museum, the monastery complex will be adapted once again to house an Andalusian center

The Andalusian Center for Contemporary Art (Centro Andaluz de Arte Contemporáneo). Courtesy Archivos del Centro Andaluz de Arte Contemporáneo y Juan Carlos Cazalla.

for postgraduate studies in addition to its other functions already in place. The museum will no doubt, given its stated purpose to meet the standards as defined by the International Council on Museums, promote a clear, logical, and inclusive understanding of the creative spirit by means of its collections and exhibitions. With its advanced museography, superb explanations, and lucid didactics, it will satisfy the needs of those who find their way to this beautiful complex across the river.

La Cartuja, adapting once again to new societal needs continues to be a vehicle for communicating the true essence of life in Spain — or perhaps of life anywhere in the modern world: that change can be endured if it is presented in such a way as to be demonstrably useful to those it is meant to serve. The monastery, having done this repeatedly for centuries, may be Spain's least known but most apt metaphor as it metamophosed repeatedly in its long journey from a spiritual place of silence for a select group of monks to a worldly communicator of recent trends and ideas to the masses.

CONCLUSION

The primary need in the first twenty years of the Spanish democracy was for society to transform itself. Beyond new rights and freedoms, promises of prosperity, modernity, and autonomy, and the powerful momentum toward full integration into the larger world a new way of envisioning themselves had to be made acceptable to the majority of the citizenry. For that to happen society had to reinvent itself. Spain's various populations had to see it as desirable to picture themselves as contributing members of a heterogeneous, multidimensional, and tolerant country. Furthermore, they had to be willing to live in solidarity with those whose definitions of civic virtue differed considerably from their own. A reeducation process began that permeated communal and personal existence. Across class and regional lines Spaniards revised and rearticulated their national value system as they absorbed democratic ideals. Along with new ideals came the belief, and the rhetoric to accompany it, that the country's diversity was an advantage rather than a handicap to the general welfare.

Spain's reeducation process was both direct and indirect and it did not happen overnight or in a vacuum. Even before Franco died Juan March, Joan Miró, and many others were working behind the scenes to prepare the ground so that society could move forward when the time was propitious. Furthermore the memory of progressive thinking that characterized the second republic that preceded the civil war had never been entirely snuffed out. And, finally, the economic progress and heavy tourism begun in the 1960s had already cracked the totality of totalitarianism long before democratic principles took hold. Thus, when it became possible to move forward full throttle, modernized schools, an uncensored press and media, a weakened military, a general secularization of society, and the change in women's status and potential all had an immediate influence. These were some of the most direct forces driving Spain's reconstruction of self identity. Culture, in all of its manifestations, was a major educational tool. Not just the state, but also regional and municipal government bodies were infused with the funds to promote their traditional and contemporary patrimonies, both internally and externally.

Museums played a special role in Spain's process of democratic identity construction during these formative years. As expected, the state museums mounted international exhibitions at major venues, especially in Madrid. It published and distributed catalogs that encouraged an interest in European art, art from the United States, and occasionally even art from Asia. At the same time, regional museums played prominent roles in the periphery of Spain, encouraging local cultures as they attempted to define or redefine their past and future. And, the private sector, through foundations and friends' groups, built and supported museums as they had not done since before the civil war. Spain's museums thus showed themselves to be effective sources of indirect, informal education. They were understood by the country's political leadership, both regional and national, to be places where all kinds of people would cross paths, where the media would promote issues museums were engaged in, and where visitors, especially if they ventured into a number of museums throughout the country, could experience a variety of interpretations of Spain's past and present. A number of museums were granted significant budgets for the roles they would play in preparing the citizenry for the vicissitudes and shifting realities they were confronting. At the same time, other institutions were left to struggle when they did not suit the prevailing political atmosphere. To the consternation of museum professionals, there seemed to be no consistent intellectual rationale for the levels of support the various museums received. Those museums with missions coinciding with the political and social goals of the party in power or those that were seen as able to attract the largest audiences received the most money—hence, the poverty of the Prado and the relative wealth of the Reina Sofía during the socialist years. When the parties changed, or the agendas of the parties in power shifted, so too did the financial support shift. And, the Prado's fortunes did improve with the election of the conservatives in 1996. This has been of concern to contemporary art museum directors as well as directors of historical museums. They worry that their access to international creativity is in some way linked to what they perceive as political policy: the socialist being considered the more international and the conservative the more dedicated to *españolización*. Politics and art are certainly linked in Spain, but, because it is now a democratic country, profound mistakes can be rectified at election time.

Notwithstanding the major political change from the socialist to conservative parties in 1996, museums of all types had real impact on Spanish society, during the transistion to and consolidation of democracy. They were one of the instrumentalities that proclaimed in no uncertain terms the new nature of Spain. Every time a museum was opened or renovated or one museum received more attention than another, related issues of city, provincial, regional, or state identity surfaced and inspired vigorous public debate. The questions raised by the debate always seemed to swirl around basic identity issues: What does the Guggenheim Museum Bilbao mean about who the Basque Country is in relationship to Spain, Europe, or the United States? Does the neglect of the Prado in Madrid affect Spain's reputation in the world at large and prove that the country does not care about its historical identity? Is it important for Spain's public image that it buys the Thyssen-Bornemisza Collection? What does the Sephardic Museum in Toledo reveal about Spain being a truly Catholic country? Will creating a major contemporary museum in Valencia show the region to be sufficiently cosmopolitan, and will that attract more business to the region? Will having a fine arts museum in Oviedo help alter the provincial image of Asturians? Is Spain losing its cultural roots as it opens itself evermore to globalization? Can Catalonia convince the world that it is a "nation" by creating MNAC? Answers to these questions are site-specific. But, if they are answered with the site of Spain in mind, if the context is thus enlarged, the answers must be given differently. The museums can be seen as an accumulation of layers of significance. Layer upon layer of rich identity construction, layers contradictory of each other adding to the new national portrait. By the mid-1990s Spain's museums demonstrated a wide range of aspirations that reflects the populations' own increasingly cacophonic and kaleidoscopic sense of itself. One had only to go beyond the Prado—to any randomly chosen museum anywhere in any of the seventeen regions—to grasp the power of this phenomenon.

Museums not only affect the people who go through their doors. In any country with a free press, they affect every one who hears or reads about them. If well over 800,000 people went to the Thyssen-Bornemisza Museum and over one million to the Guggenheim Museum Bilbao in the first year of operation, one can be sure that word of their activities spread throughout Spain to many millions more. They triggered arguments and ideas about the nation, about modernity, and about identity in conversations countrywide, even worldwide among the art-interested. Although these two museums represent the extremes of attitude toward nationhood and peoplehood, on a smaller scale attitudes were also being shaped by hundreds of other museums and their projects. Not unlike the United States where the *Enola Gay, Harlem on My Mind,* and *West as America* exhibitions brought to the fore simmering and contradictory points of view about American identity that had never before had so public a forum, Spain's many museums became sites for challenging and occasionally confirming issues of ongoing significance to the Spanish public.

The role of the museum as *institution* in constructing the identity of the present-day Spaniard is richer, more reciprocal, and more varied than it has ever been before. Together during the years of transition and consolidation of democracy the sum total of Spain's museums played a more significant and influential role than could ever have been played by any single museum alone. All of the museums of the country contributed to the larger projection of one crucial message to Spaniards and foreigners alike: Spain is a country that welcomes discourse, allows for its own multifaceted, even fragmented identity, permits competition between central and local governments for cultural dominance, and accommodates the progressive and conservative points of view. While at least some tiny piece of every Spaniard's cultural identity remains lodged in the Prado in Madrid, other perhaps more meaningful pieces of it can be discovered for that same Spaniard in one or more of the other museums throughout the country. And for those who do not live in Spain but only visit as tourists, its configuration of museums teaches that Spanish identity has been forever changed and forever enlarged.

The role of Spanish museums in the democratizing of the identity of the citizens of that country was, during the first twenty years after Franco, largely a function of socialist values. Museums fulfilled the people's most pressing needs for both internationalism and regionalism coexisting in a constructive dynamic tension. The success was phenomenal. Now, the dominant conservative party is primarily committed to capital development and improvement of infrastructure while strengthening the values of the center. The conservative promises are being kept, and the people's voice continues to be heard. Another book will judge the degree to which the conservative response was successful when their time is over. One can only wonder what subsequent elections will do to change the map of Spanish museums. That Spanish museums are as yet imperfect institutions is a reflection of the imperfection of democracy—a system that thrives on contradiction moving forward and backward simultaneously. As it fulfills one constituency's dreams, another's is put on hold. Slowly, though, the museums strengthen and gain coherence. And we watch in admiration from the United States as the process in Spain takes its course—knowing that there are lessons for us to absorb as we, too, plot our own museological futures for the next century, amid both strife and optimism—those twinned companions in any profoundly democratic society.

INTRODUCTION: CENTER VERSUS REGIONS AND THE HISTORI-
CAL STRUGGLE FOR CULTURAL AND POLITICAL IDENTITY

1. See Fernández de Sanz-Pastor Consuelo y Piérola, *Museos y colecciones de España* (Madrid: Ministerio de Cultura, 1990), and *Museos de titularidad estatal y del sistema Español de museos* (Madrid: Ministerio de Cultura, Dirección General de Bellas Artes y Archivos, 1993), for lists of museums of Spain. See also María Bolaños, *Historia de los museos en España: memoria, cultura, sociedad* (Gijón [Asturias]: Ediciones Trea, S. L., 1997), an invaluable book on the history of the widest range of the museums in Spain.

2. "Spain, a 'nation of nations' as some have described it, has also had to devise a solution to the complex problems of containing nationalisms with a state structure, and to do so within a democratic framework. . . ." and "The process of decentralization must conform to four basic principles. First, regional autonomy must not undermine the unity of Spain. . . ." Kenneth Maxwell and Steven Spiegel, *The New Spain from Isolation to Influence* (New York: Council on Foreign Relations Press, c. 1994), vii–viii and 75.

3. A mass liberal democracy, as defined by Enrique A. Balorya, *Comparing New Democracies* (Boulder and London: Westview Press, 1987), 54, and as accepted by most political scientists, consists of "a set of institutions and rules that allow competition and participation for all citizens considered as equals. Empirically, such a political arrangement is characterized by free, fair, and recurring elections; male and female universal suffrage; multiple organizations of interests; different and alternative sources of information; and elections to fill the most relevant offices. Behind such a set of institutions lies an accommodation, a compromise among social and political actors on the method and the rules for peaceful conflict resolution. Mass, liberal democracy also means the acceptance of opposition; acceptance of the possibility that lower social

groups may mobilize; and acceptance of uncertainty regarding the outcomes of conflicts of interests."

4. Such autonomy statutes for select regions had been one of the goals of the short-lived second republic preceding the Spanish civil war. Nevertheless, all progress in the direction of regional autonomy was lost as a state ideal during Franco's dictatorship.

5. Robert P. Clark, *The Basques: The Franco Years and Beyond* (Reno: University of Nevada Press, 1979), 301–2. See pages 1–77 for a full discussion of the history and sense of difference experienced by the Basque people.

6. For example, Manuel Fraga, a prominent minister under Franco became president of Galicia, a position he retained throughout the 1990s. He so revised his Francoist personality that he spearheaded the construction of the Centro Galego de Arte Contemporáneo in Santiago de Compostela, which has proudly featured avant-garde, international art exhibitions that would have shocked Franco and his followers.

7. See Paul Preston, *The Politics of Revenge* (London and New York: Routledge Press, 1990), 782, for an elaboration of this strategy.

8. Ministerio de Cultura, *Cultura y sociedad: una política de promoción sociocultural,* a conference in the series "Cultura y comunicación," no. 24 (Madrid: Ministerio de Cultura, 1983). With respect to Europe, see Finn Jor, *La desmitificación de la cultura,* a conference in the series "Cultura y comunicación," no. 3 (Council of Europe, 1979; reprinted and translated, Madrid: Ministerio de Cultura, 1984).

9. Surveys taken by the Spanish Ministry of Culture support this whole heartedly. These surveys are discussed in some depth by John Hooper, *The New Spaniards* (London: Penguin Books, 1995), 295 and 327.

PART ONE: THE LONG ARM OF THE CENTER

1. Other key institutions might logically include state defense forces, a national library, a countywide radio or television network, and a national university.

2. These statistics were gathered from the Centro de Investigaciones Sociológicas, for the purposes of gaining a better understanding of the concepts of Spain, the state, nation, autonomy, regionalism, independence, and flags. "España," *El Pais* (January 23, 1997, Internet edition).

3. See Donald Preziosi, "Museology and Museography," *The Art Bulletin* 77 (1995): 13–15. Preziosi also remarks in his unpublished manuscript, "Collecting/Museums," that "the modernist ideologies of nation-statism, with all their terrors and salvations, are naturalized and 'demonstrated' through the apparatus of the museum and the disciplinarity of art. . . . It is in this sense that museology, and museography have so very profoundly *enabled* identity and allegiance of all kinds. . . ."

4. See Paul Preston, *Franco: A Biography* (New York: Basic Books, 1994), 414 and 424. Preston notes that on December 7, 1940, Franco had expressed his displeasure to the new Vichy ambassador to Spain, François Piétri, regarding the lack of "territorial adjustments" with respect to Spanish claims on French Morocco. Franco said, "Friendship cannot exist without justice, and there are all too many injustices to repair for this friendship to become real." Alicia

Rodero Riaza points out, in her superb essay, "El regreso de la dama a España," in *Cien Años de una Dama* (Madrid: Ministerio de Educación y Cultura, 1997), 43–49, documenting the diplomatic history of this exchange of works of art, the agreement between France and Spain was signed on December 21, 1940, after several months of denials by France of Franco's territorial requests. This gesture was intended to appease Franco, but more to the point, to "put the brakes on Franco's territorial claims on Hitler" (author's translation).

5. Marlisle Simons, "The Lady of Elche," *New York Times* (West Coast edition), 23 January 1997, A4.

6. It would be a mistake to assume that the Spanish state museum system is rigidly systematic. There is no inviolable scheme that determines just what fits into the category of a state museum and what does not. Still, the tentacles of the state reach much deeper into the country than would appear on the surface. For example, there are museums with contents and buildings owned by the state, but managed by other ministries—including the whole panoply of military museums managed by the Ministry of Defense. There are also museums owned by the state but managed by universities, banks, academies, and what is known as the Royal Patrimony. Finally there are other museums connected to the Spanish museum system by means of a variety of agreements not mentioned.

7. Personal interview with Andrés Carretero, March 27, 1994. He enthusiastically favored the trend of his government toward diminishing the presence of the state in what he felt ought "properly" to be regional museums.

8. None of the directors of those museums, it should be stressed, were supportive of the idea of losing state status. The prestige of being a state museum was, they believed, critical to the efficacy of their work, to their ability to function in an international arena, and to their ability to have credentials to represent the nation at international conferences.

1. INSIDE MADRID

1. Manuela Mena, "175 años del museo del Prado," *ABC* 18 November 1994, 40–41. See other statements throughout the article registering grave concern about the state of the Prado by Felipe Garín, a former director of the Prado, Matías Díaz Padrón, chief curator of the Prado, and Jonathan Brown.

2. As quoted by José Luis Alvarez Alvarez in "Reflexiones sobre el Museo del Prado," *Razón y Fe* 230 (September 1994): 158 (author's translation).

3. Ibid., 158–66.

4. That such a reconciliation is possible, although expensive and representative of an entirely distinct disposition of financial resources, is evident when Spain's neglect of the Prado is compared with France's dedication to the remodeling of the Louvre—also under a socialist government.

5. "Puddles at the Prado," *Economist* 331 (1994): 95.

6. Ibid. Specifically, between 1991 and 1996, there were five directors of the Prado: Alfonso Pérez Sánchez was dismissed for signing a petition against Spain's involvement in the Gulf War; Felipe Garín, a convenient scapegoat, was fired because of raindrops leaking near the Velázquez masterpieces in 1993; Francisco Calvo Serraller resigned in 1994 over a "scandal" about

designer chairs photographed in the Prado for a magazine run by his wife; and, José María Luzón Nogué Luzón, appointed in 1994, was succeeded by Fernando Checa after the Conservative Party won the elections in 1996.

7. Alan Riding, "The Prado Finds Out What It Has and Where," *New York Times* 1 August 1990: B3(N) pC11 (L). Riding interviewed Alfonso Pérez Sánchez about the lost paintings. Of the original transfer to the Prado in 1819, out of 3,067 paintings, 109 were destroyed and 51 were missing. Of religious works and other acquisitions received by the Prado in 1872, around 500 were lost. Many more pieces were in poor condition, some had actually disintegrated. Pérez Sánchez, who is publishing the inventory of the *Prado disperso*, points out that since the inventory was begun hundreds of these works have been treated and restored. He also said: "it is remarkable that so little has been lost."

8. José María Aznar, *Una política cultural para España* (a published lecture on the platform of the "Comisión Nacional de Cultura del Partido Popular") no. 3 (Madrid: n.p., 1994), 5. This position was elaborated upon by Miguel Angel Cortés and his associate, Borja Adsuara Varela, on May 17, 1995, before Cortés was appointed secretary of state for culture by Aznar after the Conservative Party won the national elections.

9. Royal Decree 1142/1996, May 25, 1996. BOE núm 127: 17836–17840.

10. See María de Corral, et al., *Museo Nacional Centro de Arte Reina Sofía* (n.p.: Minsterio de Cultura, 1992). See also Bolaños, *Historia de los museos en España*, 404–11, for an unofficial history. Both sources were used to reconstruct this history of the Spanish Museum of Contemporary Art.

11. Personal interviews with Tomás Llorens, May 18, 1995, and June 7, 1996.

12. This is not to say that *Guernica*'s stay in New York was uneventful. During the Vietnam War, it became the centerpiece of an infamous protest by the Art Workers Coalition demanding that the museum remove the painting because the United States had no right, given the behavior of its soldiers at My Lai, to be, as was suggested by its hanging in Museum of Modern Art, morally indignant. For full discussion of the political implications see Francis Frascina, "Meyer Schapiro's Choice: My Lai, *Guernica*, MoMA and the Art Left,1969–70." Parts 1–2. *Journal of Contemporary History* 30 (1995): 485–511; 31 (1995) 705–28.

13. Personal interview with José Guirao, June 20, 1996.

14. See *Memoria, 1992–93* (Madrid: Colección Thyssen-Bornemisza, Ministry of Culture, 1994), 63, for discussion of the public relations implications of the purchase.

15. Ibid., 32. *Memoria, 1992–93* is currently the most detailed source of information about the foundation and the museum.

16. Without making a judgment call as to which is the finer collection, there is no doubt that Norton Simon was Thyssen's only competitor after World War II for great master works on this scale.

17. See Michael Kimmelman, "A New Broom Sweeps the Prado Museum," *New York Times*, 21 November 1993, 42.

18. As further evidence of the dynamic and positive nature of the Thyssen-Bornemisza Museum–Spanish government relationship, one year after the original agreements had been signed in Madrid, a similar set of agreements brought

another branch of the Thyssen-Bornemisza Collection to Barcelona, to the Museum of the Monastery of Pedralbes (Museu Monestir de Pedralbes). Seventy two old master, mainly pre-Renaissance paintings and sculptures were placed on display in a restored medieval monastery—once again not only preserving a significant site, but adding present-day value to it as well. These works were selected not only for their coherence as a group within the collection, but also for their links to Catalan art. In 1999 plans were revealed to expand the Madrid site and to enhance its holdings with art from Lugano.

19. *Memoria, 1992–93*, 25.
20. *Memoria, 1994–95* (Madrid: Colección Thyssen-Bornemisza, Ministry of Culture, 1996), 85–87, reports in 1994 income of 792,932 million pesetas and expenses of 1,016,182 million pesetas; and in 1995 income of 792,932 million pesetas and expenses of 954,373 million pesetas. These figures are combined for the Madrid and Barcelona branches (separate figures were unavailable).

2. OUTSIDE MADRID: THE SEPHARDIC MUSEUM IN TOLEDO

1. The exceptions in Spanish history occur most notably during the republic of 1868 and the ill-starred, extremely progressive second republic of 1932. Notwithstanding the reprieves the country had long endured authoritarianism and was well prepared for the difficulties that followed on the heels of the Spanish civil war.
2. See Michael Kimmelman, "Culture and Race: Still on America's Mind," *New York Times* (West Coast edition), 19 November 1995, A1, A40, for his twenty-five-year retrospective look at the exhibition. His article is the basis for my summary of the controversies surrounding *Harlem on My Mind*.
3. The majority of comments in the comment book were definitely unfavorable. I thank the curator of the exhibition, William Truettner, for having made the unpublished books available to me after the exhibition closed. They were subsequently studied in a public symposium I organized at the University of Southern California on "Museums and the New Art History." The following is a typical negative entry: "The show is very biased against Western culture. It has absolutely nothing good to say about America. . . ."
4. It should be noted that a small private institution, the Autry Museum of Western Heritage in Los Angeles, has successfully demonstrated how American museums might challenge outmoded mythologies without alienating their audiences. For example, their newspaper ad for a 1996 exhibition on General Custer reads as follows: "The man. The myth. The legend. The exhibit. Was he a hero or a villain? Genius or lunatic? Controversy and speculation have been General George Custer's legacy since the dramatic battle he lost 120 years ago. We invite you to form your own opinion as you view *Inventing Custer: Legends of the Little Bighorn*."
5. Juan Ignacio de Mesa Ruíz, "Amigos del Museo Sefardí de Toledo," *Boletín Informativo* (December 1993) (author's translation).
6. Santiago Palomero, "Poemas de amor," (working paper read at the conference "Museo/Museum," Barcelona, Spain, May 20–22, 1996).

7. I have turned to Santiago Palomero and Ana María López Alvarez for much of the historical information relayed in this chapter, along with *Museo Sefardi* (Madrid: Ministerio de Cultura, 1995) and *La vida judía en Sefarad* (Madrid: Ministerio de Cultura, 1991), in addition to the regular, ephemeral announcements for the *Curso de Verano* (Toledo: Museo Sefardí and Universidad de Castilla-La Mancha) from 1991 on.

8. The 1988 seminar organized by the author focused on international museum training and was sponsored by the Borchard Foundation at La Bretesche.

9. The recognition of Israel as a state, among much pro-Arab sentiment in Spain, was another indication that the democracy could sustain contradictions.

10. Copy written for the Ministry of Culture brochure for a 1993–94 course (author's translation).

11. See C. Sanz-Pastor, *Museos y colecciones de España* (Madrid: Ministerio de Cultura, 1980), 566. Sanz-Pastor describes the Museum of the Visigoths in Toledo as predicated on the presentation of that "decisive" time in the "birth of the unitary conscience of the Spanish people" (author's translation).

3. MILITARY AND ECCLESIASTICAL MUSEUMS INSIDE AND OUTSIDE MADRID

1. Preston, *Franco: A Biography*, 782.

2. This brief history of the Army Museum has been abstracted from the official *Guía de museos militares Españoles* (Madrid: Ministerio de Defensa, 1995), 13–22.

3. See Preston, *Franco: A Biography*, 555. Speaking about the event, Preston wrote: "In his speech in the galleries Franco described himself as the sentry who protected Spain against international hostility, 'the one who is watchful while others sleep.'"

4. Personal interview with Leticia Azcue, May 18, 1995.

5. *Guía del museo del ejército* (Madrid: Ministerio de Defensa, 1984) and *El museo del ejército Español: poesía y grandeza de una patria inmortal* (Madrid: Ministerio de Defensa, 1983).

6. *Guía del museo del ejército*, 73 (author's translation).

7. Ibid., preface.

8. See the exhibition catalog *Las reales fábricas de sargadelos, el ejército y la armada* (Madrid: Ministerio de Defensa and the Real Patronato de Patronato, 1994).

9. Santiago Palomero Plaza and Jesús Corrobles Santos, "Una propuesta utópica para el Alcázar de Toledo," *Revista de museología* 13 (1998): 103–6.

10. See Norman B. Cooper, *Catholicism and the Franco Régime* (Beverly Hills, Calif.: Sage Publications, 1975), for a review of the trajectory of the Catholic church from 1939–45 to what he frequently terms a "climactic point of alienation" from the state in 1971.

11. Stanley G. Payne, *Spanish Catholicism: An Historical Overview* (Madison: University of Wisconsin Press, 1984), 202–17.

12. Ibid., 230.

13. See Bolaños, *Historia de los museos en España*, 386–92, for a complete history of church and church-related museums during the Franco era.

14. *Guía de museos de la comunidad Valenciana* (Valencia: Generalitat Valenciana, Consellería de Cultura, Educació I Ciencia, 1991), 99, describing the Diocesan Museum of Sacred Art (Museo Diocesano de Arte Sacro) in Alicante (author's translation).

4. PROGRESSIVE PRIVATE FOUNDATIONS LEGITIMIZED BY THE STATE

1. See *Fundaciones culturales privadas Registro y protectorado del Ministerio de Cultura Registros y protectorados de las comunidades autónomas* (Madrid: Ministerio de Cultura, 1993) for a listing of private foundations registered to the state and to the autonomous regions.

2. See "Cuadernos de investigación cultural," *Nuevo marco legal de las fundaciones y del patrocinio y mecenazgo en España: ley de fundaciones y de incentivos fiscales a la participación privada en actividades de interés general* (Seville: Junta de Andalucía, Consejería de Cultura Sevilla, 1995), for the complete law and an introduction to the discussion surrounding the law's aim to advance the support of philanthropy and patronage in Spain.

3. *Una política cultural para España*, 21.

4. A sample of influential foundations especially active during the socialist period includes: La Fundación Arte y Tecnología, founded in 1983 and devoted to contemporary and technologically advanced art; Amigos del Museo del Prado, organized in 1980, a desperately needed organization that tries to help the Prado; Argentaria, founded in 1992, which supported contemporary and past art; Fundación Banco de Vizcaya, which supported art exhibitions, often collaborating with the Reina Sofía, the Hayward Gallery in London, the Foundation Gala-Dali, and the Metropolitan Museum of Art in New York; Coca Cola; Tabacalera, which collected art, including photography, and supported major realist painter Antonio López's controversial exhibition at the Reina Sofía; Caja de Madrid, which made significant contributions to the Thyssen-Bornemisza Collection's and the Prado's didactic materials, to the creation of a guidebook of Madrid's important buildings, and to the restoration of monuments in Toledo and important Spanish-Roman mosaics; and the Central Hispano, which sponsored exhibition of old master paintings and collected extensively.

5. Bringing Spaniards to America, the Fulbright Act also played a similar role, which, to this day, receives a great deal of credit in Spain for having generously supported travel and study grants during that period.

6. See *La Fundación Juan March (1955–1980)* (Madrid: Fundación Juan March, 1980), 11–31, for a brief official history of the Juan March Foundation. In the unnumbered pages of the "presentación" Juan March Delgado, grandson of the founder, writes, "Perhaps it is unnecesary to point out that the Juan March Foundation has never proposed to invade the territory of political life. . . ." Because by 1981 Spain's democracy had not been consolidated (the defining 1981 attempted military coup was an event yet to be endured), it is quite understandable that the Juan March Foundation would downplay the political ramifications of their activities throughout the dictatorship.

7. The Juan March Foundation's activities, including invaluable contributions to the sciences, and its continuing patronage of contemporary and traditional music are detailed in their monthly publications and in their yearbooks.

8. See Preston, *Franco: A Biography*, 681, for a full history of the Franco and Eisenhower incident. The president even, according to Preston, "naively speculated later whether Franco might not win free elections in the unlikely event of his ever holding any." George Steiner, in his review of Preston's *Franco: A Biography*, "Franco's Games," *The New Yorker* 70, no. 33 (October 17, 1994): 120, adds: "Surely this charming, modest host would win a free election—particularly when he could deal so efficaciously with malcontents. The Communist Party official Julián Grimau, after being horribly beaten and tortured, was thrown out the window of the national police headquarters in 1962. He survived to be condemned to death. A wave of international revulsion, of appeals for clemency proved vain. Grimau was executed in April 1963."

9. Preston, *Franco: A Biography*, 755.

10. Lucinda Barnes, unpublished interview with Antonio Saura, November 22, 1988.

11. Steven Schiff, "Milan Kundera: Testaments Betrayed," *The New Yorker* 71, no 40 (December 11, 1995): 101.

5. SEEKING BALANCE WITH THE CENTER

1. Carol Duncan, *Civilizing Rituals inside Public Art Museums* (London and New York: Routledge, 1995), 133, writes that "Exhibitions in art museums do not of themselves change the world. Nor should they have to. But, as a form of public space, they constitute an arena in which a community may test, examine, and imaginatively live both older truths and possibilities for new ones. It is often said that without a sense of past, we cannot envisage a future. The reverse is also true: without a vision of the future, we cannot construct and access a usable past. Art museums are at the center of this process in which past and future intersect. Above all, they are spaces in which communities can work out the values that identify them as communities."

2. Preston, *Franco: A Biography*, 166.

3. James Michener, *Iberia* (New York: Random House, 1968), 91.

4. In a conversation with a staff member in the Badajoz tourist office in 1996, I asked her to locate on a map the exact location of MEIAC in relation to the old bullring. She made a point of telling me that the bullring was closed and a new one a little farther from the museum was opened. She said a garden would be built at the site of the old bullring because of its history. I wondered aloud if it would be a memorial, and she responded that it would not be, people just wanted to forget.

5. See Miguel Logroño, "Geografía del arte. Centro y periferia," *Museo Extremeño e Iberoamericano de Arte Contemporáneo* (Extremadura: Consejería de Cultura y Patrimonio, 1995), 246ff.

6. Antonio Franco Domínguez, "El Museo Extremeño e Iberoamericano de Arte Contemporáneo," in *Espacios de arte contemporáneo generadores de revitalización urbana,* ed. Jesús Pedro Lorente (Zaragoza: Universidad de Zaragoza, 1997),

85–91. See also for a complete description of the prison and his perspective, as founding director, of MEIAC's goals.

7. Antonio Bonet Correa, "Perennidad del panóptico," *Museo Extremeño e Iberoamericano de Arte Contemporáneo,* 226.

8. See Fernando Castro Flórez, "Espacios exteriores. Memorias del lugar," *Museo Extremeño e Iberoamericano de Arte Contemporáneo* (Extremadura: Consejería de Cultura y Patrimonio, 1995), 235–46.

9. Bonet Correa, op. cit., 233.

10. Castro Flórez, *Museo Extremeño,* 245.

11. The history of the Museum of Fine Arts of Asturias is summarized from *Museo de Bellas Artes de Asturias, antecedentes históricos, y memoria, 1980–1982* (Oviedo: Junta de Gobierno de la Fundación Centro Regional de Bellas Artes, 1983) and from a number of conversations with the museum's director, José Antonio Fernández-Castañón Carrasco, and secretary, Emilio Marcos Vallaure, in 1995 and 1996.

12. The Center/Conservative Party ceased to exist after the 1981 election. The museum was such a success that the Socialist Party remained supportive.

13. Personal interview with Emilio Marcos Vallaure, May 24, 1995.

14. Evangelina Rodríguez Cuadros, *Guía de museos de la communidad Valencia* (Valencia: Consellería de Cultura, Educacío i ciencia, 1991), 15 (author's translation).

15. The history of IVAM as reported here is based on conversations with former chief curator Vicente Todoli; the museum's first director, Tomás Llorens; and former director J. F. Yvars.

16. Letter to the author, September 11, 1995, from J. F. Yvars: "As a result of the recently held elections, the Conservative Party has taken over Valencia's regional government, and changes have taken place in the departments of cultural policies. In consequence, I have resigned from my position as director of IVAM. . . ."

17. Rafael Marí Sancho, *Eduardo Zaplana* (Barcelona: Rafael Marí Sancho, 1995), 104.

6. NEGATING THE CENTER IN BILBAO

1. See Jean-Claude Larronde, *El nacionalismo vasco: su origen y su ideología en la obra de Sabino Arana-Goiri,* trans. Lola Valverde (San Sebastián: Ediciones Vascas, 1977), and Beltza, *El nacionalismo vasco, 1876–1936* (San Sebastián: Editorial Txertoa, 1976), for in-depth discussions of Basque language, ethnicity, and nationalism.

2. From personal interview with Teresa Casanovas i Llorens, a highly placed official in the region's (Duputation's) Department of Culture, Service of the Historical Patrimony, in Bilbao, October, 1, 1996.

3. Tomás Uribeetxebarria, diputational head of culture in 1989 and president of the Guggenheim Consortium through the opening of the Guggenheim Museum Bilbao, discusses the lack of museums in the region and his plans to rectify the problem in the regional newspaper *El Correo Español-el pueblo vasco,* 29 June 1989, 3.

4. Javier González de Durana, "La invención de la pintura Vasca" in *Centro y periferia en la modernización de la pintura Española 1880–1918* (Madrid: Ministry of Culture, 1993), 395–402, and Mireia Freixa and Maria del Carmen Pena, "El problema centro-periferia en los siglos XIX y XX" in *Actas VIII Congreso nacional de historia del arte* a conference in Cáceres (Mérida: Editora Regional de Extremadura, 1992), 371–83, have written two of the best summaries of the complex problem of Basque essentialism in the visual arts, both of which have contributed greatly to my understanding of this history.

5. See Juan J. Luna's "El Museo de Bellas Artes de Bilbao: historia y actualidad" in *Tesoros del Museo de Bellas Artes de Bilbao, Pintura: 1400–1939,* (n.p.: Fundación Rich, 1989), 13–28, for the complete history of the Bilbao Museum of Fine Art. See also Bilbao Museum of Fine Art yearbooks, especially *Urtekaria anuario 1993 (and 1994) asterlanak-albistak estudios-cronicas* (Bilbao: Museo de Bellas Artes de Bilbao, 1994 and 1995).

6. Paul Delaney, "After Centuries in Turmoil, a Region's Culture Seems on the Brink of a Revival," *New York Times,* 7 June 1987, H43.

7. Freixa and Pena, "El problema centro-periferia en los siglos XIX y XX," 383, speak about the convoluted subject of Spanish center-periphery relations in the postmodern era. Fears about loss of identity must be kept in mind as intense reactions to the Guggenheim Museum Bilboa set in and fears of the Basque Country losing autonomy, once to Madrid and now to New York City, surfaced. This identity anxiety occurred after it became evident that there would be no subjection to the Spanish state in this project—but that subjection to the "international" was imminent.

8. Kim Bradley, "The Deal of the Century," *Art in America,* 85, no. 7 (July 1997), 48ff, for details.

9. Fernando Savater, *El País* (November 27, 1996, Internet edition). Savater, writing on nationalism as discussed in his book, *Contra las patrias,* said, "The Basque problem is nationalism, and ETA is one of the consequences of that problem. . . . The nationalist essence is incompatible with democracy: there are nationalistic democrats, but nationalism is not democratic. . . . Nationalisms call for pluralism in the Spanish state but deny pluralisms wherever they exercise their power" (author's translation).

10. For series by Ramón Zallo, see his articles in *El Mundo:* 12 February 1992, 52; 14 February 1992, 52; 16 February 1992, 60; and 17 February 1992, 61.

11. Jorge Oteiza, in an open letter printed in *Egin* (May 13, 1993, "data edition").

12. Personal interview with Javier González de Durana, May 25, 1995.

13. *Museo Guggenheim Bilbao estudio de viabilidad* (Los Estados Unidos: Diputación Fora de Bizkaia and Solomon R. Guggenheim Foundation, 1992), 1.2 and 1.3.

14. Personal interviews with José Ignacio Vidarte, May 27, 1994, and May 25, 1995. See also Bradley, "The Deal of the Century," for an account of the negotiation and its resulting budgets and stipulations.

15. Ernest Lluch, letter to the editor, *El Correo Español-el pueblo vasco,* 30 June 1992, 63.

16. Personal interview with Thomas Krens, August 1995. See also Joseba Zulaika, *Crónica de una seducción: el Museo Guggenheim Bilbao* (Madrid: Editorial Nerea, 1997).

17. This statement demonstrates that Krens picked up an obvious, stereotypical trait of many Spanish museums. But it clearly shows that he had not realized the special character of the Bilbao Museum of Fine Art whose directors' tenures have always been long-lived, dedicated, and highly professional.

18. Richard Gunther and John Higley, *Elites and Democratic Consolidation in Latin America and Southern Europe* (New York: Cambridge University Press, 1992), 77.

7. A NATION WITHIN A NATION: CATALONIA

1. Personal interview with Rosa María Malet, May 29, 1995.

2. Preston, *Franco: A Biography*, 766 and 775. See also Paul Preston, *The Triumph of Democracy in Spain* (London and New York: Methuen, 1986), 30.

3. Daniel Solé i Lladós, et al., *Cens de museus dels municipis de Barcelona 1987–1995* (Barcelona: Centre d'Estudi i Recursos Culturals, Diputació de Barcelona, 1995). This census also contains an invaluable survey of Barcelona museums, including opening dates, budgets, administration, and personnel.

4. Josep M. Carrete Nadal, "El museo de Gavà," *Revista de museologia* 6 (December 1995): 63-67.

5. Concern about the neglect of the infrastructures of major museums was widely expressed at the conference, "Culture, Museums and Philanthropy before the Year 2000," sponsored by the Spanish Federation of Friends of Museums, Madrid, January 20–21, 1995.

6. Ramón Carrasco, *De Museus* 3 (November 1992): 40 -41.

7. See Garry Apgar, "Public Art and the Remaking of Barcelona," *Art in America* 99, no. 2 (February 1991): 108-21.

8. Robert Hughes, *Barcelona* (New York: Vintage Books, 1993), 41ff.

9. Preston, *The Triumph of Democracy in Spain*, 679.

10. Unfortunately the Ethnology Museum (Museu Etnològic) and the Decorative Arts Museum (Museu d'Arts Decoratives) were not included under the general umbrella. The city remains responsible for them, and they have received less financial support as a result.

11. Pere Duran I Farell, "El MNAC, exponente de la identidad y la universalidad catalanas," in *El Museu Nacional d'Art de Catalunya (MNAC)*, Cuaderno Central no. 23 (Barcelona: Ayuntamiento de Barcelona, n.d..), 66, (author's translation).

12. Catalan antiquarians had arranged the purchase and organized the export of the apses for the Americans by buying off civil or ecclesiastical authorities. See Xavier Barral I Altet, "Las colecciones del MNAC," Ibid., 96.

13. Duran I. Farell, "El MNAC," op. cit., 66.

14. Eduardo Folguera Caveda, "Los estudios y la formación de profesionales de los museos," *Revista de museología* 6 (December 1995): 13 (author's translation).

15. Detailed information about the museum's collection can be found in *MACBA Memoria d'activitats 1995–1996* (Barcelona: Consorci del Museu d'Art Contemporani de Barcelona, 1996), 76-94.

16. See Daniel Giralt-Miracle, "Metamórfosis del museo contemporáneo, forma y fondo," *VII Congreso Internacional de la Federación Mundial de Amigos de los Museos* (Córdoba: Junta de Andalucía, 1990), 40, for early collecting strategies.

17. Personal interviews with Miquel Molins in Valencia, March 16, 1998, and Manuel Borja-Villel on the telephone, September 3, 1998.
18. Personal interview with Luis Monreal, May, 21 and 22, 1996.
19. The history of the La Caixa Foundation and its activities is based on the above interview with Luis Monreal and Fundació La Caixa, *Yearbook 1994* (Barcelona: Fundació La Caixa, 1995), 12–15.
20. See María de Corral and Dan Cameron, *Tropismes, Col·lecció d'Art Contemporani Fundació "la Caixa"* (Barcelona: Fundació La Caixa, 1992), 134ff.
21. See Daniel Sole Elados, "15 anys despres. . . ." *Revista de museología* 6 (December 1995): 4–5 (author's translation).

8. VISIONS AND REVISIONS IN ANDALUSIA

1. *Plan general de bienes culturales de Andalucía* (Sevilla: Consejería de Cultura y Medio Ambiente of the Junta de Andalucía, 1985), 15–20 (author's translation).
2. Ibid., 26, refers to article 12.3 of the Statute of Autonomy
3. Ibid., 82, refers to chap. 6, pt. 2, "Plan for Museums."
4. See *Guía de museos de la comunidad Valenciana*, 12.
5. Personal interview with Bartoloméo Ruíz, June 1994.
6. See *La Cartuja recuperada Sevilla, 1986–1992* (Seville: Junta de Andalucia, Consejería de Cultura y Medio Ambiente, 1992), for history of the La Cartuja Monastery.
7. José Ramón Sierra Delgado, "Rehabilitación de la zona de monjes," Ibid., 93 (author's translation)
8. Francisco Torres Martínez, "Recinto y pabellon," Ibid., 149.
9. *Guía de museos de la comunidad de Valenciana*, xiv, op. cit., chap. 5, note 14.
10. Ramón Sagúes i Baixeras, (unpublished paper read at the *DEAC* conference, Bilbao, Spain, September 30, 1996).
11. James Clifford, *The Predicament of Culture* (Cambridge, Mass., and London: Harvard University Press, 1988), 264. Clifford quotes Edward Said: "It seems a common human failing to prefer the schematic authority of a text to the disorientation's of direct encounters with the human."
12. Ruiz, interview, May 1996.
13. As per *Plan general de bienes culturales de Andalucía, 1996–2000*, 2d ed. (Sevilla: Consejería de Cultura y Medio Ambiente de Andalucía, 1997).
14. Ibid., 177–79.